Government Issu

Government Issued Opinion

The Dark Science of Manipulating Perceptions and Policies

Dennis F. Poindexter

McFarland & Company, Inc., Publishers
Jefferson, North Carolina

LIBRARY OF CONGRESS CATALOGUING-IN-PUBLICATION DATA

Names: Poindexter, Dennis F., 1945– author.
Title: Government issued opinion : the dark science of manipulating
perceptions and policies / Dennis F. Poindexter.
Description: Jefferson, North Carolina : McFarland & Company, Inc., 2022
| Includes bibliographical references and index.
Identifiers: LCCN 2022009214 | ISBN 9781476687124 (paperback : acid free paper) ∞
ISBN 9781476645544 (ebook)
Subjects: LCSH: Social influence—China | Social control—China |
Information warfare—China. | Propaganda—China. | Social
influence—United States. | Social control—United States.
| Information warfare—United States. | Propaganda—United States.
| BISAC: POLITICAL SCIENCE / Propaganda
Classification: LCC HM1176 .P65 2022 | DDC 302/.13—dc23/eng/20220223
LC record available at https://lccn.loc.gov/2022009214

BRITISH LIBRARY CATALOGUING DATA ARE AVAILABLE

ISBN (print) 978-1-4766-8712-4
ISBN (ebook) 978-1-4766-4554-4

Front cover images © 2022 Shutterstock

Printed in the United States of America

*McFarland & Company, Inc., Publishers
Box 611, Jefferson, North Carolina 28640
www.mcfarlandpub.com*

Table of Contents

Preface

When I was in the Air Force, we were told during five days of training how to survive a nuclear blast and continue to do our jobs. None of us took it very seriously. We had already seen those films of mushroom clouds and read about the different ways the explosion would destroy our enemies. The blast wave moved across houses, bending the treetops almost to the ground, just as they disintegrated. We were mostly young second lieutenants and enlisted airmen—young but not stupid. We could not imagine being on the other end of that. We would not survive long after the air burst, fire and radioactive debris. But our bosses in the Strategic Air Command (SAC) thought it would be nice if we believed we could—our motivation was important to whether we did our duty in wartime. There seemed to be a finality to nuclear war that was not very inspiring. When you get training on that kind of conflict, the glamor is gone soon after. We all wished for something not quite so destructive as global incineration. We should have listened to the old adage: Be careful what you wish for.

Before the U.S. presidential election in 2020, both party factions believed that a win by the opposing side would cause "lasting harm" to the country. Not since the 1800s has a U.S. election been so sharply divided in almost every aspect of society, from energy policy to immigration, tax policy, foreign policy, policing, crime, racial justice, the response to the COVID-19 pandemic.[1] This led *Dimock and Wike* at the Pew Research Center to point out that politics begins to feel like a zero-sum game, where one side's gain is inherently the other's loss.[2] In the U.S., the country is divided along sharp lines, marked by signs that read Republican or Democrat.

In a number of different subject areas unrelated to politics, the two parties line up according to their leadership's stance on policy. For example, there are detailed differences in how to handle COVID-19, mask wearing, data and recommendation from scientists, contact tracing, whether to get a vaccine, or life when the pandemic is over. About the only thing most agree on (77 percent) is that they are sharply divided.[3] Why do we look to

1

politicians to decide what we should do in these matters? Surely, they do not know more about COVID-19 than the usual lineup of epidemiologists.

When the 2020 presidential election was over, more than ten thousand people walked to "Black Lives Matter" square, just across the street from the White House, to protest the vote count. Many believed they had been cheated and started a group called "Stop the Steal." Facebook and Twitter, it seemed overnight, banned the group on their platforms "to protect the conversation on our service from attempts to incite violence, organize attacks, and share deliberately misleading information about the election outcome."[4] This after riots tore though many U.S. cities in the months before, when the social media platforms did little to censor any groups causing the violence.

The marchers started peacefully but were disrupted later in the evening by a few Antifa and Black Lives Matter activists who hurled insults at families with children and disrupted diners on the sidewalks outside of D.C. restaurants. Most of the people on both sides were peaceful, but a few are not. The contrast with the ones who were not is stark. Both sides were frustrated with their government—neither is getting what they want from it.

Influenced by different issues, they turned out to protest, or counter-protest, for the same core values—free speech, freedom of assembly, causes worth getting on the Metro and riding downtown to demonstrate. We share those ideals of both sides because they are foundations of democracy. Both groups are tolerated, though less so where they turn to violence and property destruction. They believe in a cause that is created for a purpose that they can support. They organized though their own communication channels and handle their own logistics. They make signs, slogans, and demonstrate solidarity with each other. It is, in most of their minds, the democratic way.

When the final votes were counted in Georgia, and Congress belonged to the Democrats and the Oval Office to President-elect Biden, President Trump addressed his supporters, among them many of those same Stop-the-Steal protesters and told them they had been cheated. They marched on the Capitol rotunda and the House chamber in an unseemly end to the Trump administration. Early on, a woman and a police officer died in the mayhem; the woman, Ashli Babbitt, was shot dead by a member of the Capitol Police. The medical examiner's conclusion of her cause of death was homicide, but no charges were filed against the officer who shot her, who was found to have acted within his duty. The officer's family awaits a murder investigation—which was still not concluded four months later. The FBI Director was asked about this in March 2021 and declined to give a cause of death for the officer, nor the reasons for the protracted investigation.[5] (Of the four police officers who died immediately surrounding

January 6, all were eventually found to have died of natural causes.) Some of those arrested are still in pre-trial confinement as this book goes to print, over one year after the events occurred.

I worked in the U.S. House of Representatives for over four years, and I could not conceive of anything like that ever happening. It is a peaceful place in the midst of a city that often is not. I got chills when that news came in.

Demonstrations like the ones in Washington were peacefully held in Minsk in 2020, and looked much the same, with two deaths initially among the protesters. There were even more demonstrations afterward.[6] The main difference was the 6,000 people who were arrested there protesting the election results which put President Alexander Lukashenko back in office for his 26th year. He has outlived the patronage of the Soviet Union but carries on with Russia the same way he always has. If you believe his vote counting, he got 80 percent of the vote in the last election. The demonstrators, like those in Washington, D.C., do not believe that. Only one person remained to battle Lukashenko in his election, after two other candidates fled the country. Since then, the last candidate has been exiled and her husband jailed.[7] A person who really gets 80 percent of the electorate has no reason to jail the opposition's relatives or his opponents, does he?

After the election in Belarus, tens of thousands of protestors were in the streets of Minsk, and they did not stop coming back every Sunday since the August 9, 2020, election. After 18 weekends of demonstrations the arrests continued and two journalists are arrested just for covering the events.[8] More and more of them are arrested every week, and many complain of beatings and overcrowding in jails, but they keep coming. The marchers in the U.S. and in Belarus share a cause but do not recognize each other for it. Nobody knows how long this can go on, but Russia backs President Lukashenko as they backed Viktor Yanukovych in the Ukraine. Eventually, Yanukovych became a liability that was allowed to exit to Russia, a fate the demonstrators in Belarus could hope to repeat.[9] It is a long road to get there.

Neither side, in Minsk or in Washington, D.C., have convincing arguments that the seated governments accept as truth. Lukashenko's government claims a mandate to rule since 80 percent of voters voted for him. The protesters believe that mandate is suspect. But his government cracked down hard on the largely peaceful demonstrations, the biggest of which attracted up to 200,000 people. Police used stun grenades, tear gas and truncheons to disperse the rallies. Water cannons, armored vehicles and military trucks were seen in the center of Minsk. Several subway stations were closed and internet access restricted. At least four more journalists have been detained in Minsk and the western city of Grodno, according to the Belarusian Association of Journalists. The European Union imposes sanctions on Lukashenko and U.N. High Commissioner for Human Rights Michelle Bachelet said the situation with human rights in Belarus is getting worse.[10, 11]

> Social media disinformation in Belarus often originates from the accounts of state-controlled outlets and groups. State-controlled media harass political opposition and minority voices and deceive the public into believing this disinformation. Up to 77.27% of news content broadcasted by three leading state-controlled television channels—Belarus 1, ONT, CTV—in November 2019 contained signs of propaganda and manipulation (Media IQ, 2020). This content mostly covered domestic politics such as the parliamentary election. These state-controlled outlets also try to present Belarus as the only stable country in the region, while framing its political system as the only credible one. Common narratives that mention foreign countries include presenting the EU institutions as "weak" and promising an imminent collapse of the West (Chulitskaya, 2019). Many of those narratives align with storylines propagated by local junk news outlets that are linked to Russia, such as vitbich.org and mogilew.by (Chulitskaya, 2019)....
>
> A key foreign player in the Belarusian disinformation market is Russia. Belarus might be one of the most vulnerable countries to the influence of the Russian state propaganda. More than 40% of the population considered the Russian state-controlled television channels their main sources of information (Laputska & Papko, 2017). Two thirds of all the content that is being broadcasted in Belarus originates from Russia (Laputska & Papko, 2017). Chulitskaya (2020) identified 64 actors—mostly junk news websites—that disseminated pro–Russian narratives online. These actors operated 149 social media groups, pages, profiles, and websites. A Warsaw-Based research center EAST identified at least 40 news outlets that are based in Belarus and focus on local agenda but are openly or covertly supported by Russia....
>
> Trolling tactics rely on human users who spread pro-government information in the comment sections of leading independent media. Over the past decade, trolls praising the regime and denouncing the opposition have increased their operation significantly (Freedom House, 2019). Their purpose is to mobilize public opinion and to criticize any type of regime opponents. Several popular independent outlets claim that they have become victims of troll farms. According to the editors of leading news outlets that include Nasha Niva and Tut.by, these farms target comment sections on their websites to attack pro-democracy activists and regime opponents and to promote progovernment narratives (NN by, 2015, 2020). There are also some signs of troll farms operating on social media platforms. However, it does not appear that they function as the major source of misinformation on social media. The platforms most impacted by disinformation are Facebook, OK, Telegram, VK and YouTube.[12, 13]

President Biden's party claims a much smaller percentage of the vote than Lukashenko's 80%, but his party wins a majority of the U.S. House of Representatives and the U.S. Senate giving him party unity of the Executive and Legislative branches of government, much more important to enacting legislation. After the election is over a single, one-time demonstration in Washington, D.C., is held on the steps of the U.S. capitol building. That is characterized as a "riot," "mob" or "insurrection" and the FBI launches a manhunt for almost anyone involved in planning the event, but only a few hundred compared to those 6,000 arrested in Belarus.

The FBI Director calls the riot an act of domestic terrorism which has a particular meaning in law that the director would know well.[14] This is a potentially wide swath of people who attack government buildings or attempt to intimidate people who work in them.

18 U.S. Code § 2331
(1) The term "domestic terrorism" means activities that—
(A) involve acts dangerous to human life that are a violation of the criminal laws of the United States or of any State;
(B) appear to be intended—
(i) to intimidate or coerce a civilian population;
(ii) to influence the policy of a government by intimidation or coercion; or
(iii) to affect the conduct of a government by mass destruction, assassination, or kidnapping; and
(C) occur primarily within the territorial jurisdiction of the United States....

To deter this kind of activity from happening again, large fences reinforced with barbed wire and National Guard troops are temporarily placed around the Capitol building. They put a pall over that part of D.C., which is strangely quiet. There are few demonstrators or tourists. Unlike the Belarus demonstrations, the Washington event is not repeated every Sunday. Those fences and National Guard troops are a deterrent.

The Trump administration futilely tried the courts as a last resort, bringing a dozen lawsuits alleging voter fraud or disqualification of ballots. His campaign holds a series of press conferences with anecdotal evidence of widespread manipulation of ballot results, none of which proved substantial enough to move a court to disqualify any voters. Four of these cases were dismissed within days for various reasons but one remained until the end to be considered by the Supreme Court. The court declined to hear that case on the grounds that the state of Texas "has not demonstrated a judicially cognizable interest in the manner in which another State conducts its elections."[15] None of the cases are likely to change the outcome of the elections they challenge.[16] They are, overall, an embarrassment to the Trump campaign and, at this time, serve little purpose in changing voter laws in states. Ex-President Trump cannot let go of the idea that his campaign lost the election because they were cheated by state administrations, and he said so in his first speech after leaving office.

Mr. Trump followed up with an extended rant, claiming "this election was rigged and the Supreme Court and other courts didn't want to do anything about it." Instead, they "used process and lack of standing" to avoid the controversy. That's deeply misleading. Judges in all six contested states found the Trump lawyers didn't produce sufficient evidence.[17]

There is disinformation and misinformation on both sides of the political fence, which should come as no surprise to anyone. Increasingly, research shows those forms of manipulation of public opinion are used by the major political parties around the world. The forms of government, like dictatorship, democracy, communist or socialist do not seem to matter with regard to the type of manipulation being used. We have to decide if this is what we really want from our governments.

The marchers in both Belarus and Washington, D.C., believe in democracy and they believe demonstrating will make a difference in restoring democracy they can believe in. Simon Jenkins at *The Guardian* called street demonstrations "democracy's ultimate freedom." But, at the same time, he rightly questioned the benefit of them. China's Tiananmen Square, Turkey's Taksim Square, the protests in Hong Kong were *photogenic* but did not achieve their objectives.[18]

Jenkins is right, though we might not want to admit it. The demonstrations go on but the policies that create them do not change. Influence campaigns in those places normalize existing divisions and amplify them. That may not be their objective. We have not developed an effective way to achieve the objectives of either side of these demonstrations because the governments that surround them will not allow it.

While we observed these street demonstrations, we saw two related, chilling warnings within a year of each other:

> We are concerned about ongoing campaigns by Russia, China and other foreign actors, including Iran, to undermine confidence in democratic institutions and influence public sentiment and government policies. These activities also may seek to influence voter perceptions and decision making in the 2018 [mid-term elections] and 2020 U.S. elections.[19]

The second was this: In November 2019, Duncan Lewis, former head of the Australian Security Intelligence Organization (ASIO), said China was using "insidious" foreign interference operations to "take over" the Australian political system.

> Espionage and foreign interference is insidious. Its effects might not present for decades and by that time it is too late…. You wake up one day and find decisions made in our country that are not in the interests of our country.[20]

Russian campaigns have been trying to interfere in elections in Europe and the U.S. There is no doubt about that, but how successful were they? Before each of the last two elections, the U.S. intelligence services said China, Russia and Iran were trying to influence who won, yet said almost nothing about how successful they were. After the elections were over, we should have heard what China and Iran did, but all we heard about was Russia. That was curious, but in researching what happened during that time, it turns out influence campaigns are much broader than most of us knew and may be a good bit better than anyone thought.

A few weeks after I submitted this book for pre-publication review to the Director of National Intelligence, the same office published a formal analysis of what other countries besides Russia did, and a rationale for not publishing that information sooner. That explanation is Appendix A of this book. It includes some of the things Iran did to influence our elections but not much about China.

The Chinese are the capable of influencing a whole population to adhere to policies of the Chinese Communist Party (CCP). What they do internally is an influence campaign which is part of a government program to alter beliefs and its citizens' core values to fit those of the leadership. It is not always subtle, as the Uighurs can testify, but it works. It takes patience to make these work because influence of core values does not happen quickly. It works because the Chinese can match any country in the world for persistence and detail. It is not only the detail of their techniques we worry about; it is how they are applied:

> China has already begun to experiment with metrics and quantification of the value and virtue of its citizens, going beyond the function of measuring workplace performance and health-related self-tracking to measuring one's purchasing and consumption history, interpersonal relationships, political activities, as well as the tracking of one's location history. China has also already begun to apply a reward and punishment system that rewards those who comply with the Chinese government's ideals and punishes those who deviate from them.[21]

What we should realize when we evaluate the social media in our society is that the information the Chinese use to measure their own citizens is the same information that social media collects on its platforms. Social media have so much data, even they do not realize how much of it is being collected and sold. Most of it is used for some kind of influence from advertising to political influence campaigns.[22]

In Chapter 1, I show a range of different influence campaigns, and my definition of the term. Some of these countries are our allies and some are our enemies, but the techniques are much the same. Politicians tend to think of these campaigns in terms of elections, but influence campaigns are pervasive, covering everything from validation of territorial claims to what kinds of steel we should allow into a given country. The Chinese use personal relationships between families in senior management to influence one another at the top level of other institutions.[23] Hundreds of groups exist for the sole purpose of influencing senior leaders all over the world.

The Chinese are open about the purpose of these groups. These are like the groups the Soviets used to establish as fronts for Russia's Communist Party.[24] The Chinese are subtle and do much more than just influence by persuasion.

They carry that softness over to their influence campaigns. Those too are soft, giving people what they want in exchange for what the Chinese need. People like that. They take care of each other, so their children get good jobs and rise to the top, or they benefit in other ways that seem to be harmless to others. There is comfort there with little conflict.

The Russians use a kind of brute force politics, releasing embarrassing information, trying to manipulate voting machines, and heavy-handed removal of any political opposition to the point of disfiguring a candidate in the Ukraine, or poisoning one in their own country.

Clive Hamilton and Mareike Ohlberg have some of the best examples of how China runs their kind of influence campaign without calling it by that name. The incestual relationships between U.S. business and China is not new, so that part of influence campaigns is familiar to most. The model that J.P. Morgan used in Hong Kong shows how Hunter Biden could have gotten involved in Chinese finance, but most institutions working in China know it is the Chinese way. J.P Morgan was unlucky enough to be caught by U.S. regulators because they paid $264 million to the Federal Reserve Board and Justice Department for their hiring practices.[25] They would have never been looked at the same way by the Chinese regulators.

Chapter 6 is a case study of an influence operation that did not go well. We do not see those often. The U.S. indictment was sealed until after the U.S. mid-term election in 2018 and unsealed to prosecute two years later. It was exposed by two different countries and the Russian agents who ran those operations were finally indicted. There was enough in the public domain to put this campaign together without that sealed indictment to document it. We will never see these Russians in court because they worked for the Russian intelligence services who will not allow their representatives to appear for trial.

I came away enamored with Anne-Marie Brady, a professor at the University of Canterbury, Christchurch, and a prolific writer. Brady focused her works on the Chinese influence campaigns, which were aimed the 200,000 Chinese immigrants living in New Zealand (pop. 4.5 million). She named names of some local professors who were working with the Chinese, making her less than popular with some of her peers. In her paper, "Magic Weapons: China's Political Influence Activities Under Xi Jinping," she managed to stir up so much trouble for herself that she nearly lost her academic job in New Zealand. But that shows what clout the Chinese have and how little the academic communities of the world want to challenge it. The New

Zealand professor puts that kind of conduct together in a way that is difficult for the Chinese to deny. She speaks Mandarin and follows the Chinese in her country and China. She exposed the organizations and people involved, telling what they are trying to do. Her writing has elements of a spy novel.

> [The Chinese] United Front Work Department personnel often operate under diplomatic cover as members of the Ministry of Foreign Affairs, using this role to guide united front activities outside China, working with politicians and other high-profile individuals, Chinese community associations, and student associations, and sponsoring Chinese language, media, and cultural activities.... The organization most closely connected with the PRC authorities in New Zealand is the Peaceful Reunification of China Association of New Zealand (PRCANZ), founded in 2000.... The name of the organization is a reference to the "Peaceful Reunification" of mainland China and Taiwan.... The PRC also relies on "patriotic" businesspersons—Red Capitalists—who are always prominent in such organizations, to provide further funding. This is a longstanding practice of CCP united front work....[26]

She and Keven McCauley (*Russian Influence Campaigns Against the West*) are analysts like those of the old days.[27] McCauley is a great Russian analyst. They live their work, sometimes in places only they can go.

"Analyst" has a special meaning in the intelligence community. It refers to someone who has immersed themselves in a subject for their professional life and they know the technical and linguistic language of the places they write about. They work for the government sometimes. There are Chinese analysts, Russian analysts and cyber analysts, among many. They are very focused on their subjects.

My life's work over the last forty years has been in cybersecurity, and information war, both of which evolve rapidly. Twenty years ago, they were completely different than they are today. This book is about the lowest rung in the information war chain. I am looking at these influence campaigns from the perspective of government cyber operations, mostly post Internet, where they are growing exponentially. But the Russians and Chinese were in them long before computers were ubiquitous. These campaigns are very closely aligned with political warfare.

Influence campaigns are a new area of study to some, but they have many names, so they are deceptive in their own right. The tactics have been around for a long time. Disinformation, misinformation, propaganda, psychological warfare were commonly used terms associated with it early on, and lately computational propaganda (Bradshaw and Howard).

I think the first four of those are products of the campaigns. We usually lose sight of what a campaign really does. A campaign manages changes to human behavior. The targets of those campaigns come to believe or act in a certain way. The tactics used, like disinformation, produce that result. They are intended to change core values and beliefs when applied broadly, but they can focus on a single action, like changing the behavior of law enforcement officers or preventing Germany from buying more natural gas from Russia.

Influence campaigns have a paucity of evidence on measures of effectiveness (MOE). These have always been used to describe the effectiveness of certain elements of conflict in an outcome on the battlefield. For example, the injection of information at certain points increases the effectiveness of combat operations.

> In Cyber operations that assesses changes in system behavior, capability, or operational environment that is tied to measuring the attainment of an end state, achievement of an objective, or creation of an effect. … This can be very complex if we are talking about influence operations or information operations.[28]

This kind of information war is still waged by military, in military environments, all over the world but it has been around longer than what is happening today. We need to see influence campaigns as a different kind of warfare in its own right, and the battlefield as our core values and individual beliefs. That is not war in any sense of the word, but it has altered war by replacing it. That may be temporary.

Every politician ever born says how closely their personal values line up with the values of their country, and they cite examples of how that linkage is expressed by their "fighting for" their constituents who have those same values.

When I was finished with this book, I found that we know almost nothing about the effectiveness of these campaigns. We can accurately describe the techniques, but we need to know much more about how effective they are or who benefits from them. This speaks to the information we have and the effectiveness of applying it:

> In October 2017, Facebook revealed that approximately 80,000 pieces of content published by the now infamous Russian-operated Internet Research Agency were introduced to 29 million people between January 2015 and August 2017. Their subsequent likes and shares increased the reach of the posts to 126 million Facebook users. This is indeed a big scary number. But what we don't know is how much user attention this content commanded among the many billions of stories and posts that comprised the news feeds of U.S. voters, or if it changed any minds or influenced voter behavior.[29]

In 2020 there was a substantial increase in the variables in influence campaigns. The effects of hacking voting system components, the impact of censorship by social media companies, changes in the law that impacts money in elections, the effects of artificial intelligence on information stolen by governments. But like social media we have little evidence of the effectiveness because we have not had the kinds of investigations required to determine those things. To a great extent, our governments do not want to know who actually benefited from these campaigns.

It turns out that the Russian campaigns are the place to find out how influence is done at the lowest levels. For a country run by a former KGB officer, they do not protect their programs very well. Even if they fail, they can always deny they did anything they got caught doing. President Putin can look right into the camera at Helsinki, for example, and tell his version of a story that most of the world knows is not true. He can say with a smile the Russians did not interfere in the U.S. elections in 2016. Fox News' Chris Wallace's Emmy-nominated interview with him gets to that issue quickly, when he asks why Putin's GRU officers were being indicted if they did nothing wrong during the U.S. national election?[30] Putin answered several questions Wallace did not ask, but not that one.

The Chinese do not take criticism well. They censor things like this away just like they did with COVID-19, then start a trade war when we dispute what they say. That points out that the Chinese, Russians and Iranians do not do the same kinds of campaigns. They are similar in certain elements, but they are unlike each other in major ways. When they seem to work together, which is more and more, they can do things that we should be afraid of.

What many books covering this aspect of information war (Chapter 2) lack is a focus on the human interpersonal communications (Chapter 4) and what we should do to try to stop some of these efforts from achieving more success (Chapter 9). We think we know about influence just from our life experience, but there are some surprises that pertain to the non-intuitive nature of influencing large groups, and why foreign campaigns are not doing that as often as we might think.

When I started writing this book, I got the impression they had been unsuccessful. In reading all the indictments, thousands of pages of Congressional testimony and articles about what happened in 2015–20, it did not look like they had much to show for their campaigns. But then, like Duncan Lewis, I woke up one of those days and said, "Oh, this doesn't look good." It was the day after the 2020 election was over and there were complaints about the election being stolen. The immediate reaction from the press and social media channels was that *just saying* it might have been stolen was a *misstatement likely to cause violence.* That was odd. There was no reason at that time to suspect then that any violence would result from these events any more than there was reason to believe that marches in Portland, Oregon, would result in violence after they got to their destination. Yet, those trappings of violence still remain—the fences and troops—long after the threat of violence is gone. The prosecutions of those guilty of violence are far from happening even though there is substantial evidence of crimes. We are left with the impression of a constant, sustained threat which we must be protected from.

Every state of the United States named as part of this alleged vote-stealing had logical reasons why voters might have misinterpreted what happened in their state, and they have continued to respond to those claims long after the election was over. The press and social media used the same terms to describe their censorship. There was nothing illegal about it and censorship was necessary to reduce violence. The Attorney General of the United States said, "nothing was severe enough to overturn the election," a qualifier that got my attention because that is not the same thing as saying nothing nefarious happened. Shortly after, he resigned his position and that was odd. President Trump's reelection campaign put a team together to investigate and go to the courts. The courts, almost everywhere, said … "Nothing here" … and that was that. But it did not feel like anything was over.

Most of us believe in a myth that benevolent democracy provides for the welfare of citizens, giving them freedom to choose a course, providing accurate information to them which can be digested, analyzed and congealed into a belief system that supports a set of public policies. Most of us believe that our system of government would not allow anyone to be elected that was not the choice of the people who are citizens of our country.

The ideal, often mouthed by politicians, is the creation of a broad belief structure that is recognized as the correct approach and brought to the front by an intelligent leadership that believes similarly to those they represent. Even the most rigid and restrictive governments give lip service to this idea. President Xi of China and President Putin in Russia both give standing to it, yet we think their countries are nothing like ours.[31, 32]

Some countries are different than democracies that allow people to make up their own minds about how they want to be governed. A few like Iran, North Korea, Cuba, and Venezuela control their own populations in ways most of us agree are oppressive and even destructive. We allow that because it is an "internal matter" for each country. As long as it stays that way, we have a difficult time justifying interference.

A 2018 Hoover Institution study states clearly that it does not agree that China has ever tried to interfere with a U.S. election, but qualifies that statement with an elaboration:

It is important not to exaggerate the threat of these new Chinese initiatives. China has not sought to interfere in a national election in the United States or to sow confusion or inflame polarization in our democratic discourse the way Russia has done. For all the tensions in the relationship, there are deep historical bonds of friendship, cultural exchange, and mutual inspiration between the two societies, which we celebrate and wish to nurture. And it is imperative that Chinese Americans—who feel the same pride in American citizenship as do other American ethnic communities—not be subjected to the kind of generalized suspicion or stigmatization that could lead to racial profiling or a new era of McCarthyism.

However, with increased challenges in the diplomatic, economic, and security domains, China's influence activities have collectively helped throw the crucial relationship between the People's Republic of China (CCP) and the United States into a worrisome state of imbalance and antagonism. Not only are the values of China's authoritarian system anathema to those held by most Americans, but there is also a growing body of evidence that the Chinese Communist Party views the American ideals of freedom of speech, press, assembly, religion, and association as direct challenges to its defense of its own form of one-party rule.[33]

That belief has influenced our understanding of the Chinese people for a long time, but not our beliefs about the CCP. The same can be said for the Russians.

Just a few years later, the problems faced by governments are much more difficult to manage and much more personalized to the individuals who influence policy. Governments should learn to pay attention. A new study by Samantha Bradshaw and Philip Howard at Oxford showed they are doing this—if only they were doing it for the right reasons:

> Organized social media manipulation campaigns were found in each of the 81 surveyed countries, up 15% in one year, from 70 countries in 2019. Governments, public relations firms and political parties are producing misinformation on an industrial scale…. It shows disinformation has become a common strategy, with more than 93% of the countries (76 out of 81) seeing disinformation deployed as part of political communication.[34]

Bradshaw and Howard suggest social media are the go-to choice for influence campaigns. That view takes the focus away from some of the other methods of modifying the core values of people in other countries, but social media is still close to the most significant vehicle. These types of campaigns are multimedia and multimethod events. Nothing has shown that better than national elections in several countries, that influence campaigns are partly driven by national political parties and other governments interfering with the conduct of those elections.

What democratic governments are doing instead of reacting to the methods being used against them, is emulating them. It has become the *modus operandi* for political campaigns.

The U.S. intelligence community assessed in 2016 and 2020 that the Russians, Iranian and Chinese directly aimed at disrupting democracy and reducing confidence in it.[35] Do we assume, because there are many indicators of disruption, that they were successful? We should not. Not yet.

Although we are, for example, told by U.S. political parties and the press that there were no credible instances of voter fraud, there is evidence that the Russians did everything in the 2016 election, and again in 2018, to demonstrate that they were trying to learn how to impact the voting infrastructure in the U.S. They were developing intelligence on each aspect of the voting infrastructure, something cyber analysts find alarming. The U.S. Department of Justice (DOJ) indictments document the Russian actions in great detail. Several states managed to achieve extremely close results that arrived in those late-night hours in just the right amounts. But should we believe it was the Russians? We should not, but neither should we disregard what they are trying to achieve by this intelligence gathering.

The Chinese and Iranians are mentioned in both intelligence assessments, but we know next to nothing about what either one actually did in 2016 and 2018. U.S. intelligence sources and Congressional investigations tell us almost everything the Russians did. There were no leaks of Chinese activity. There were no criminal indictments of any Chinese for what they were said to have done. Do we know if any of their actions influenced the elections? We do not.

We should be asking ourselves why.

Author's note: In this book, I put my own stories
with a rule above and below text.

1

Defining Influence Campaigns

In World War II, the U.S. ran a successful operation that proved effective in changing behavior of some Japanese citizens in their own country. The Office of War Information (OWI) was focused on influencing the Japanese people to mistrust their leadership, discourage them from war participation and encouraging surrender. At that point in the war, the U.S. was considering the dangerous invasion of the Japanese mainland. The media at that time were radio and paper leaflets, though radio was more widely used near the end of the war when the U.S. got closer to the heart of Japan.[1]

In the last three months of the war, OWI prepared and delivered 63 million leaflets to 35 cities targeted for destruction. Postwar surveys indicated the Japanese believed the accuracy of the leaflets, which contained news, warnings, and directions to leave their homes.[2] Many did leave immediately, because what followed was bombing, often firebombing. There was a motivating consequence of not paying attention to those leaflets. The program was successful because people actually did mistrust their leaders and some surrendered. It was a monumental achievement for the pre-internet days.

We have to wonder why a people like the Japanese would ever think to disregard what their Emperor has told them and leave their homes and lay down their arms. Influence campaigns have a lot to do with it. Like the one in Japan, they are often run by intelligence services.

Australian Prime Minister Scott Morrison had been having more than his fair share of trouble with the Chinese when he decided the world should investigate the origins of the virus we all know as COVID-19. Australia has been in a trade war with China ever since.

That war had significant impact on trade, as well as consequences beyond that. Morrison was suspended from WeChat, China's version of Twitter, about the same time President Trump was banned from Twitter. Neither one of them were very happy about it. Right at that time, it so happens, Australia was starting to look into rising concerns about Beijing's ability to export its brand of censorship overseas through technology groups.[3] That is something every country should be looking at.

Tencent-owned WeChat claims Chinese Twitter says Morrison, hoping to get talks back on track to settle the trade war, wrote a "conciliatory message" to Chinese officials but that it was "contrary to objective facts." That was the reason they gave for suspending him. Some Australian commentators said the censorship of Morrison's message to people living in Australia highlighted the need to regulate the influence of Chinese technology companies in the country.[4]

If it escaped our notice the first time around, this is a social media platform deciding what the facts of the Prime Minister's note should be when he publishes another text to make up for his previous bad behavior. It hardly even makes sense that WeChat thought they could do that. We might find it difficult to tell the difference between WeChat's comment to him and diplomatic notes from the Chinese embassy. The language is almost the same. Given the way things have been going between the two, the PM is not likely to reply the way WeChat thinks he should, and the standoff continues. China and Australia, to this day, are still in a trade war which COVID-19 has not helped to resolve, and WeChat still acts like it is speaking for the Chinese government.

What happened to Australia has had a backlash. The PM's original challenge was over COVID-19. The number of infected still goes up and down but is not going away. Quite a bit of the world is tired of sitting at home pretending to work and looks at how and why China let the virus run amok when it first got started. After a year, the World Health Organization finally investigated and waffled over its own findings, even delaying its interim report. China has enough censorship to make investigative results go away most of the time, but not this time. It affected too much of the world's people and too many aspects of our lives. Now that we have vaccines, the fight turns to which ones are best.

China's vaccine from Sinovac has had varying degrees of success from 91 percent in Turkey to 50.4 in Brazil, which is enough to justify using it, but not nearly as good as its four main competitors in the world market. China wants to argue with Pfizer over the way they calculated those better results.[5]

It was a sure coincidence that within a few days of this argument getting started, hackers stole information from the European Medicines Agency (EMA) that included the data those Pfizer numbers are based on.[6] A few days after later, an altered database appeared on the dark web. A day or so later the altered data was leaked.[7] This data is stolen, altered, then leaked in an effort to undermine trust in certain types of vaccines, but not the Chinese vaccines. So, we might conclude the data was stolen by China, but the State Department's Global Engagement Center which tracks disinformation around the world says it is Russia that wants to discredit all the other vaccines.[8] We should consider that both Russia and China have vaccines and neither of them does as well in the principal world markets. It is easy to get lost in the science and forget that all we want is to have one that works and won't kill us.

When someone steals the data, alters the results, and give that data to the public, it is an influence campaign at work. Nobody pointed a finger at China or Russia to say they hacked the data. Proof of influence does not exist until we discover those hackers were hired, or acted on behalf of another country. We will eventually get around to it, but there is hardly any rush. There are indications that hackers stole and altered the data from Russian-language computers[9] but that does not prove Russian government responsibility. There are plenty of other campaigns that are more important to look at. We know influence campaigns exist, but we do not know how effective they are. Do people actually believe that Pfizer does not have a better vaccine than a vaccine from Russia or China? We can see the techniques being used, but governments shy away from investigating further to measure the effectiveness of those techniques. It almost seems like they do not want to know.

Influence campaigns, in this context, are government-sponsored programs often managed by intelligence services, to generate an effect on the core values or beliefs of select populations to influence policy decisions or act in a way beneficial to the originating sponsor.

There are some campaigns that are not government-sponsored, especially those of minor political parties, but my main purpose is to highlight ones that are. Those are the ones that document the conflict between ideas of governance between the main superpowers.

Other countries, and groups with regulatory authority over aspects of society, do not like the idea of foreign powers interfering with their manner of governance. They fight back by publishing supporting papers, sponsoring research, and personally influencing members of their own side. If they are not suppressed, they appeal to the public of their own country. So, countries that have these programs have to tread lightly to avoid arousing the opposition to their ideas. They have learned to hide how they go about influencing others. Unlike the fluttering of leaflets from the skies of Japan, these campaigns are hidden behind a wall of secrecy and deception.

The wrapper around these influence campaigns is covert operations— the kind that brings James Bond to mind. But while Bond had influence campaigns in his time, there were rigid controls on who might run them, and social media did not exist. To manage a program like this there are many special rules, mostly for our own protection. We would not want some rogue James Bond deciding it would be a good idea to start influencing China on his own. Every country worries about the same thing and has regulations similar to the U.S. restraints.

> In the US, covert action *is codified* in Title 50 *U.S. Code* as an activity or activities of the United States Government to influence political, economic, or military conditions abroad, where it is intended that the role of the United States will *not* be apparent or acknowledged publicly.
> It does not include:
>
> - activities with the primary purpose of acquiring intelligence, traditional counterintelligence activities, traditional activities to improve or maintain the operational security of United States government programs, or administrative activities;
> - traditional diplomatic or military activities or routine support to such activities;
> - traditional law enforcement activities conducted by United States government law enforcement agencies or routine support to such activities;
> - activities to provide routine support of any other overt activities of other United States government agencies abroad.[10]

The complication is that government agencies have both Title 50–like programs and Title 10–like programs. Covert and clandestine programs are separately funded. Most influence campaigns are covert and are under Title 50, but some have elements from both Title 10 and Title 50. For example, if the FBI is after a drug lord in the U.S. it has to do so in secret. It cannot drive around in the neighborhood in an FBI vehicle, so it must use cars and trucks that are licensed to look like other vehicles where they are driving. People who go into the neighborhood cannot wear suits nor appear to look like most FBI agents. Although the rules are somewhat different, the operations would normally look like covert programs from the outside. But where things become more complicated is when intelligence assets are being used covertly, under Title 50, to discover that a drug lord is, for example, hiding his assets in several companies owned and operated covertly by associates in another country. We might discover the rest of the drug operation using Title 10 funds with overt programs that do not hide their sponsorship. In the same way, every country makes distinctions between its intelligence operations and its clandestine operations. China can run several types of overt and covert programs that try to influence leaders in the U.S. using more than one type of overt and covert program:

China has a chain of Hong Kong organizations that start with China-United States Exchange Foundation (CUSEF), which also funds the United States Heartland Association and has links to the PLA [People's Liberation Army] sponsored front organization the China Association of International Friendly Contact. CUSEF's representative to the U.S. is Fred Teng who is also the president of America China Public Affairs Institute which promotes knowledge, understanding and more accurate perceptions about China within the U.S. government among key policy and opinion leaders.

It works closely with the Chinese Communist Party (CCP) and encourages a security partnership with U.S. anti-terrorism, cybersecurity and law enforcement.[11] This is just one example and there are hundreds more.

A view of this closer to the ground is given by a person who has a different view of influence. Indian Army Brigadier General (retired) Anil Gupta, on a thrilling assignment in the disputed territories between India and China, reminds us that the People's Liberation Army is, like most armies of the world, part of influence campaigns as well:

> Adhering to Sun Tzu's dictum of "winning without waging a war," the Communist Party's Central Committee and CMC has laid out the concept of "Three Warfares" (sanzhongzhanfa) as a set of codes for the PLA to conduct political warfare. Referred to as the "Political Work Guidelines of the People's Liberation Army," three warfares strategy entails: public opinion (media) warfare (yulunzhan), psychological warfare and legal warfare (faluzhan) with their main focus on; control of public opinion, psychological warfare to include blunting an adversary's determination, transformation of emotions, psychological guidance, collapse of (an adversary's) organization, psychological defense; and, restriction through law (legal warfare).[12]

This puts the PLA into almost anything connected to the business of warfighting, from manufacturing weapons to propaganda. Facing an enemy in a contentious area, Gupta tells the story of a video sent out right before the Indian Army had their Corp Commanders meeting:

> The video released by *Global Times* showed a duly grouped Task Force practicing "infiltration drills" operating at night crossing the border with switched-off lights and guided with laser to avoid detection, destruction of enroute threats by using drones, when approaching the target behind enemy lines a sniper team was deployed to destroy enemy spotlights, a fire strike team was used to neutralize the enemy's light armored vehicles with anti-tank rockets.
> Thus, the enemy's defenses were neutralized and thereafter the task force launched the final assault on the enemy headquarters, in which vehicle mounted infrared reconnaissance system was used to guide the troops to accurately lock on the targets and destroy them.
> The exercise as per the propaganda mouthpiece [Chin's] *Global Times* was done at 4700 meters simulating border with India but much farther in depth in the area of Tanggula mountains. The video had glaring mistakes apart from not

displaying the timeline, the troops participating in the exercise were wearing summer combat fatigues and not the extra winter clothing essential to survive at that altitude. Doesn't it remind the readers of some Hollywood thriller?[13]

Among countries, there is an undercurrent of activity on both the influence and counterinfluence that is usually out of sight. That is a good thing. We could have seen that video, glancing at the news of the day, but we would not know what it was really about. It was not prepared for a mass audience. It was probably not even seen by very many. This was the PLA doing what the Chinese central government directs. The video is part of something larger, the expansion of China into areas it has claimed for centuries that we have long forgotten—Hong Kong, Taiwan, and this forgotten region in India. It is conducted by military units, intelligence services, political parties, and social media.

What makes it successful is the inability of third parties to recognize such actions as attempts to influence the public in the target country. These programs can be as big as influencing a national election, or very limited, as the video was. It may have only been used once, but it is part of something bigger. The Chinese put time and effort into making this movie to influence the army they were facing across that border. That shows that they believe it is effective when all the parts are put together. China and Russia are expansionist countries, and this campaign helps them with that objective.

In a different part of the world, in 2020, Iran had a fire in a building at the nuclear facility in Natanz. Two hours after that fire was disclosed, some journalists, like Jyar Gol at the BBC, were notified via email that a group, the Homeland Cheetahs, were responsible for setting it. They claimed that the Iranian government had covered up previous acts committed by the group and could not do so this time. Iran's government denied this incident was anything other than an accident. Gol concluded that the author(s) of the email certainly knew details of the fire very quickly after it was disclosed, adding:

> But there is also the possibility that the email was an elaborate attempt to mislead us as to who was behind the attack, and could actually be the work of foreign agents posing as opponents of the regime in Iran.[14]

Do we know if the Homeland Cheetahs carried out the attack? Maybe, but since almost nobody had heard of them before, we may never find out for sure. The vast majority of people around the world do not care who did it. There may not even be such a group, but we know there was a fire, and very few people even care about that. Governments often claim terrorists, who can be stateless, carried out attacks, or just take at face value what they are given.

But what about a scenario where the delay in attributing the attack to a specific group or country then delays retribution or retaliation? When a government runs these kinds of influence operations (the attack, or the attempt to attribute it to a terrorist group), there are certain constants in how they are conducted. The limitations are tied to the inability to manage the kinds of campaigns being run. They are expensive and complicated, with hundreds of participants. Here are some of the characteristics of the programs:

1. A high-level leader of the sponsor country must approve the campaign, i.e., these kinds of activities create risks that many governments agencies are not willing to accept without cover from above. The more difficult the task, the higher the risk of exposure. The higher the risk of exposure, the higher up that risk is accepted.

2. They are covert, so the sponsoring country cannot be seen as involved. Covert programs may have both overt elements (the government or sponsor within the government is known) and covert.

3. Official press and government outlets change stories associated with these programs to fit a narrative, not necessarily the facts of a case. The first to respond has opportunities to influence that following stories lack. Some democracies have favored press outlets to release ideas to, but many national governments have their own media outlets.

4. Social media outlets and Internet trolls are used to repeat press and government stories and suppress counter-views.

5. Sometimes, specific individuals, for and against an issue, are targeted and statements issued in their names, and/or

6. Specific individuals favoring the sponsor's point of view can be targeted for directed persuasion or given special assistance to propagate their favorable ideas.

Spreading false or misleading information to masses of people is being done commercially by businesses that specialize in it and they have customers that are both commercial businesses and governments. So, parts of influence campaigns are being contracted out on a massive scale. That does not mean they are not managed by intelligence services because intelligence agencies contract out a good bit of their work.

> Our report shows misinformation has become more professionalized and is now produced on an industrial scale. Now, more than ever, the public needs to be able to rely on trustworthy information about government policy and activity. Social media companies need to raise their game by increasing their efforts to flag misinformation and close fake accounts without the need for government intervention, so the public has access to high-quality information.[15]

In 2019, the Chinese were accused of running an influence campaign about the demonstrations taking place in Hong Kong.[16] While the Chinese have denied doing any such thing, Twitter deleted over 900 accounts, and alluded to there being another 200,000 accounts that were part of a large government program to characterize the demonstrators as "cockroaches" (as they were labeled in tweets) and malcontents. The language used was consistent across platforms and public media. Twitter and Facebook also ran paid advertising characterizing the demonstrators the same way. Social media is making money on both sides of the politics. The ads were funded by state-owned media outlets in China. Google, late to respond, eventually found similar ads running on YouTube. Governments pay companies to run these campaigns and the social media corporations benefit.

China had an influence campaign pointed at President Trump that Graphika—a social media analysis firm—called "Spamouflage Dragon." It used mainly the same techniques employed by Russia in the 2016 U.S. presidential election.[17] Before the November 2020 election, Spamouflage began to attack the Trump campaign, but switched its target to Hong Kong shortly after. A combination of fictitious accounts on Facebook, Twitter, and YouTube have been taken down and reappeared, sometimes using the same named accounts, and the same terms, e.g., "cockroaches," to describe the demonstrators.[18] It is possible this is a Russian campaign attempting to look a Chinese one; they have used deception for centuries. Some covert programs are not as straightforward at trying to influence world opinion about a group of demonstrators. Some use smoke and mirrors.

The Yemen–Saudi Arabia conflict has been a continuing "proxy war" by Iran and Saudi Arabia, with both having "allies" fighting with them. Nobody liked the idea of missiles being fired from those Yemini territories. By June of 2019, Houthi rebels in Yemen had fired more than 135 missiles, many intercepted by Saudi missile defense systems. The Houthis enthusiastically referred to these missiles as "Houthi missiles," even telling Al Jazeera they were manufactured in Yemen and allowing the missiles to be photographed.[19] If the intelligence services of the world actually knew what missile manufacturing capability Yemen had, they did not say. If those services believed Yemen could make its own missiles, they might reduce interdiction of Iranian missiles going into Yemen. This kind of disinformation is aimed at a specific action to reduce interdiction of those missiles.

In fact, as almost all the intelligence services knew, these missiles were seized in raids on Sana'a in September 2014, so they were controlled but not manufactured by them. The Houthis claimed the early missiles were manufactured in Yemen, but they were really purchased from the Russians and North Koreans by the previous administration in the south of Yemen.[20] The Saudis tried to destroy them in a series of raids but were probably not entirely effective.

After that, Iran began supplying longer-range missiles, some made in China, and the myth that they were made in Yemen quickly dissolved. Some of the missiles that were shot down in Saudi Arabia were examined in detail and found to be made in Iran.[21] Some even had components stamped with the names of the companies that did the manufacturing, making it difficult to deny that these were Iranian missiles. So why maintain a myth of Houthi manufacturing of missiles with stamped parts clearly showing their manufacturing origin? The Iranians were either careless or thought identification would be difficult once a missile exploded. In any event, they were willing to accept the consequences of having the world know the missiles came from Iran. Covert influence operations are less successful when the lie that sustains them is not supported or can no longer be denied.

Covert operations often have multiple branches to hide their true purpose. In 2015, when the United States and many of its allies came to agreement with Iran on the development of nuclear weapons, the world took a deep breath and relaxed. It was foolish.

The U.S. knew what would happen if they did not stop progress on an Iranian nuclear program being conducted clandestinely. There was precedent for Israel responding on its own if no agreement was reached. Israel had twice before, in Iraq and Syria, destroyed nuclear programs before they became operational. Israel does not want nuclear weapons in the hands of its sworn enemies, which is understandable, though perhaps not quite a justification for some of the actions that were taken to meet that objective. There was room for a number of influence campaigns in this kind of situation.

In June 1981, Israel bombed the Osirak nuclear reactor being built for Iraq by French and Italian contractors.[22] That bombing was announced by Israel, thus not covert, but was influential nonetheless. However, that was the second bombing attack on the facility. The first, allegedly encouraged by the Israelis, took place September 30, 1980, a year after the Iranian Revolution during the Iran-Iraq War, with two aircraft the Israelis said were Iranian F-4 jets.[23] The lack of success of that mission dictated a follow-on in June. We might wonder how the Israeli military was able to persuade one of its declared, arch enemies to bomb another country during a declared war between Iran and Iraq.

On September 6, 2007, the Israelis bombed the nuclear facility at Al-Kubar in eastern Syria. Few outside Israel knew it was their jets that destroyed the building, and the Israelis did not claim the attack. Afterwards, there was speculation it might have been the Israelis, but not until March of 2018 did they admit it.[24] One might wonder how a country can keep such a secret for eleven years, yet suddenly give it up. They had a reason for breaking their silence—influence.

The Israelis kept the secret until they needed to warn Iran that they would not be allowed to develop a nuclear weapon. The Iran Nuclear Agreement with the Joint Comprehensive Plan of Action did not relieve Israel of its concerns about the development of a nuclear weapon.[25] But a deterrent strategy relies on a credible threat of retaliation. That stance is difficult to find credible if a country is denying it has ever acted as it threatens to. The Israelis were now saying, "We have done it twice and would do it again." That message would not be lost on Iran. It is a not very subtle reminder of the past, and a credible warning for the future.

But it was also a reminder of why Iran put some of its development capabilities in underground facilities, something they have admitted to the IAEA.[26] That lets Israel in on a secret, at the same time the rest of the connected world learns of the underground facilities. Israel makes its warning and exposes a few secrets kept by Iran. Each is trying to influence the ability of the other to take action. Exposure is an important element of disruption of influence campaigns. It makes these operations less effective.

Since 2003, the Israelis had been running a large, sophisticated, covert operation to stop Iran from developing nuclear weapons.[27] The operations included a range of activities, from international diplomatic pressure, economic sanctions, support to Iranian opposition groups, disruption of equipment and raw materials needed for production of the weapons, sabotage of production facilities, and the targeted assassination of key persons in the development program. The U.S. did not agree to participate in the assassinations. The objective was to influence Iran to stop its development of these weapons.

Israel kept quiet about the raid on Al-Kubar, but they were far from inactive during that seven-year period. Besides the killing of Iran's chief nuclear experts who were assassinated in broad daylight, in 2010, there was evidence that somebody was launching a cyber weapon that speeded up, then damaged a thousand or more centrifuges Iran was using to produce nuclear material. The U.S. and Israel had teamed up to produce this weapon as a part of a bigger covert program called, on the U.S. side, Olympic Games.[28] In 2020, a similar thing began. This time, Iran accused Israel of killing a scientist, Mohsen Fakhrizadeh, who founded the Islamic Republic's military nuclear program in the 2000s.[29] For Iran, Israel is always the enemy of choice, so there is trouble with attribution. It would not matter who actually killed Mohsen Fakhrizadeh, because the Iranians would believe Israel did it, even if they did not. The accuracy of attribution is important to countering operations on both sides.

The Russians have not changed very much from the days of the Cold War, but they have adapted their techniques to the Internet and social media. What makes that important is that the tools of persuasion lie in the ability to change the attitudes and beliefs of a few people who use the Internet to suit Russia's political positions. The Russians are not the best at this, and they are not as patient as the Chinese. Their haste makes exposure of their methods easier. To some extent, the Russians are learning new network attacks from the Chinese, but they started from a different place. In the 1990s they were the first and best at hacking, though they have less of a lead today. They can advance their trade much faster, even at the risk of antagonizing almost any country they try to influence.

We see similar things today with accusations that the Trump administration actively collaborated with the Russian government to favor Trump over Hillary Clinton in the 2016 U.S. presidential election, a matter now settled since the Mueller Report found little evidence the Trump campaign did so. There is little question the Russians did Donald Trump a favor in the 2016 election, but in 2018 it appears they hacked Republican websites and locations, something withheld from the public until 2020.[30] The U.S. Department of Justice (DOJ) found prosecutable crimes and indicted twelve Russian intelligence officers for interfering in the election, but no Americans were indicted on counts pertaining to dealings with Russian agents.

However, indictments are normally not the way governments react to this kind of incident. In that respect, the U.S. reaction was unusual. Intelligence services do not like to ask for prosecution of one another very often. There are exceptions when they are caught spying inside another country, but even that can be ignored on occasion. We did not find until months later that the Russians did spy—inside the U.S. Other indictments were coming, and the DOJ did not want to expose those before they were finished with the investigation. Indictments are sealed in part to protect other cases and indictments that may follow from them, one of the reasons somebody engineered an attack called Solarwinds on the U.S. court's computer system, attempting to steal those sealed indictments.

In February of 2018, thirteen Russian citizens were charged in the U.S. District Court of the District of Columbia with crimes related to their attempt to influence the election in 2016. Eleven of those charged were Russian government intelligence officers working for the Main Intelligence Directorate of the General Staff (GRU). The Russian government denies any involvement but there are indicators they ran covert operations using cover organizations, layered financial payments, and false names. The incredible story from the Russian government is "It wasn't us," while multiple sources say it is (Chapter 6).

The indictment claims the Internet Research Agency, LLC, which employs "hundreds of people ... is an organization engaged in operations to interfere with elections and political processes," and which, since 2014, carried out "interference operations targeting the United States.... Defendants, posing as U.S. persons and creating false U.S. personas, operated social media pages and groups designed to attract U.S. audiences. These groups and pages, which addressed divisive U.S. political and social issues, falsely claimed to be controlled by U.S. activists when, in fact, they were controlled by the defendants."[31] IRA had support staff that developed graphics, did translations and analytical support, search engine optimization and service for its internal equipment. Some of their targets were countries other than the U.S. and included domestic audiences in Russia. They combined their activities with outright spying to support their operations.[32]

The Russian press outlet *Russia Today* supported the other operations by publishing stories that reinforced stories that the IRA had developed. The DOJ filed a criminal complaint against Elan Alekseevna Khusyaynova, who is alleged to have been the chief accountant for IRA's Project Lakhta, a Russian campaign to influence the 2018 midterm election in the U.S.[33] She had billing for the operation in the range of $13 million and operational budgets of around $10 million a year.[34] Many transfers of funds were done with Bitcoin.[35] The complaint alleged that the operation's goal was to sow division and discord in the U.S. political system, including by influencing the 2018 midterm election through "information warfare against the United States," conducted through fictitious U.S. personas on social media platforms and other internet-based media. In one example they employed individuals in Ghana (without Ghana's direct knowledge), fed them news articles each day, and had them write comments on certain issues related to that topic. There was a matrix of types of responses they were supposed to make for each one.

Over the last four years, the Department has brought several other cases against Russian actors exposing influence activities. Eventually, the Russian operations became redundant. They use the same tactics, sometimes the same GRU agents, in different countries and different targets.

The Russians ran these operations covertly, but not very well. The DOJ indictments say they provided cover jobs for leaders of the IRA, so it appeared they worked in other places rather than at the IRA. They moved money to the operating locations in businesses created just for that purpose, or used existing subsidiaries of registered Russian companies not known to be associated with the IRA. IRA and GRU agents personally came to the U.S. under various pretexts to engage in spying that was used to support expansion of the program.

In this case, "Russian news services prepared a number of alternative explanations of what the IRA actually did and social issues, falsely claimed to be controlled by U.S. activists when, in fact, they were controlled by the defendants to Russia, as part of that denial."[36] The Russians denied it all.

But perhaps the most dramatic denial came from Vladimir Putin himself in Helsinki, Finland, after a two-hour private meeting with Trump in July 2018. Trump, in a live television broadcast, said Putin repeatedly denied that his government had been involved in interference with the U.S. election.

Trump said Putin privately stated his denial in a room where only interpreters were present. In a press conference afterwards, Putin publicly denied any interference.[37] But there have not been cover stories offered that would explain why it was another entity that did these activities, except for the minor references to the Ukraine taking those actions. In that respect, given the amount of evidence to the contrary, it is not wise for Putin to make that claim because it is not very credible. It does not help his cause to repeat incredible data points that can be easily refuted. That does not seem to bother him.

In a joint press release in October 2016 the Department of Homeland Security and the Office of the Director of National Intelligence on Election Security had this to say about the leadership aspect:

> Such activity is not new to Moscow—the Russians have used similar tactics and techniques across Europe and Eurasia, for example, to influence public opinion there. We believe, based on the scope and sensitivity of these efforts, that only Russia's senior-most officials could have authorized these activities.[38]

In October 2020, a sealed indictment was unsealed and filed in the Western District of Pennsylvania. They named six GRU agents as involved in

> …the destabilization of the Ukraine, Georgia (the country), France's elections, efforts to hold Russia accountable for its use of weapons-grade nerve agent on foreign soil, and the 2018 Winter Olympics after a Russian government-sponsored doping effort led to Russian athletes being unable to participate under the Russian flag.[39]

The complexity of Congressional investigations and their aftermath have not helped to produce conclusions that are satisfactory to either the right or the left of the political spectrum. The Russians are denying any such involvement and without their cooperation, none of the accusations in the indictments will ever be proven. But what the Russians have shown is an ability to cause disruption of the political process inside governments, by inserting their intelligence services into social media, political parties, the free press and governance processes. In order to stop them, we must do a little more than we have been. The EU, Australia, Southeast Asia, Canada, and the U.K. need to consider the same types of actions.

Over the past three years, there has been more interest in how these kinds of campaigns are being carried out. Brexit, and national elections in France, Germany, the Netherlands, the U.S. and Australia have all raised questions about outside interference, with each citing very similar tactics. Many reports have been written about the attempts at influence using the methods described, but few of those mention how successful any of them are. We can identify the techniques that are used, and their outcomes, but not their effectiveness.

It is almost like we are afraid to know.

2

Examples of Influence Campaigns

Governments try to prevent other countries from making nuclear weapons, attacking critical infrastructure like energy or telecommunications or deterring those kinds of attacks, sabotaging supply chains, stopping or reducing interference by a particular form of government, like the Chinese Communist Party, or using technical cyber-attacks to meet national objectives.[1] These are all subjects for influence, which are not acknowledged by the country trying to do them.

There are other campaigns that are narrower and focused on just a few people affecting policy in a given area, but they all start by identifying who to target. The Chinese might look for their U.S. groups to seek out people that are their friends. But China and Russia can find out through hacking. In 2018, the Czech Republic accused the Russians of hacking into their government network in 2016, looking at the positions of leaders on issues pertaining to their relationships with the Russians.[2] In 2020, the Czech security service told reporters a national security agency warned them that the Chinese hacked into their government network looking for Czech Republic leaders' opinions about issues sensitive to Beijing, such as Tibet, Taiwan and Hong Kong.[3] The world public only recently discovered some of those efforts are being made by foreign countries getting involved in influence campaigns in their countries, but some governments have known it for a long time.

Working in the U.S. Senate and House of Representatives, I had the opportunity to informally talk to many individuals trying to influence national policy. Most were lobbyists, who are a peculiar breed, under intense pressure to be successful and to stay out of the press for activities that could embarrass their customers or their own companies. They are very private people. I was a member of a lobbying group after I left the government and worked on draft legislation, point papers, press releases and issue papers. This was a lot of work for us because we had real jobs to do at the same time, and we did not have the experience that a formal lobbying group would have.

The real lobbyists clobbered us on the issues we were trying to influence, which were largely related to technology. They would show up at a working meeting of a bill mark-up. We would not know who they were, or where they were from, but they were representing someone with influence and their opinions seemed to carry more weight with the group. They watered down our drafts and deleted portions of what we had written. We really could not understand how this was happening and usually never found out the" why" of what was being done.

The professional lobbyists were considerably better than we were because they are paid to influence public policy. When they were not attending fundraisers or sitting in a congressman's office, they were more relaxed and open about their work. They knew everybody and what issues they specialized in. Influence campaigns are like that too.

Each of the major businesses I worked for had large staff functions on the Hill working on various technology issues; it is very hard work, and the hours were horrendous. One of the keys to this is that Congress has only a handful of members who know technology well. The rest rely on those experts and staffers who are the targets of those lobbyists. They know what motivates others to do what they want, and they do their best to do what is needed. They did not have to do it for everyone, just the ones who were the leaders in tech issues. Most of the ones I knew thought of their work the same way lawyers do about theirs, partly because most were lawyers. They represent their clients' interests and try to separate personal judgments about the issues they are asked to support. They did not necessarily personally agree with the positions they supported but they knew how to influence.

Countries are more complicated targets than political leaders. Governments often adopt different ways of going about their covert programs based on tradition, culture or history.[4] That is molded into today's foreign influence campaigns that are part advertising and marketing, news exploitation, diplomacy, and national security initiatives with an objective of countering policy of another country. Countries differ in those capabilities, so they have to adapt their influence to their strengths. They align with policies important to them, but not necessarily their allies. Their allies may be targets of their influence campaigns too. They may also be inwardly directed, supporting changes being proposed by policymakers inside their own countries. They can be, as we have seen, used to attempt to influence national elections of other countries, or their own. They involve influence campaigns, intelligence gathering, intelligence analysis, and intelligence operations that directly support the campaigns. Government and private businesses are both targets and participants.

So, we do not see the same kinds of campaigns coming from Russia and Iran as the Chinese would use. Influence campaigns are not going to be the same, so they are harder to recognize and categorize, though they have many similar techniques. They are harder to counter because they are so different. And we are almost always playing defense against their offense, which puts us at a disadvantage. In the last chapter I discuss some suggestions on how to change that.

Among all of the influence campaigns that were ever run, we probably know the most about the Russian campaign in the U.S. national election in 2016. Russian influence, and whether the Trump administration colluded with them to improve their effectiveness, were points of political dispute that in part led to the attempted impeachment of a sitting president, Donald Trump. We should have been focusing on 2018 and 2020 as a result.

Usually, it is not enough that the people being influenced are persuaded to adopt a particular view; they must act in a particular way, even if that means remaining neutral. The clouding of the existence of an obscure terrorist group may be enough in some cases, but not for a national election. Bigger operations are more difficult to hide, and probably will eventually be discovered. They are denied when they are.

> The actual term involves the creation of *plausible deniability*, the possibility of denying a fact, especially a discreditable action, without arousing suspicion; the method of achieving this.[5]

We have used this concept since the 1600s when privateers, who were employed by countries that did not want to be named, sailed the oceans attacking ships from other countries, but it became more popular in modern times.

The influencers involved in these kinds of operations know proof is hard to come by and denial is effective. Draw out the time it takes to accurately attribute the campaign to a specific country, invent new stories to change the narrative while the investigations continue, and the world waits to take action. Putin's Russia will deny even the most obvious attempts and will change their narrative as false ones are discovered. In his interview with Chris Wallace on Fox News, Putin was handed an indictment filed by the Justice Department that indicated which agents of the GRU were hacking the U.S. election systems. Putin put it down and did not read it. He then not only denied Russia was doing this, he claimed the indictment was a political document to undermine relationships between the U.S. and Russia. He said they did not have the resources to run this kind of operation in a country as big as the U.S.[6] The denials are too often incredible to observers outside Russia, but the Russians do not seem to care.

While influence campaigns are not new, Russia and China have refined them into mechanisms to disrupt the U.S. and influence the outcome of its elections. They have done much the same thing in Europe and, separately, elsewhere in the world. While they disrupt their rivals, they use the same techniques to manage their own policies through controls over their own populations. They are not alone in trying to influence policies of other countries, but elections are not the only areas targeted in their operations (see Chapter 6).

> We found evidence of organized social media manipulation campaigns in 70 countries, up from 48 countries in 2018 and 28 countries in 2017. Some of this growth comes from new entrants who are experimenting with the tools and techniques of computational propaganda during elections or as a new tool of information control. However, journalists, academics, and activists are also better equipped with digital tools and a more precise vocabulary to identify, report, and uncover instances of formally organized social media manipulation. Over the past three years we have been able to refine our language and search terms for identifying instances of computational propaganda, and we found that many countries have displayed elements of formally organized social media manipulation for the past decade. As a result, we suggest that computational propaganda has become a ubiquitous and pervasive part of the digital information ecosystem.[7]

Some of these operations have focused on social media, where Bradshaw and Howard excel.

The French recognize the 2016 campaign as one that benefited them in how they handled similar attempts against their national election the following year.[8] In that case, the Russians made tactical errors that reduced the influence of a large quantity of data stolen from Emmanuel Macron's presidential campaign. It was released so close to the actual election that the benefit of exposure was reduced.[9] Thus, the campaign was less effective as it might otherwise have been. In the same way, the Russians ran some U.S. influence operations after the 2016 election was over.[10] They might have been preparing for 2020, or they may just have not planned their operations very well. We will probably not know which for many years.

The French have a robust national intelligence capability and would have been able to identify those responsible for hacking Macron's campaign. Nonetheless, the U.S. told them where to look. In testimony before the Senate Armed Services Committee in 2017, Admiral Michael Rogers, director of the National Security Agency (NSA), said the U.S. had warned France about Russian activity surrounding the election.[11] Security firm Trend Micro also observed that the same group that hacked the U.S. Democratic National Committee were setting up a phishing domain on Microsoft servers used by Macron's party. The servers were running on software using Russian language configurations.[12] The exposure was so blatant, there was speculation at the time that Russia was trying to blame someone else for the attack by making it look like an unsophisticated attempt. In the post-election detailed analysis Jean-Baptiste Jeangene Vilmer described the operation this way:

> There was a coordinated attempt to undermine Macron's candidacy, through a classic 3-dimension information operation: (1) a disinformation campaign consisting of rumors, fake news, and even forged documents; (2) a hack targeting the computers of his campaign staff; (3) a leak—15 GB of stolen data, including 21,075 emails, released on Friday, May 5, 2017—just two days before the second and final round of the presidential election. This leak was promoted on Twitter by an army of trolls and fake accounts (bots) with the hashtag #MacronLeaks—even though none of the leaked documents actually came from Macron, only various sources related to him.[13]

While we might believe that these kinds of campaigns are new, just another part of the Internet Age, they are far from it. The Internet provides new levels of access to influencers, but there were people who attempted to influence policy in similar ways during the Russian revolution in 1917, long before there was any thought of electronic global communications.[14] Those campaigns were less effective and took a long time to play out, but they had roots that are growing today in influence campaigns run by national governments. Their actions must be affected in time for the campaign to be successful. The Russians should have learned from Chechnya, where they failed to engage with the local population, leaving the advantage to those they were most interested in influencing. That mistake cost them dearly and is not one they wish to repeat.[15] In spite of that, they made the same mistake in France.

We do not know how many influence campaigns there have been, or how many have been successful, because we are seldom able to see those that are not. In the last few years, it seems the Russians have been exposed more than other countries. We assume they are more active than others in running these kinds of programs, but that is not an accurate measure of the number of programs. The successful ones are seldom discovered or accurately attributed to a specific country. The difficulty is defining what success actually means.

> In July 2020, a statement by the Director National Counterintelligence and Security Center, William Evanina, said in his approved remarks that the intelligence community assess that China prefers that President Trump—whom Beijing sees as unpredictable—does not win reelection.[16] ... At the same time, Russia is using a range of measures to primarily denigrate former Vice President Biden and what it sees as an anti-Russian Establishment. This is consistent with Moscow's public criticism of him when he was Vice President for his role in the Obama Administration's policies on Ukraine and its support for the anti-Putin

opposition inside Russia. At the same time, Iran seeks to undermine U.S. democratic institutions, President Trump, and divide the country in advance of the 2020 elections. Tehran's motivation to conduct such activities is, in part, driven by a perception that President Trump's reelection would result in a continuation of U.S. pressure on Iran in an effort to foment regime change.[17]

In the U.S. we might believe that these campaigns were effective since former Vice President Biden did win, and the Chinese were said to favor his election; but we really have no idea whether the influence campaigns were effective, nor if the Chinese ran them. In Appendix A there is evidence of disagreement in the U.S. intelligence agencies about what China actually did. We know what tactics they probably used because they used them in other operations against other countries. We can only speculate on their success. The Russians are charged with a growing number of influence campaigns, but one of those operations was certainly not successful, possibly more. Only the Russians, Iranians and Chinese know, and they are not likely to tell us how they assess their own campaigns. That is very sensitive intelligence information that is a state secret.

There is one aspect that *only* the three countries know: the success of recruitment programs that ran in conjunction with the influence campaigns of 2016 and 2018, and how those were applied to 2020. Social media contacts, business leaders, affiliates of political parties, writers, the press, even potential spies or political allies can be used again in other operations. They keep their names and contact information until they are needed again. They stroke their egos, pay them to write articles that live on, and make plans for future engagements. The sponsors keep large quantities of collected information on their "friends." There is a hidden value in this that is difficult to quantify, but generally makes it easier to run another operation. The use and effect of these individuals is cumulative, since more and more of them can support the next operations.

Spying, and these kinds of information campaigns, use a different calculus to decide whether the costs are justified by the return; it used to be called work factor analysis. This looks at what it costs to collect a specific kind of information or achieve a broad objective. How much that information is worth to the country collecting it, a speculative prediction of information value verses cost of collection. These are really educated guesses because of the myriad of variables that go into evaluating the value of information and the costs, some of which are already sunk costs of operating an intelligence apparatus. It is a kind of pseudoscience to justify budgets.

There are many more examples of Russian influence programs, not because the Russians are more prolific, but because the Russians are not careful about how they protect their operations. Being discovered is not usually a sign of a successful program. We hear almost nothing about the influence campaigns of China or Iran, the two other countries the Director of National Intelligence said were trying to influence the U.S. national election. Those two countries have not been publicly identified with their operations, for reasons that are worth investigating. The Russians stomp around making lots of noise and get caught. The Chinese say: Don't look over here, and for some reason we do not.

The 2016 election was followed by an almost identical statement about the 2020 election by the U.S. ODNI.[18] But, neither the current statement, nor that of 2016–18, is very clear on what influence campaigns really are, nor the range of activities they are applied to. They are used for many more purposes other than to try to persuade voters to vote for a particular candidate. In fact, that is seldom the reason they are run. The Russian interference in the U.S. was well documented by several Congressional Committees, attributed to the Russian government (see Chapter 9), and private Russian businesses which were indicted by the U.S. Justice Department (DOJ). Those indictments tell us what the participants are alleged to have done and, until they are convicted these are just statements of what the U.S. Justice Department (the FBI agents testifying in these cases work for the DOJ) believe happened. It does not reflect all of what actually took place. There are many things that have happened that the FBI does not want to make public.

The FBI knows more than it can tell in open court and they do not need to tell the Russians everything they know to get a conviction. There is a tricky balance there. The DOJ has to look at what sources and methods (their investigative methods in this case) will be disclosed to help prove an element of the case. If they used an informant, they need to protect that person from being discovered. If they have evidence from surveillance or raw intelligence from the intelligence services, they might not want to say where the Russians were when that surveillance was conducted or what mechanisms were used to collect it.

In 2020, the election resulted in a number of accusations of voter fraud by the Trump campaign, which the U.S. Attorney General said was not significant enough to change the outcome of the election.[19] We do know from the indictment of the Russian principals that, in 2015, the Russians stole over 500,000 voter registrations (possibly more) from key battleground states in the 2016 election and hacked voter tabulation and validation equipment.[20] They improved their processes and tried again for the 2018 elections. They stole more and different types of information about parts of the voting infrastructure in each of the elections in 2016 and 2018. The 2016 remarks by the ODNI should have formed the outline of the types of responses to threats that were known at that time, but there is scant evidence of any response to China or Iran.

In my first book, *The Chinese Information War*, I looked at how the Chinese managed their own population and tried to influence the behavior of others. The Chinese are by far the best at this form of information war because they are willing to resource their approach in ways that make them successful, and hide their skills so their actions cannot be attributed to them. In other words, they usually do not get caught conducting influence campaigns that can be attributed to them. That is all the more reason for governments to look more closely at what they are doing. We seem to be reluctant to formally examine what the Chinese have done and continue to do, probably because of the people who benefit from them.

We see those differences visibly as China absorbs Hong Kong. China's form of government, managed by the Chinese Communist Party, helps them with that success, but the price the people of China pay for it is constraining for individuals in their country. In Hong Kong, politicians are replaced; dissent is stifled, and political representatives removed; leaders of street demonstrations are arrested and jailed; censorship is tightened; media is managed. There is a slow strangulation of those who do not favor CCP rule. It involves denigration of critics, limiting access to political processes, arrest and confinement, press controls, and occasionally, roughing up people who do not agree with them.[21] The actions they have taken creates a startling contrast between China and other free world countries.

Hong Kong was part of China before being seized in the Opium Wars in the 1840s. For China, that timeframe is fairly recent in their long history, so they have desired to recover it since then. The lease for Hong Kong was given in perpetuity originally, but China, after its revolution, was able to convince the British to take a 99-year lease, knowing that someday it would be returned. China then negotiated for the turnover, adding a clause in the Basic Law for the Hong Kong Special Administrative Region (SAR), which gave guarantees for Hong Kong's separate identity under the "one country, two systems" formula, lasting some 50 years.[22] As with other agreements made with China, the Chinese subsequently said they had a "different understanding" of the agreement and started to move on Hong Kong, culminating in the situation we have in 2021. Still, nearly 150 years has gone by since China lost Hong Kong and they eventually achieved their objective. The Chinese, if nothing else, are patient.

I have written previously of the Russians in Ukraine and the dislike shown by Vladimir Putin towards Hillary Clinton when she was U.S. Secretary of State, blaming her for disruptive demonstrations during his own election.

> With the protesters accusing Putin of having rigged recent elections, the Russian leader pointed an angry finger at Clinton, who had issued a statement sharply critical of the voting results. "She said they were dishonest and unfair,"

Putin fumed in public remarks, saying that Clinton gave "a signal" to demonstrators working "with the support of the U.S. State Department" to undermine his power. "We need to safeguard ourselves from this interference in our internal affairs," Putin declared.[23]

However, in the 2016 case, there was little proof that the Russian campaign in the U.S. benefited Donald Trump or affected Hillary Clinton's vote count. Special Counsel Robert Mueller's investigation was not very much help in this regard because it was not established to find out if Russian measures were effective in deciding the election. Nor did it investigate China or Iran, even though those campaigns were both known at the time. The report, and congressional reports which preceded it, point to methods and tactics of the Russians but not to effectiveness of the measures in influencing the popular vote. In the end, only the Russians know how effective their campaigns have been.

In the Ukraine, Russia ran a series of operations that included such things as direct attacks on candidates (including disfigurement), attempted sabotage of the vote aggregation computers, the moving of demonstrators from one place to another to simulate larger sentiment than existed, raising gas prices, distributing a flyer that said "Jews Must Register," billboards favoring annexation by Russia, harassing and jailing reporters, and many others.[24]

In Crimea, the Putin and the Russian Defense Minister denied that Russian troops were involved in military operations even though both participated in the preparations and deployment of Russian Special Forces.

> There were persistent (rather than plausible) denials of Russian operations, even in the face of photographic evidence and firsthand testimonials.[25]
> ...as battalions of Spetsnaz (elite infantry) units and Vozdushno-Desantnye Voyska (Airborne Forces or VDV) left their bases, while others were airlifted close to the strait separating Russia from Crimea.[26]

Similar to the Mueller report, a long-awaited study of Russian interference in British politics turned out to be very disappointing in its scope. The world press often mentioned this coming report as a look at Russian influence in the Brexit campaign vote, but the report notes the intelligence services were never tasked with doing that kind of analysis.[27]

The lack of documented evidence of effectiveness in both the U.S. and Britain is curious. Any result would be politically volatile and seems to have been avoided by the intelligence services and politicians who do not want to know how effective these programs really were, and who benefited from them. The final report was even delayed until after the election in Great Britain, yet it still said nothing in it related to the most important thing to many British citizens.[28]

Russian operations in the French election of 2017 are best known for failure to either influence the public or sway the national election.[29] The French capitalized on the many reports done in the United States about previous Russian influence campaigns and modified their own internal operations accordingly. For the Russians, that temporary setback will hardly be a deterrent in future endeavors. The U.S. had two years after 2016 to prepare for the 2018 mid-term elections. The tactics they faced in 2020 have yet to show success or failure in any form. The glowing reports from the FBI, Homeland Security, and CISA would make anyone skeptical of such an optimistic assessment, given their past performance in previous elections.

> "It's come a long way," said a second top leader, a senior Homeland Security official. "In 2018, a lot of this kind of effort was going on, and it's evolved substantially since then. Going back four years, we have substantially better positions at the federal level and the state level."
>
> The cyber-troopers of U.S. Cyber Command, which operates under the Defense Department, are able to "hunt forward" and surveil the work of Russian and other foreign cyber-operatives. That helps American authorities identify the targets they've selected within the United States, take note of their practices and even study the malware they use, which helps bolster cyber-defenses at home, officials say.[30]

Up until 2020, very little was written much about the most recent campaigns run by the Chinese or Iran, but the Brookings Institute did a broad report of the types of influence China attempted in Hong Kong, Australia, New Zealand and the U.S., citing a number of known methods the Chinese used. Those included "sizeable donations" to political parties, support to research institutions in those countries, harassment of the overseas diaspora, monopoly of Chinese-language media, and miscellaneous other types of interference.[31] Aside from the support to research and educational endeavors, few of these activities have been investigated in open sessions by congressional committees, nor has there been much interest from the news media in any of these campaigns.

Attorney General William Barr cited interference by the Chinese in domestic affairs but gave few examples of political interference in the U.S.[32] Often the Chinese effort looks like it is legal in the laws of the home country, even where it is not. Where China has proven effective is in providing money to political parties through businesses, while avoiding attribution to China, per se. The U.S. intelligence community cites the intentions of China to influence the U.S. elections, but does not indicate how that would be done, nor specifically who benefited. The Chinese hide those linkages well, but not so well that they could not be discovered by U.S. intelligence.

The Chinese and Russians both use front companies or shell corporations to appear legitimate. The U.S. has more anonymous shell corporations than any other country (see Chapter 9). President Xi himself was ensnared by the Panama Papers, which showed which family members and other Politburo members made use of them.[33] The leading politicians who do benefit from those donations usually ask what proof we have that any foreign country has given them money? In general, the most successful influence campaigns cannot be attributed to their sponsors, and in that the Chinese excel. They seldom leave proof.

Despite the occasional slip, both Russia and China have been changing their approach to improve effectiveness. The Russians adapted their previous efforts through what they called "...reflexive control, [...] designed to influence an adversary, with or without his or her knowledge, to make decisions and take actions that are predetermined and advantageous to the friendly side."[34]

As an example, during the McCarthy era, which was widely criticized for its oppression of individual rights, the Russians had been developing groups in the U.S. that favored their positions. These were called "front groups" and were formed by "trusted sympathizers who obey the party's orders to issue a call to form an organization targeting a particular organization and cause." There were several famous groups like this including the World Federation of Trade Unions, World Peace Council, Christian Peace Conference, and Generals for Peace and Disarmament. They populated the leadership of these organizations with people they controlled.[35]

> A former high official of the Communist Party of the USA provided a guide to establishing front groups. Trusted sympathizers who obey the party's orders were directed to form a nucleus that issued a call to form an organization targeting a particular audience and cause. The nucleus included Communist Party members, clandestine members of the Communist Party, and individuals willing to accept party discipline and instructions....
>
> Among what is called "agents of Influence" are people specializing in managing and manipulating certain areas of public discussion like journalists, writers and artists who are persuaded to promote particular policy positions favorable to the Russians.[36]

In the case of the Russian influence campaign in 2016, the methods have expanded to technical support for imagery, signage, hacking, computer support, and funding for salaries of other types to include meeting and function planning.[37] The U.S. DOJ indictment in 2016 mentioned instances of support that took place in 2014 and 2015, indicating the U.S. government was aware of their operations much earlier than was publicly disclosed, which is not surprising. It was this information the French benefited from. This led to criticism of President Obama for failure to take action to prevent further abuses.[38] A Senate Intelligence Committee report is quite clear that the Obama Administration did not respond with sanctions until after the election of 2016 was over. The claim in the report is that

...senior administration officials told the Committee that they assessed that their warnings to Russia before the election had the desired effect, and that Russia undertook little to no additional action once the warnings were delivered.[39]

So, while the Obama administration might have believed it was effective in curbing the Russians with warnings, in retrospect, that assessment was wrong. The Russians just hid those operations a little better.

Note that these areas combine cyber operations with economic and political warfare. The Chinese Belt and Road Initiative is almost exclusively about using these three together. The cyber operations determine which countries and leaders are the best candidates, the economic operations build infrastructure and the leverage of repayment of loans influences how the countries respond to political positions the Chinese favor. The Chinese even influence equipment standards, then include those in Belt and Road agreements. The Chinese loan money for massive infrastructure projects built with Chinese labor, companies and technology. They leverage the inability of some countries to repay these loans or accept property, like ports, in exchange. That provides influence over the country's leadership and trade infrastructure assets for China.[40]

What is more important though is that sponsor countries seldom evaluate the success or failure in objective ways. Carrying them out is often not science, but the investment of large sums of money can be justified only on the presumption that the programs are successful. Success then becomes defined by the ones running the operations and they have a vested interest in being able to say they are successful. Objective measures may say otherwise. Since these programs are often state secrets, they cannot be openly evaluated. There were no unclassified reports of how effective the Russian campaign was to influence voters in 2016 in any of the countries the Russians were said to be targeting.

On the other hand, the same can be said for the success or failure of U.S. operations to counter these programs is governed by the same logic. We know very little about what the U.S. did to counter the aggregate of programs run against Russia, China, and Iran, let alone how successful they might have been. If there were any such things, at least they are secrets that have been kept. When the Brooking Institute says the Chinese were pouring money into elections, and the U.S. intelligence services say they favored Joe Biden in that election, there should have been an investigation into where the money went. We see almost nothing of the kind in the news media, or public briefings to congressional oversight committees. There were no leaks to favored press outlets.

Part of the difficulty for any country is the complexity of these kinds of operations, which generally leads to their being compromised. I was involved in many covert programs over the years, and all of them relied on not being discovered, even though almost all eventually will be. We spend a great deal of time protecting aircraft like the SR-71 so our adversaries cannot see it while it is being produced, but we know it will not take long after it flies for someone to find it and start looking at what it can do. Accidental discovery before a program is intended to be made public must be planned for and publicly explained, usually with plausible cover stories. We all know the stories of night flights of weather balloons being mistaken for really fast airplanes when intuition should tell us the two are dissimilar enough to not be confused. Even with cover stories, there are many ways that covert programs fail to remain a secret.

In complex covert programs, there are so many associations of people, businesses, political leaders, and other entities that it becomes difficult to hide attribution and protect the components from public disclosure. There are many paper-thin stories tying them all together. Today, there is too much information on the Internet that exposes associations. Not all online communication is accurate, but that seldom matters to those running these programs. A government or contracted participant in one of these programs cannot publicly deny false information, nor confirm correct information being spread by journalists, politicians, or social media. National security policy in every one of these countries prohibits the discussion of references to classified national security programs (state secrets).

These types of campaigns are uniquely human-centered and unlike many military operations to influence command and control of a battlefield, these have broader objectives. Informants and spies upset the linkages between the delicate web of campaign activities, putting sunlight on things growing in darkness. Insiders turn against people they once worked with and upset the best of plans. Whistleblowers inside government often start their own kind of trouble. Politicians talk too much, trying to score votes and gain support for constituents. On the other hand, there are many willing participants who may not even know they are part of an influence campaign. They join groups that were formed, funded and managed by campaign participants.

We have several modern examples of how these operations are discovered, but the best known is the Russian meddling in the U.S. presidential elections. Some of Project Lakhta's operations were conducted in 2015 before they were discovered.[41] Some were conducted up until 2018. The Russians have to be concerned about what is known about their operations after they were discovered.

There are many contrary arguments that qualify success in different ways, but exposure and attribution are powerful arguments against the benefits of any programs being realized. Discovery creates its own reaction by those who must make decisions about the subject of the influence campaign. If we discover the Chinese are supporting a particular political candidate by illegally funneling money through U.S. support groups, the candidate will suffer from the association with criminal activity, even if he or she does not know about it.

When Fox News' Chris Wallace asked Speaker of the House Nancy Pelosi about the dichotomy of reporting, she said the Chinese side of interference was "not significant" but the Russian activities were.[42] Pelosi was opposed to the Trump administration, which Russia was said to favor, and downplayed the Chinese influence campaign favoring her political party. The Chinese campaign was never investigated to the extent that Russia's was so she could not say if it was significant or not.

Weeks before the U.S. national election in 2020, a "foreign interest" sent emails to the Democrats from a pro-Trump group called the Proud Boys, claiming that it was acceptable to vote in ways that are illegal under U.S. law. There were some experts who claimed the individuals were selected from voter registration information similar to what the Russians stole during the 2016 election, and were sent to disrupt the vote if voters associated the letter with Trump's team.[43] This used to be called a "dirty trick," but when nations do it they use intelligence services to steal or solicit voter rolls and political affiliations, then target voters directly. It is no longer an internal political matter.

3

The Doctrinal Dimension

In a hierarchy of complexity, influence campaigns since the 1980s have been the lowest level of a broader subject called political warfare, with political warfare at the top. Just below that is a more limited aspect, information war. The difference was posed by Linda Robinson and Todd Helmus, et al., from RAND Corporation:

> The techniques Russia, China and Iran employ are a subpart of a larger Information War is called Political Warfare. While Information War was a military creation, Political Warfare was not part of it, thus not mentioned in that doctrine. Political warfare in modern times was defined by George Kennan as: "...the logical application of Clausewitz's doctrine in time of peace. In broadest definition, political warfare is the employment of all the means at a nation's command, short of war, to achieve its national objectives. Such operations are both overt and covert. They range from such overt actions as political alliances, economic measures (as ERP—the Marshall Plan), and 'white' propaganda to such covert operations as clandestine support of 'friendly' foreign elements, 'black' psychological warfare and even encouragement of underground resistance in hostile states."[1]

These are very subtle differences, and difficult to separate. Some researchers would define all such aspects as political warfare and some, particularly those in the military, would say it was information war. My first lesson in drawing this distinction was explained as information war by an intelligence analyst working on targeting for the Strategic Air Command. He said it like I would understand it and I didn't want to show my ignorance by asking him what that was. It brought home the complexities of dealing with a subject spread across so many disciplines.

For many years, we had meetings on information warfare without being able to clearly identify what made it up. We have a similar problem with the integration of artificial intelligence (AI) in modern information war. There is no agreed upon definition of AI or IW, yet we discuss it in books and business applications as if everyone understood what makes them up.[2]

From those early days, wherever one sat, information war seemed simple, but that was because we seldom took stock of the whole thing, or accurately defined it. At that time, it was extremely sensitive and rarely talked about in the press. We have few secrets like that anymore.

In the early 1970s, I talked to an official who had the job of deciding which enemy targets were going to have nuclear weapons dropped on them. Almost every one of these people took their jobs seriously, since the number of people who would die in a nuclear explosion would be massive.

My unsolicited idea was to bomb Moscow first, since we believed the Russians were our main enemy and were vulnerable to direct attack on their command-and-control structures. They were centrally managed and reliant on their command structure to maintain their combat capabilities. Cutting off the head of such a centralized system seemed to be simple logic.

I was young.

The targeting guy said, "OK, we bomb Moscow, and they bomb Washington, so then where are we?"

Too easy, I thought. "Well, it seems like we leave it to the dispersed locations to carry on the rest of the war and bomb all of their targets. We have pretty good capabilities there and we should win."

"You would be right if bombing targets was all there was to it. Who is going to surrender if both of the capitals are gone, and half their infrastructure is blown away?" That caught me off guard because I thought of war in terms of the efficient use of weapons to cause more damage than the enemy could. But surrender is a political decision that requires damage assessment, political will, and command authority to negotiate conditions. Those are all things that require information and some communications that cannot be denied to the enemy or the war will continue long after it could have been over.

The longer he talked, the more I knew that war was not just about who dropped the most nuclear weapons or killed the most people. It was more complicated than that. If we want to win, we have to have a way for the enemy to digest information about damage to their military capability, assess their political and military response, while communicating with someone with sufficient authority to decide when and how to stop the war or continue it until it meets certain objectives. It might even be possible to influence those individuals before the fact of a war. It is sometimes hard to imagine nuclear war under any circumstances, but these kinds of decisions would be made under extreme pressure and in terrible operational environments. Most everyone involved with nuclear weapons thinks it is better to not use them in war.

In a way, information war and political war are much the same. In their current form, they are more about preventing traditional forms of war than propagating them. The early aspects of information war come from military doctrine almost 40 years old, from a time when computer networks were just being formed and the Internet was not yet a dream. In those days it was seen as an augmentation of conventional military warfare. When it began to form, very few computers were in the hands of private individuals, most of them were centralized, and were huge by today's standards. Given those conditions, it is not hard to imagine how the doctrine of information war came to use computers to attack other computers or target professionals to put computer centers on their target list.

By the early 1990s, U.S. doctrine pertaining to information war was a jumble of things that already existed in the military, adapted to the Information Age.

1. *Economic Warfare: the manipulation of information exchanged in trade (either denial or exploitation) as an instrument of state policy.* China is the best example of a country that manipulates its economy to the disadvantage of other countries. China claims it has an economy that is better prepared and competitive, but as a matter of practice, it steals other technology from countries, licenses it and enforces patents based on stolen ideas. In *The New Cyberwar*, I described the methods used, and they have only become more brazen in the years since.

2. *Command and Control Warfare (C2): the use of conventional or enhanced methods to attack the enemy's ability to issue commands and exchange them with field units, while protecting that of our own forces.*

3. *Electronic Warfare: the use of specialized methods to enhance, degrade or intercept radio, radar, or cryptography of the enemy.*

4. *Intelligence-based Warfare: the integration of sensors, emitters, and processors into a system that integrates reconnaissance, surveillance, target acquisition, and battlefield damage assessment.* For two years I worked on a program that was doing this kind of integration. It was amazing, and at times amusing, to see so much parochialism among the intelligence services. We overcame it by having the deputy directors of the larger intelligence services meet every month to resolve problems as they came up. They cut through the red tape, kept the program going in spite of resistance on many fronts.

5. *Psychological Warfare: the use of information to affect the perceptions, intentions, and orientations of others.* The Russians have promoted their capabilities in this area particularly in Europe and the U.S. combining aspects of cyberwar with specific targeting of individuals in political and social leadership positions. In 1977–78, a Russian Special Operations unit was assigned to assassinate Afghan helicopter pilots trained in the U.S.[3]

   6. *Cyberwar: the use of information systems against the virtual personas of individuals or groups.* The Russians used two methods during the 2016 U.S. election: (1) first, they used the names of existing, known individuals and published communications in those names, without the knowledge or participation of that person[4] (2) They invented personas that claimed to have expertise and used those to support or undermine Hillary Clinton.[5] Cyberwar, for a time had begun to replace information war as a term of reference, but the Russian use of the term, discovered during the investigation of election tampering, has brought the term "information war" back to into vogue.

   7. *Hackerwar: the use of techniques, like specialized software, to destroy, degrade, exploit, or compromise information systems, both military and civilian.*

Information war has changed considerably since these doctrines were written, with economic warfare elements becoming much more important. Indeed, we can see how these same elements are used today as part of broader programs using different elements of information war to achieve objectives. The new version of information war is more refined, subtle, and even less oriented to military use. At a simple level, this kind of war means both the control and use of information to manage the will of people, mostly using the various military-defined aspects of information war while doing it. Those targets are domestic audiences and foreign ones.

   Today, many of the warfare aspects have been dropped and overtaken with political motivations generally changing the definition the way the Congressional Research Service did in March 2018:

> While there is currently no official U.S. government definition of [Information Warfare] IW, it is typically conceptualized as the use and management of information to pursue a competitive advantage, including offensive and defensive efforts…. In this sense, IW is a form of political warfare, where targets include a nation state's government, military, private sector, and general population.
>
> Taking place below the level of armed conflict, IW is the range of military and government operations to protect and exploit the information environment. It consists of both offensive and defensive operations: the protection and assurance of one's own information (information security), and information operations to advance interests. It is conducted not only in crisis, conflict, and warfare in the operational sense, but is ongoing in peacetime as well. Whether attacking government agencies, political leadership, or news media in order to influence public opinion or to compel decision makers to take certain actions, ultimately the target of information warfare activities is human cognition….[6]

Note that some of areas of information war are totally computer on computer, where human beings cannot react soon enough to be of any benefit. We now talk about information war in a broader context, closer to the meaning of political war. The Chinese method of stealing private information from wide areas like health care, insurance providers, banking and financial institutions and government records to identify specific individuals in a population and using artificial intelligence to directly target individuals may be effective, but we will never know until we investigate the Chinese campaigns to find out. But it is a broader approach that includes theft of proprietary and privacy information, protection of domestic infrastructures, supply chain manipulation, and both the protection of voting infrastructures and vote totals and other interference in the country's political processes. Countries use collected information to bribe, extort or expose people who do not favor their positions. Information war is now more about information which can be manipulated, analyzed, and used for purposes never thought of by the people who originally collected it. These totally different data points are related in the concept of political war.

China has a broader view of public opinion than Russia, more suited to political warfare. Doctrinally, the Chinese believe in public opinion warfare:

> ...the first to sound grabs people, the first to enter establishes dominance (*xian sheng duoren, xianru weizhu*). Essentially, the objective is to establish the terms of the debate and define the parameters of coverage.... Chinese military writings emphasize the importance of influencing global public opinion so as to coerce opponents into compliance without having to go to war and to influence an enemy's leadership, domestic population, and military in the event of conflict, as well as to garner international support.[7]

But the Chinese have taken the idea and applied it to the integration of the economic, diplomatic, military, and commercial operations in China that are centrally managed and messaged as if it were under the direction of a single person. Every aspect of communication to publics is directed, managed, and loosely coordinated. Guidance is issued daily. Ultimately, the goal is to persuade a global audience of opinion leaders to follow a path set out by China. They wear down opponents that way.

We should remember that these are government actions, done overtly and covertly, to influence public policy, sometimes even the policies of the countries running these operations. Usually, if they work as they are supposed to, those influenced by these actions will never know who did them, nor what was done to influence their targets. What has made the Russians infamous for their actions is their *inability* to do covertly what a few countries do very well. In short, the Russians get caught when a few others do not. That is a measure of their programs, but not one that defines their success.

They do, however, learn from their mistakes. In October 2020 the National Security Agency and MI-6 issued similar warnings about a newly uncovered tactic the Russians were using.[8] Their intelligence service was hacking Iran's elite hacking unit and using those links to attack the Middle East and Great Britain. So, do we know that Iran's influence programs are on the rise, or is it the Russians using Iran's network links? Matthew Rosenberg, a reporter for the *New York Times*, speculated that the U.S.:

> And those charged with protecting American elections face the same central challenge they did four years ago: to spot and head off any attack before it can disrupt voting or sow doubts about the outcome.[9]

The Russians began moving their attack servers to locations in the U.S., so they were less likely to be discovered by the National Security Agency, which is prohibited from monitoring U.S. entities. They "closed down" or repurposed its state-run intelligence assets, such as public servers carrying their internal correspondence. (Russian Intelligence Service) Cozy Bear webservers "went dark," i.e. moved their operations to other networks and used new operators identified with different names, including their host websites. They moved their Internet trolls to encrypted sites where they are more difficult to identify and track.[10]

The Russians referred to their operations in the U.S. national election of 2016 as information warfare.[11] This kind of warfare runs counter to military visions of what war is and how it is to be fought, though it has been part of the doctrine of military forces since the mid–1990s. As it is practiced today, it is almost unrecognizable from the founding principles that brought it to where it is now.

What the Russians called information warfare was not exactly new to the governments of the world, but Russia's application of it has helped change the definition from the one we had in 1980, and the one the Congressional Research Agency has now. Today Iran, Russia, China, North Korea and a host of others, like Venezuela, and even the Catalonia region of Spain, have joined in some aspects of this concept.[12] It is no longer an exclusive club, though the degrees of participation vary widely, as does the understanding of the complexities of this kind of war, which is more the influence of human beings than kinetic attack.

An earlier study by Bradshaw and Howard notes influence campaigns run by a handful of countries in 70 different target nations.

> Private firms increasingly provide manipulation campaigns. Over the last year, we found forty-eight instances of private companies deploying computational propaganda on behalf of a political actor. Since 2018 there have been more than 65 firms offering computational propaganda as a service. In total, we have found almost US $60 million was spent on hiring these firms since 2009.[13]
>
> … Facebook and Twitter attributed foreign influence operations to seven countries (China, India, Iran, Pakistan, Russia, Saudi Arabia, and Venezuela) who have used these platforms to influence global audiences.[14]

None of the free world countries like the UK, the U.S., France, Germany, Israel, Canada, Australia—without exhausting a longer list—are mentioned, yet we should assume even these have some influence campaigns. Vladimir Putin was said to be furious at Hillary Clinton because he blamed her directly for street demonstrations in Moscow criticizing his government for rigging elections in 2011. Either Putin was misinformed, or the U.S. had operations of its own.

> Putin fumed in public remarks, saying that Clinton gave "a signal" to demonstrators working with the support of the U.S. State Department; to undermine his power. "We need to safeguard ourselves from this interference in our internal affairs," Putin declared.[15]

From a person like Putin, having a great deal of experience with manipulation of similar types of activities in the Ukraine, Estonia, Georgia and elsewhere, we might surmise his ability to know how to run this kind of operation. If it takes one to know one, he was certainly capable of that identification.

The obvious problem with identification of countries with influence campaigns is that there is really no way for researchers to know that the attribution to a given country is correct in these kinds of activities. The operations are largely covert, and countries go to some lengths to hide the country of origin or give false clues that cast blame on another country. The behaviors might be observed in many countries but are spoofed by governments that know how to hide their true identity.

The Russian influence in the 2016 U.S. election were far from that sophisticated. Fake news outlets also popped up in many on-line venues and they were not all for political gain. A few were in it for the money. Fake news pays as the citizens of Veles, Macedonia, have come to find out. Several sites have been tracked to this small town and a few of the sites employ 11–14 writers to keep them producing. They make money from advertisers who measure their worth by mouse clicks. These were mostly supporters of President Trump and occasionally Hillary Clinton, but their allegiance was far from political, playing instead to the value of each article they could produce.[16] This type of activity certainly helped the Russians with their objectives, even if monetary goals and no political affiliation was at its root.

The Russian motives were less entrepreneurial, supported positions on both sides of contentious issues through social media, press reports, and the release of sensitive information obtained by theft. In an unclassified assessment of Russian involvement, the Director of National Intelligence (DNI) said:

> "We assess Russian President Vladimir Putin ordered an influence campaign in 2016 aimed at the U.S. presidential election. Russia's goals were to undermine public faith in the U.S. democratic process, denigrate Secretary Clinton, and

harm her electability and potential presidency. We further assess Putin and the Russian Government developed a clear preference for President-elect Trump. We have high confidence in these judgments.

We also assess Putin and the Russian Government aspired to help President-elect Trump's election chances when possible, by discrediting Secretary Clinton and publicly contrasting her unfavorably to him. All three agencies agree with this judgment. CIA and FBI have high confidence in this judgment; NSA has moderate confidence."[17]

In his most recent statements about the Russians, the ODNI pointed out that there were three countries, maybe more, that were involved in trying to influence the outcome of the U.S. mid-term elections in 2018.

"Russia, and other foreign countries, including China and Iran, conducted influence activities and messaging campaigns targeted at the United States to promote their strategic interests."[18]

President Trump posted an accusation on Twitter that China was manipulating U.S. midterm elections by taking out advertising in the *Des Moines Register*, mostly pointing out the impact of U.S. tariffs on Iowa farmers. When the U.S. increased tariffs in August of 2019, the Chinese stopped buying many of the U.S. agricultural products.[19] This was a decidedly pointed act against part of the political base in the Midwest of the U.S. and certainly constituted interference in the internal affairs of the U.S. The Chinese are quick to point out that the U.S. should not interfere with such internal issues as the Uighurs or human rights in Hong Kong, but should consider whether this kind of interference was good for China.

What complicates research into this kind of activity is that, even in the face of overwhelming evidence, every country denies its own actions, and sometimes the actions of allies who cooperate with them. But we can look to its statements by other governments, and investigations, after the fact, to follow a series of events.

Over time, it becomes more difficult to deny these actions, though many governments still maintain the fiction because they can. For example, it took almost two years to confirm that the Reagan administration had an agreement to supply small arms to the Contra rebels trying to overthrow the Nicaraguan government. Congress had passed legislation that limited support for the rebels, even though the Cubans and Russians gave arms to the government the U.S. was trying to undermine. That congressional legislation was bypassed through an agreement to allow funding of the rebels—on the condition that the aid was not used to overthrow the existing regime.[20] It was a ridiculous restriction that was impossible to enforce.

Governments are always trying to get their stories disseminated before any opposing positions can be announced; it is often obvious that not all stories are consistent. In one simple example, Mohammed Reza Kolahi

Samadi, a mild-mannered electrician from Iran, in 2015 lived in Almere, a city near Amsterdam. By local accounts, Samadi was killed by two men hired by Naoufal Fassih, a notorious gangster.[21] We all have ideas about what happens to people who get involved with organized crime, unintentionally or through business connections and go on to get killed. We can relate to why and how that might happen.

Although Samadi's wife told the police on the way to the hospital that the Iranian government had been behind the attempt, to the casual reader, the story could have easily fit into that "killed by organized crime" index. Except for Dutch investigators, few people remembered, or knew about, her comments about Iran.

Unfortunately for the Iranians, the Dutch are fairly good at getting their versions of stories in the press, though sometimes slowly, and this case was not as it appeared to be. In 2018, the Dutch expelled two Iranian diplomats for hiring the killers, indicating they suspected more than they were letting on in 2015.[22] The Iranians were part of something more than the killing of this one man. They had killed a number of dissidents in several countries, using criminal gangs for that purpose. We might remember that Iran attempted to do the same thing to the Saudi ambassador to the U.S. several years earlier, using gangs in Mexico.[23] The Dutch put it all together and linked several cases to Iran. Iran denied repeatedly that its Quds Force had anything to do with this attempt. We now have a new index: people killed by the Iranian government using criminal gangs as front organizations. Iranian denials carry less weight when so many stories of a similar type can be pieced together.

Sometimes, very complicated stories can seem obtuse to the casual reader. This characterizes the case of Huawei Technologies Co., Ltd., a Chinese multinational telecommunications equipment and consumer electronics manufacturer, headquartered in Shenzhen, Guangdong, China. What is unique about the story of Huawei is the basis for its classification as a Chinese state secret. If China required Huawei to do the kinds of things that the U.S. suggests they are doing, they would make that fact a Chinese state secret that very few in China, or anywhere else, would know about. At the same time, the U.S. efforts to expose Huawei are U.S. state secrets. None of these secrets should be made public, but they have been. I call this the dichotomy of secrets: We talk about things in public that we know to be secrets that should not be talked about in public. We do that because some secrets must be made known to have the influence required to make policy changes, especially where other countries or particular political groups have to make those changes. In the case of Huawei, countries have cut their purchases of their equipment because they have new information about that equipment. We do not know specifics about what that new information is because that was never made public, but we do know that the U.S. government has some facts about Huawei that the public does not.

In May of 2019, President Trump signed an Executive Order, widely described in the press as a ban on Huawei equipment in the U.S. infrastructure. In fact, the EO does not mention Huawei at all:

> "I further find that the unrestricted acquisition or use in the United States of information and communications technology or services designed, developed, manufactured, or supplied by persons owned by, controlled by, or subject to the jurisdiction or direction of foreign adversaries augments the ability of foreign adversaries to create and exploit vulnerabilities in information and communications technology or services, with potentially catastrophic effects, and thereby constitutes an unusual and extraordinary threat to the national security, foreign policy, and economy of the United States. This threat exists both in the case of individual acquisitions or uses of such technology or services, and when acquisitions or uses of such technologies are considered as a class."[24]

For over 10 years, the U.S. government has restricted access to Huawei in the U.S., especially in technology areas it was trying to purchase (see *The Chinese Information War*). Those restrictions have been gradually ratcheted up, even while Huawei denies spying for the Chinese central government. What makes the U.S. suspect that Huawei was involved in intelligence collection? Michael Hayden, former director of the National Security Agency and the Central Intelligence Agency:

> "I stand back in awe at the breadth, depth, sophistication and persistence of the Chinese espionage campaign against the West.... God did not make enough briefing slides on Huawei to convince me that having them involved in our critical communications infrastructure was going to be okay. This is not blind prejudice on my part. This was my considered view based on a four-decade career as an intelligence officer."[25]

Most of the information needed to assert that Huawei is acting for the Chinese government is in the public domain. Certainly, people like General Hayden, who has had access to some of the most sensitive secrets about China, are only one aspect of the belief structure surrounding Huawei. Another is media coverage, such as David Sanger's March 2014 article in the *New York Times*, written after Edward Snowden disclosed the existence of a U.S. program, to find out if Huawei was working for the People's Liberation Army.[26] So, some might wonder if Huawei was doing that. NSA is not saying.

4

The Human Dimension

The ability of any country to influence human cognition is not as simple, or effective, as many believe them to be. We are not sheep. We are not stupid. Eighty-six percent of the world is literate and can read and understand what is being said to them.[1] If they lived in countries that allowed them freedom to choose a course and pursue it, they could prove their independence. That seems to be the catch for much of the world's people.

What we think we know about policymaking is not correct, and influence campaign sponsors know it. The person in the street may sometimes wonder why public sentiment can favor actions like immigration controls, exiting the European Union, or background checks on gun purchases in the U.S., yet politicians fail to bring bills that favor those controls or vote with public sentiment when they are brought. Lobbyists are certainly part of that, but not all of it. We may believe that what the public favors will eventually become policy, but research in policy formation indicates that any apparent connection between policy and the preferences of the average citizen "may be largely or entirely spurious."[2]

The blunt truth about who influences policy, from Gilens and Page:

> The central point that emerges from our research is that economic elites and organized groups representing business interests have substantial independent impacts on U.S. government policy, while mass-based interest groups and average citizens have little or no independent influence.[3]

Those lobbyists did know what they were doing. As discouraging as that may be, it certainly expresses our frustrations with government inaction. What governments and lobbying groups have in common is that they push narratives that fit their political beliefs into packages of products that are used to reinforce positions they favor. They often do try to influence large groups, but usually only to pressure others who have the ability to write policy or proclaim it. The individual no longer has the same ability to influence a policy by organizing people of the same policy persuasion and pushing that agenda towards a political solution. It is possible they never had that ability. Social media, which touts this capability as a given, makes us believe in "influencers" who get paid for publishing, may be overrated as a mechanism to move changes in policy. We want to believe that our opinions count, but we may be disappointed to find out how often they do not, no matter how many Facebook friends we might have.

Our perception of how government decisions about national policy are made is therefore wrong in dangerous ways. The influence of a few policymakers can make a big difference. In that respect, those influencers understand how to use that to make money. Russia and China have learned to identify and target these specific individuals and influence them in ways advantageous to themselves. This is something we know about in a more abstract way.

The first element of an influence campaign requires the country carrying out a program to disrupt the stability of related core beliefs and values of a small part of the target population. These two things, and their stability within a population, define *public opinion*.[4] However that kind of disruption is not easy, and it can easily backfire on those trying it.

Philip Converse, in 1964, wrote a widely cited description of belief systems in mass publics that describes the problems involved in launching major influence campaigns across many nations around world. The grand subject Russia and China are attempting to disrupt is democracy. Neither have it, and it interferes with their manner of governance. They do not want it. If we ask Xi Jinping or Vladimir Putin, they would say they want to coexist with those other forms of government, denying they would ever interfere in another country's internal affairs, even though the evidence is overwhelming that both of them do.

Converse said belief systems are "…*a configuration of ideas and attitudes in which the elements are bound together by some form of constraint or functional interdependence.*"[5] He said that all belief systems are constrained and maintain themselves. In a way, they are kind of like Newton's first law of motion applied to human interaction: An object at rest stays at rest and an object in motion stays in motion with the same speed and in the same direction unless acted upon by an unbalanced force. It is a little more complicated, but not significantly.

> On a broader canvas, such findings suggest that simple "thinking about" a domain of idea-elements serves both to weld a broader range of such elements into a functioning belief system and to eliminate strictly logical inconsistencies defined from an objective point of view.[6]

However, as part of the research done to support his theory, Converse managed to correct one major misconception of his day: *belief systems are not based upon an assumption of shared information*, i.e., if we take a broad base of people who share a common belief, only a few of them will have used the same information to make a judgment about that belief. Remember that his research was done before the Internet. It was a simple idea that would become much more important today.

What the Russians and Chinese capitalize on is their understanding that we believe ourselves to be more sophisticated than history or social research has shown us to be; we have extensive access to information that should debunk any false narrative, but we seldom use it.

There are few people in the world who know more about narratives that governments tell than Roger Schank, a noted researcher in artificial intelligence. One of Schank's books, *Tell Me a Story*, explains why stories, as examples of content, worked better than raw content and logic alone. Schank lists the types of stories as official, invented (adapted), firsthand experiential, second hand, and culturally common.[7] We have all heard these stories without even thinking about them.

We are focused here on the official stories told by governments, though influence campaigns mix these up. They often try to represent themselves as one of the other types, so they call a Facebook posting from a woman in Iowa a first-hand experiential statement by an eyewitness, when in fact that woman is really a statement about how Moscow or Beijing wants us to believe about what she is describing. One of their trolls made it up, pushed it out and posted it or gave it to an automated system that did all that for them. The inability to separate the real issue proponents from the fake ones is a major obstacle for governments. A government can support writers who say they were present on the ground and saw a missile fired from an aircraft, writing about what they saw; they can say that assassins sent to kill a former intelligence operative were "on vacation" in the U.K. and not there to kill someone; they can have press conferences that have government officials testify to the accuracy of statements made by the state controlled press; or have paid performers supporting their position picket outside a government official's house.

The Chinese are better at this than any other country because the Chinese Communist Party is the singular manager of ideas in China. It has become the centerpiece of defense against criticism of Communist ideals and a shift away from criticism of China per se.

> China seeks to promote views sympathetic to the Chinese Government, policies, society, and culture; suppress alternative views; and co-opt key American players to support China's foreign policy goals and economic interests.[8]

In addition, the Chinese have shown they are willing to devote the resources needed to accomplish their objectives:

> Except for Russia, no other country's efforts to influence American politics and society is as extensive and well-funded as China's. The ambition of Chinese

activity in terms of the breadth, depth of investment of financial resources, and intensity requires far greater scrutiny than it has been getting, because China is intervening more resourcefully and forcefully across a wider range of sectors than Russia. By undertaking activities that have become more organically embedded in the pluralistic fabric of American life, it has gained a far wider and potentially longer-term impact.[9]

In the main, Russia and China, and to a lesser degree Iran, share some of the same goals, even though they go about it differently. They lead from a core group of government officials who dictate policy.

That core generates the concepts implemented by the apparatus of government and the rest of the senior leaders follow guidance from above. China seems to be a bit more refined in this.

China looks at different levels of disagreement with the Chinese Communist Party (CCP) and prescribes different responses for each:

In looking at debate and dissent, the CCP again identifies three categories of contentious issues, each requiring a different approach: academic issues, misunderstandings, (defined as problems of ideological grasp), and political issues.

Academic issues are those for which the party has not outlined a clear position. It therefore allows more open discussion and exchange on these, which represent in Mao's sense, conflicts among the people.

Misunderstandings, the second category, are issues on which the CCP has a clear stance on what is correct, for which it assumes no clear understanding or malicious or premeditated intent on the part of the person or group that voices a position diverging from it. In these cases. The CCP patiently tries to explain the correct position. In Mao's terminology, misunderstandings are a conflict among the people.

The third category, political issues, consists of those for which the CCP has an identified correct position but which "hostile forces" at home and abroad are trying to undermine by intentionally spreading falsehoods. Once malicious intent or premeditation are assumed, the person or group expressing the incorrect position falls into the "enemy" camp and needs to be repudiated firmly. Xi has moved more and more issues into the political category.[10]

None of us want a job where a disagreement is categorized as a hostile action or where our opinions about a subject are censored because they do not agree with the leadership political party. It must be difficult to go to work every day under those circumstances. But Xi has made disagreement a sin. Chinese citizens, and increasingly those living outside China, find themselves in conflict. If they cannot agree with the Chairman, they become an adversary.

If we read Schank, we might become discouraged with other governments as well. Schank says stories describing government narratives are largely official, i.e., "those we learn from an official place, such as school or church or a business or from the government ... and carefully constructed

by one or more people to tell a version of events that is sanitized and pre-
sumed to be less likely to get anyone in trouble."[11] We recognize politicians'
clumsy attempts to cover their own unpopular stances with denials, statements of "misunderstanding," and the like. Shank points out that a story
can be treated "independently of the facts." That particular observation is
only made about official stories but might apply to others as well. We occasionally embellish stories, sometimes to increase the impact, and sometimes because the truth is not always as believable as a variation based on
fact, one that is closer to a cultural norm, or broad historical beliefs.[12]

Stories are indexed in our brains, though not like computers index
items stored on their hard drives. But we can route those stories to an index
to store them. Each of those stories contributes both to memories and to
the types of indices being developed.[13] They also become parts of the col-
lective public opinion. A story, like the one shown in a video of a missile
launcher going back to Russia from the Ukraine right after the Russians
shot down a civilian airliner, manufactured a scenario that fit many existing
indices about reasons why aircraft might be shot down in war. The Russian
stories focused on what could be indexed already—attempts to assassinate
senior leaders during combat but missing the mark—or confusion during
battles as to who fires at what target, the so-called fog of war. The Ukrainians focused on the Buk transporter winding its way back to the Russian
border. The Russians had been denying they supplied any weapons to the
rebels in the Ukraine and now saw credible pictures on world-wide TV that
said otherwise.

Once a story is stored, it is more difficult to undo that as truth if that
story fits the belief structure of the person it is told to. In the same way,
Chinese sources were aggressive in publishing a story on how the original
cases of coronavirus came to be. These sources said an American soldier
originally spread the virus in China. This is about as credible as the Russians saying those GRU agents were on vacation in the U.K. when they tried
to assassinate Yulia Skripal and her father.[14] It was an attempt to deflect
blame from China for how it handled the outbreak, even though there is little scientific evidence that their story is correct.[15] However unlikely that the
explanation was true, it managed to be reported in several national news
outlets and is occasionally repeated. There is a reason for that too.

The Russians blamed the Ukrainians in both variations of their stories, and both were independent of the truth, even being made before any
facts were seriously examined by either side. They would have been stored
away in the neurons of many people who read them, before the Dutch published their report of the downing of the aircraft, two years later. That is the
purpose: get a story out before too many people hear another. Many people
might have missed the Dutch report altogether, for quite a different reason.

It is true that each person has a set of attitudes, values and beliefs that are learned, and which contribute to the success of these influence programs. Leon Festinger was the leader in describing a then little-known phenomena of attitude change called *cognitive dissonance*, which describes how opinions can be changed, even when there is an individual penalty for changing them.[16] "The key hypothesis is that when incompatibilities exist between two or more ideas or cognitions, pressures will arise to reduce the discrepancy."[17] We strive to maintain consistency, and not having it produces internal conflict, which is reduced by moving one's acceptance of an idea towards a more widely held view. This makes it harder for any contrary notion to gain currency.

But equally important is the notion that people will seek out counter-arguments that are actually *weaker* than their own well-established beliefs. That view is formulated by Richard Petty and John T. Cacioppo in their elaboration likelihood model of persuasion:

> The thought disruption interpretation holds that distraction should enhance persuasion for a message containing weak arguments (since unfavorable thoughts should dominate under no distraction and would therefore be disrupted), but that distraction should reduce persuasion for a message containing strong arguments (since favorable thoughts should dominate under no distraction and would therefore be disrupted). The predictions from dissonance theory are quite different, however. Research on selective exposure and attention indicates that people prefer to hear weak rather than strong arguments against their own position (Kleinhesselink & Edwards, 1975; Lowin, 1967), suggesting that exerting effort to hear strong counter-attitudinal arguments would induce more dissonance than exerting effort to hear weak ones. Because of this, dissonance theory predicts that for counter-attitudinal messages, distraction should enhance persuasion more for strong arguments than for weak ones.[18]

Increasingly, any country's citizens are well attuned to getting their news from biased sources, including the press and social media. This theory holds for those people who consciously watch news that is aligned with ideas they already hold, belong to groups who favor their beliefs, and are friends on-line with people like them. The idea that Democrats and Republicans are divided should be no surprise, given the research. The Russian press, like the Chinese press, largely prints what their respective states tell them to, feeding stories that would be easy to believe, even though they were not true. Both salt that effort with social media trolls and censorship. That does not mean their respective publics find their press more credible than the rest of the world; but in the absence of other stories, they may offer the only explanation. An inconsistent story, especially one published later, would not be as easy to accept. There would be pressure to resolve the discrepancy between the Russian version and the Dutch version of the story, but more than a year later, when it did not matter quite so much to many of the readers. The Dutch have the strong argument but is it really worth comparing now? Many readers would say not.

In September 2019, the Ukrainians and the Russians had a prisoner swap that exchanged one of the principal suspects in the shooting down of an aircraft in Ukraine, pro–Russian separatist Volodymyr Tsemakh. Tsemakh was in jail at the time of the negotiations for the swap and was released on bond before being included in the exchange. The Dutch complained that releasing one of the suspects was not conducive to continuing the investigation of the incident.[19] That, obviously, could be the exact point of the exchange. The release of a prisoner from jail in another country and prisoner swaps are diplomatic and intelligence operations in their own right. The Russians gain control over the possibility that the suspect will one day tell his story to investigators or write a book about the whole incident, one that might not agree with the narrative Russia is telling. They could avoid either of those things by including him in a swap, a wise move if their version of the story is to be controlled.

We would never allow mere newspaper articles to arouse us enough to want to declare war, would we? We have more media sources and many more stories to clarify almost any fact we can find. We have "fact checkers" who tell us when a person is not relaying exactly the facts as we know they should be. We believe that we are more sophisticated and educated and can tell when the media, or a government official is lying to us.

We are great believers in what used to be called, less elegantly, "crap detectors," a human being's learned ability to detect the truth among a stream of ideas that are conflicted. This was a term used in the 1960s, when it was not as fashionable to question professors in school, though the idea actually came from an interview with Ernest Hemingway talking about what it took to be a great writer.[20] He said we should be good at identifying "crap" and schools were the place to start in ferreting out complete ideas so a tale could be told. Forty years later, that almost seems naive to some, prescient to others.

Today, we have an abundance of information that we can use to make informed decisions. We have more time to read the opinions of others and have a variety of sources to get both sides of a story. In theory, we should be very good at detecting a lie among the flood of ideas that come to us by looking up the aspects of various things and sorting through them. There is a kind of Aristotelian logic that follows from this belief—a well-educated person can reach back into that knowledge and conclusions already drawn—to form new ideas. Aristotle thankfully did not have Twitter, Facebook or news broadcasts to get his information, and was better off for it, but he believed in having multiple sources. He and his students had to read and discuss among themselves what they read. What Converse's research showed was that a large part of the population of belief holders does not do that.

Some people will have absorbed massive amounts of information about a topic, absorbing some parts and rejecting others that do not fit their own perception. The sources have to be in a language the individual can understand or be translated. Some have come to the same conclusions by talking to a neighbor or friend, and/or by reading nothing. When we sit in a room of people we know and listen to their arguments, we can tell which ones are which.

To make headway against a broadly held belief structure means influencing many beliefs within a number of related issues that are bound by both social and psychological constraints in a broad population. Any influence campaign must also consider, as Converse says, that not all of those people came to the belief the same way. It is a difficult task under the best of conditions to influence different audiences with different backgrounds in the belief, but to do so covertly is even more difficult.

In covert operations there are layers and layers of visible cues and support structures that have to be developed so as to hide their real source. For example, if a foreign government is pouring money into an election in the U.S. it cannot represent those funds as coming from its banks. It must set up front companies to give the money, and similar cut-outs to those getting the money. The front companies can then give money to the campaigns or advertisers that will use it, and those may have their own front companies to receive those funds. This makes detection more difficult, but it also makes managing all of these assets harder. In the end though, complexity is part of the reason the Russians and Chinese can credibly deny their actions.

Their assertions that they are not involved in these activities become incredible only when faced with discovered facts about their operations. The sheer volume of arguments that have to be undertaken creates its own risk of exposure, and the Russians are not good at minimizing that risk, though they are adjusting to their past failures. The Chinese are better.

The Chinese Progressive Association, which was donating to a part of Black Lives Matter, is part of larger "educational" mission of the Chinese government that includes colleges and universities in the form of Confucius Institutes. There were over 100 of these in the U.S. until the Trump administration whittled them down. There are many more around the world, each one with mostly Chinese nationals teaching classes to both university and non-student classes. These same organizations teach in 519 elementary, middle and high schools in the U.S. The Chinese government approves the faculty, teaching curriculum slanted towards establishment of a belief that China is not a threat to the U.S.[21] These are vehicles that slowly turn young opinions and belief structures before they have a chance to be influenced by experience with China. These are overt operations which we can see, but we do not always pay attention to what the content of this education is really about.

Where we get our information is important to how we perceive it. To be effective, information must be perceived as rational, employ values similar to that of the reader, and come from a credible source.[22] One of the odd variables is whether or not a person has prior knowledge of the subject. The credibility of a communicator is most influential when the reader has little information about the subject.[23] Once the beliefs are established, they tend to rely less on new information. The Chinese military use this tendency to suggest that getting to the audience first is important to how that information is perceived. Get there first and follow up often. So that makes it good advice to not always make a decision when the first ideas start coming in. Wait, then read more.

When readers have little knowledge of the people making arguments, they tend to ignore those messages. For example, in the months prior to the U.S. election, Facebook removed two "inauthentic" networks, one in China and one in the Philippines, that were mostly focused on Southeast Asia but had some posts related to the U.S. election. Facebook said the U.S. part of the campaign "gained almost no following," which is not surprising since nobody had heard of them before. Their posted content for and against Pete Buttigieg, President Trump and Joe Biden indicates there was little cohesion to the campaign.[24] In the Chinese network, Facebook, which was in the middle of controversy and testifying before Congressional committees, removed 155 accounts, a very small amount. Not all campaigns will work out, especially if they are not organized, or are discovered by others.

Because there is so much information in social media and on the Internet, it is easy to lose the ability to distinguish sources. We are fooled by imitations, manufactured speech, and alterations to content. We recall our sources from lists developed from online searches and some of those have been manipulated.[25] We have not read most of the findings in those searches, i.e., we scan them, but rarely all the way to the end of the search results and remember parts but not nearly all of the critical ideas; we do not take the time to find all of the search results that are available, and seldom remember more than a small fraction of what we did read. There is too much to read, yes, but the volume is deceptive. We do not, and could not, read it all. Not everything is there. Not everything that is there is accurate. Foreign languages are not searched, although some browsers now give that option. On-line translations are becoming more useful and available, giving us much more information we could never have read before, but a mass of information about something does not always define the issue completely or accurately. The volume can be created the same way as the newspaper articles about Spain's treatment of Cubans and a ship, the USS *Maine*, exploding from unknown causes.

In the simpler times of the later part of the 19th century, William Randolph Hearst and Joseph Pulitzer were major sources of information for the dominate medium in the United States—newspapers. In their day, they had no Internet rival; the first radio station was still 22 years in the future. There was no prime-time news. There were no computers. News was delivered to the door of your home, in some places twice a day. These two leaders in newspaper publishing were used to controlling the news, so when they generated a series of articles about the then Spanish colony, Cuba, their readers took notice.

Hearst and Pulitzer sold newspapers with articles that emphasized the harsh conditions imposed by Spain after Cuba attempted a revolt in 1895. But only some of those stories were accurate about the actual conditions in Cuba. For a "revolt," there was not much fighting going on. The rebels did not have enough trained people to fight the army of 25,000 Spanish troops deployed to prevent a resurgence of the revolution. Winston Churchill got his reporting experience in this place, though he was convinced that neither the Spanish nor the rebels were very well practiced in the art of armed conflict.[26] The fighting could have gone on for years without much in the way of casualties had nothing else intervened.

As a result of January riots in Havana, the USS *Maine* was sent to harbor in the capital. In February of 1898, the *Maine* was sunk as a result of an explosion. Amid conflicting accounts of what actually happened to the ship were a number of articles claiming different possibilities, but the initial U.S. Naval court of inquiry pointed to a mine, without blaming any individual or country. Public opinion in the U.S. said the Spanish were responsible.[27, 28] By the time the Navy took another look at the photographs and original analysis, the analysts had changed their minds about what happened. The explosion was internal, and in fact, there had been other explosions of a similar nature in coal-fired boilers. By the time that observation was made, the short war was over.[29] We might have gone to war for the wrong reasons, a scenario that might sound familiar to today's readers.

Examples of the 20th century are remarkably similar in efforts to persuade individuals that a particular policy is the correct one. For those who lived through these examples, we might find ourselves victims of politicians or groups who were leading us to conclusions that were later proved wrong. Were we duped? Lied to? Actually, we were persuaded through the same kind of logic that allows us to believe that we can bring together like-minded people and persuade a government to adopt a course that we propose.

Today, a government can hire credible individuals to write articles about a subject, just as the social media elite make money writing on Twitter, Facebook, and Instagram. But they are not going to pay just anyone; these chosen ones will be people who are already known to be sympathetic to their cause. They know which ones to choose because intelligence services can identify appropriate candidates to support a campaign.

The volume of information is not a measure of what is accurate. Besides the reams of paper documents and minutes of meetings, the U.S. government has 2000 websites, with over 24,000 subdomains intended to provide information. President Obama recognized the need to reduce the confusion caused by so many sites and get the numbers under control.[30] Contrary to what governments may believe, the amount of information seldom is a measure of what is accurate.

Something similar to the *Maine* newspaper stories happened in more modern times in Iraq—hinged on a belief that Saddam Hussein was trying to develop weapons of mass destruction, like chemical warheads and nuclear bombs. We saw evidence of that in pictures supplied by the Bush Administration and, in 2003, presented at the United Nations by Colin Powell. The foundation of his speech was the U.S. Intelligence Community National Intelligence Estimate (NIE) "Iraq's Continuing Programs for Weapons of Mass Destruction," which said Iraq had and was continuing to develop both nuclear and chemical weapons and the delivery systems to use them. The pictures were from the intelligence community of the U.S. and seemed credible. What the general public could not read was the highly classified background material. Even after redaction, they only saw a small part of it.

Powell later said that when the speech was given, it took only a short time for the CIA to say the estimate was wrong.[31] If true, that would not have gone over well with him, standing before the UN assembly. Powell knew what the CIA really meant. NIEs are consolidations of the intelligence collected for the intelligence community as a whole; that view was important for its credibility with policy makers. CIA backtracking would be noted by anyone seeking support from the intelligence community for a war that suddenly looked less justified.

One year later, in a brief report by the Congressional Commission on the Intelligence Capabilities of the United States Regarding Weapons of Mass Destruction, the NIE conclusions were said to be wrong.[32] Only in the search for those weapons did the allied countries find out that the weapons were not as developed as we might have thought, nor were some of the devices intended as weapons.

In 2003, 71 percent of Americans said they favored the Iraq War. Two years later, the number favoring the war had declined by 20 percent, though that may have as much to do with the conduct of the war as public opinion about it.[33]

We can say, "Well, everybody makes mistakes," but the campaign to convince congressional leaders the war in Iraq was justified is not what most of us think of as an "honest mistake." The motivation for the Bush Administration was not honest in that sense. It was supporting a policy with a package that was credible and current, just not accurate. Press reports supported the errors in interpretation, and Congress supported the effort for war. Each campaign has momentum, and support from various sources, but that support is not always positive. Each campaign is in a fight to maintain the sponsor's position while discrediting others. Some things do not play out in slow motion in front of the United Nations.

In 2014, a more difficult story developed when the Russians saw a missile bring down a civilian airliner in the Ukraine, very visibly killing 298 people. CNN carried live, dramatic video of debris falling from the sky. The crash site was on every news outlet anywhere in the world, and fingers were pointing at Russia-supported separatists in Ukraine. This was a far more complicated issue than President Bush faced leading up to Iraq, though President Reagan dealt with the same thing in 1988 when a U.S. ship, the USS *Vincennes*, mistook an Iranian airliner for a combat aircraft and shot it down.[34] Most people have forgotten that event because there was no dispute about who did it.

The Russians faced real-time reporting from multiple countries, and photographic evidence shown on television within minutes of the event. The world public was making up its mind about what happened within hours of it occurring, and days later those sources did not make the Russians sound credible. Their guilt was solidifying.

At first, public sources did not say the Russians shot down Malaysia Airlines Flight 17, but some visual evidence supplied to the media by the Ukraine government indicated the Buk missile transporter came from Russian territory and exited shortly after the plane was shot down.[35] The on-line posting was followed by several Internet comments beneath the story that expressed reservations about its authenticity and veracity, even suggesting that the video was made by the CIA.

These counterarguments are made quickly by sources unknown who are frequently part of the influence campaign. Several global news networks ran the visuals of the Buk transporter, which appeared to be a cell-phone video, and wrote their own stories around it. Someone was beating Russia to the punch on the delivery of evidence, but it was not obvious who was doing it. As the story developed, an alternative narrative of a specialized "citizen intelligence" group began to take shape. That story expressed the view that citizens were organized and communicated to one another to find the source of the missile. They located it and took video which was released to the government and press sources.[36]

The truth of *any* of these stories is still in doubt.

Russia had its own, hastily put together narrative, repeated often by Vladimir Putin, placing blame on the Ukraine government for shooting down the plane. The Russians showed news stories, carried by news outlets around the world, with graphical tracks of aircraft shown on the wall of a "command center" in Russia that "proved" the intercept was done by a Ukrainian jet that was trying to shoot down Putin's aircraft. The graphics were crude and clearly not what we expect from any military command center. The room was large and occupied by only a few individuals. The presentation was a plausible story for anyone not viewing independent news videos and press reports flowing out of the area. Part of the Russian campaign was to restrict access to counternarrative stories, but that was already in jeopardy.

When the Russian command center story proved difficult to sustain, it changed. Truth is an unnecessary concept in these campaigns, but plausibility, especially when hiding attribution, is an aspect that carries some importance. Initially, there was no additional information that supported the Russian-invented position—no radio transcripts of pilots talking about an intercept, no recorded missile tracks on real radars, and no official statements from governments supporting their position.

The new narrative was that the Ukraine shot down the plane with its own missile. It was presented as an official statement made by the Russian government.

> First-hand radar data identified all flying objects which could have been launched or in the air over the territory controlled by rebels at that moment, Dmitry Peskov said in Moscow.[37]

The world was supposed to believe that Russia could track any missile launched over rebel territory and determine who fired it. It could not, therefore, have been anyone other than those whom the Russians blamed. It slowly became more obvious that the Russians were not set on reporting the truth, but in defining it. But in the near term, there were no other stories that supported an alternative presented by the Russian leaders.

Dutch investigators, two years later, said the missile launcher that shot the plane down came from Russia, and returned to Russia shortly after the missile strike. The Dutch report used intercepts of conversations carried on between Russian nationalists, photographs of the scene, forensic evidence from bodies and aircraft fragments, a discovered nose cone from the missile itself, and a variety of other more factual interviews.[38] It was clear in the report that the launcher was from Russian territory and was manned by Russian-speaking nationalists. So, do we think Putin made a mistake? Was he advised incorrectly by his staff? No, this kind of mistake is made with a narrative in mind and far from honest. It is storytelling with a motive. Making the evidence fit the story is a common thread in government storytelling, and in each of these events the story was made to fit a narrative that was not based on facts.

What has changed since the Russians tried to manage the story is the sophistication of the means to bias content available to the average Internet user. Today, we have much more sophisticated ways of making ideas seem credible, and making contrary ideas disappear.

Source credibility is important to how that information is perceived. We evaluate the source of what we are seeing, reading, or listening to and decide on the *competence and trustworthiness* of the source.[39] But suppose for a minute that it was possible to manipulate how other viewers of information see the competence and trustworthiness of an individual telling us something about a subject. That manipulation would reduce source credibility. We can do that just by slanting views towards that speaker or writer, by publishing articles that contradict positions taken by others, issuing denials of certain types of behaviors and the like. They can write negative reviews of books that express the view the trolls are trying to suppress. They can even start totally fictitious stories about the writer. Portions of that can be done by trolls on the Internet who are supporting influence campaigns and hiring of writers to publish articles favoring the government's position. They can filter out contrary positions.

We tend to see censorship as the evil in all this filtering, but it is not the greatest evil by any means. In influence campaigns, there is an alternative approach to defining the truth or correctness of an idea. Practitioners do not try to define what is true in the common meaning of the term. They try to define the truth in terms that a government sees as a position advantageous to itself, or to convince a person to take an action consistent with the perceived belief they might not otherwise take. There are several ways to achieve that, but they are not related to the typical ways of finding truth for an individual. It is about defining it.

First, we must define a belief through a series of similar stories that people can gather around. The Russian story that the Ukrainians tried to shoot down Vladimir Putin's airplane, hitting a commercial airliner, was such a story. The Russians denied sending troops and weapon systems into the Ukraine and thus should have no missile systems there. Having a video of a Russian BUK missile system crossing from the Ukraine to Russia was stark evidence of the inaccuracy of their story. In the same way, the story told by the two GRU officers charged by the U.K. *in absentia* gave them a news platform to claim their innocence. They claimed they were in the city to look at architecture, a paper-thin cover story that did not survive the week and never should have been uttered. Both stories were incredible, not easily believed by anyone. Yet, they remained supported even today, by Vladimir Putin himself.

The second area is to concentrate on limiting contrary arguments via search itself, i.e., to manipulate search results or interfere with them. There is little evidence the Russians did any manipulation of search results in their Ukraine activities, but they had the capability with their technical support teams. The Mueller Commission said they used algorithms that helped to improve their ability to be found by search engines.

The Chinese, on the other hand, have the reputation of doing it often.[40] They are accused of steering Android users to virtual private network (VPN) software that is modified or weakly constructed to be manipulated by Chinese intelligence.[41] They have issued fake authentication certificates through discredited certificate authorities in other countries, and, for a time, Google refused to accept anything issued by these authorities. Google said they would modify Chrome, their browser, to not accept any of China's main root certificates.[42] The certificates would make communications susceptible to man-in-the-middle attacks, which can be used to modify content in real time. The Chinese press reported this story saying it was a "security breach" when Google challenged the Chinese authorities on their certificate issuance procedures.[43]

The Chinese take these steps further with something called the Great Cannon. A concept more than a physical thing, it allows China to disrupt sites external to the Chinese domains, infect sites that China disapproves of, and inject code into a network connection of a user of one of those sites. They can disrupt sites that they disagree with. They can block them, or selectively intercept and modify content. They can censor specific individuals or specific Internet sites. They have similar mechanisms that make up a Great Firewall that blocks and filters incoming and outgoing content, including my blog.[44] So, search results can be manipulated, and not just by the Chinese but by any country with the technical skill and political will to do these things. But the Chinese excel in every aspect of information restriction.

The intent is to limit search results, remove some search items, modify source articles in subtle ways, create fake articles that propose a policy or political point of view, such as the "reeducation centers" in Xinjiang. As much as China tries to convince the world that the occupants of those facilities are being educated so they can seek employment, leaks of information about them have undone what China has tried to do.[45] The Chinese have the mechanisms to take an idea like reeducation centers and make it real to an average user who will not go further than a few references in a search.

China used diplomatic influence, pressure on public transport companies, and its own businesses to put pressure on businesses to change public views of Taiwan as being part of China.[46] With only one minor shot fired in public, the Russians had no trouble bringing in troops, establishing control, and taking Crimea. The Chinese have not done the same with Taiwan, even though some of their military would like to. China sees Taiwan as part of China, but 17 countries see it as a separate country.[47] The United States is not one of them yet does not recognize China's claim to the territory.

Nobody doubts the Chinese military's capability to take Taiwan, like Russia did Crimea, but they are just as interested in achieving that without a shooting war. Taiwan might not be as accommodating as Crimea proved to be. China knows they can influence and eventually win. They got back Hong Kong by being patient, taking small steps and maneuvering Britain into giving it up. The fact that they have not taken Taiwan indicates they do not believe they need to.

China has not stopped making different moves to enforce its claim over Taiwan using diplomacy, military threats and economic extortion. There are always aspects of support to covert programs that are overt, i.e., we can see them and attribute them. A simple example is something we seldom notice, the destination for airline schedules. China forced most airlines to re-label their destinations on schedules to reflect Taiwan as part of China.[48] This may seem like a small thing, but it strengthens China's claim when others recognize it, even in small ways.

Google takes a clever, pragmatic approach to these kind of issues by changing maps according to where the user is located. It can change borders and names of certain cities to satisfy some government claims and alters search results based on where that search originates.[49] Taiwan can be part of China and an independent country when the need arises. U.S. airlines might take note.

But at the same time the Chinese flailed the world's airlines, the Chinese, French and U.S. sent military ships through the Taiwan Strait, an area claimed by China.[50] The U.S. and France do not recognize China's claim to this waterway and those ships are very visible signs.[51] Furthermore, the U.S. agreed to sell more advanced weapons to Taiwan and China retaliated by sanctioning the three defense contractors that built those systems. In each of these escalations, the Chinese have held press conferences with diplomats and government officials espousing the official line of the Communist Party. The use of overt activities is support for covert activities that must be denied. Both may be funded out of the same program but executed differently.

Included in these approaches may be technical methods for improving the chances of being detected by a search engine and writing scripts to limit search results from certain sources. The Russians in their influence campaigns could have used these techniques to some extent, since they had a technical support unit capable of such actions. There were no reports of them doing that, unlike the Chinese.

Citizen Lab at the University of Toronto did research on how censors in China applied rules on chat during the COVID-19 pandemic.[52] The Chinese manipulated speech by removing or forbidding information more stringently as it became apparent that the virus originated in China and was reflecting badly on the government:

- WeChat broadly censored coronavirus-related content (including critical and neutral information) and expanded the scope of censorship in February 2020. Censored content included criticism of government, rumors and speculative information on the epidemic, references to Dr. Li Wenliang, and neutral references to Chinese government efforts on handling the outbreak that had been reported on state media.
- Many of the censorship rules are broad and effectively block messages that include names for the virus or sources for information about it. Such rules may restrict vital communication related to disease information and prevention.

…at least 40 people were subject to warnings, fines, and/or administrative or criminal detention around January 24 and 25, 2020. Another announcement points to a much larger number, detailing 254 cases of citizens penalized for "spreading rumors" in China between January 22 and 28, 2020…. Our results show that at least one Chinese social media platform began blocking COVID-19 content three weeks before this official announcement, which strongly suggests that social media companies came under government pressure to censor information at early stages of the outbreak.[53]

So, the Chinese used deletion of text, warnings that result in self-censorship, and actual sanctions on and arrests of its own citizens who failed to comply. Their suppression was slowly being eroded. Unfortunately, in that particular case, for the rest of the world, their censorship kept valuable information from the world public until the pandemic was out of control.

The Chinese want to control every aspect of life, including religion, family size (on occasion), travel within the country, where a person shops, what they buy, what books they read, even what Hollywood shows them at the movies.

That carries influence over the people in the movie business—actors, producers and the heads of the various studios. A major contributor to understanding how this is done is a report by PEN America, an organization that attempts to counter threats to free expression.[54] What allows China to have any say at all in the content of foreign movies is the Chinese market. It is big, having surpassed the U.S. market in 2018.

Second, access to that market is controlled by China's censors. They can require reshooting scenes of a movie, making it important to get it right the first time, another aspect of self-censorship. Third, content is important in this equation. A movie critical of China is not going to get very far in its review under the 2016 Film Industry Promotion Law, which reviews for such things as dangers to national unity, undermining religious policy, violating rights of minors and several others. While China tightens its hold on movies critical of any aspect of Chinese culture, it supports movies that criticize U.S. culture. Perhaps fittingly, control over movie censorship is in the Central Propaganda Department.[55]

The principle the Chinese have learned is that information of all types can be filtered, masked, sorted, and manipulated to deceive other countries without showing fingerprints of that activity. That is partly due to our belief that we can overcome this kind of maneuver because we are so clever. What we have found out in these last few years is that we are not as clever as we thought.

We have so much information that we are confident in our ideas, even though we may have avoided collecting articles with opinions contrary to our own. After we have formulated opinions, we look only for things that help us maintain those ideas and not for contrary ones, or weaker arguments. The Chinese have used that idea to censor what their population sees. They define those activities as a public good. They manage the press, censor what people write, translate books into Chinese when they want to, punish those who do not cooperate, and eliminate those who disagree with the Communist Party's approach.

But the most astounding part of that program is their correct insistence that it produces harmony. We may disagree with the methods used, but they generally have harmony and encourage it as a social norm. They consider the price their people pay for that harmony to be justified. Some of their foreign friends believe that too. The rest of the world may reserve judgment on that but cannot deny the results. However cynical it may be, if we believe the research, what we do individually matters little to an outcome on any policy issue. Special interests will win in the end and China knows how to influence those special interests.

Most governments know it is better to persuade their citizens, and often those of other countries, of the wisdom of political positions they take. But this is more complicated than just saying, "The United States thinks the Chinese are stealing our intellectual property." The Chinese deny any such thing, even while they talk about it in trade negotiations with the U.S. A statement by the U.S. government is not sufficient to persuade very many elite or people in the general population of any country. The denial by the Chinese does little to persuade many either.

The Russians are a little more straightforward with their influence generation.

In one case, the assassination attempts on Sergei Skripal, the Russians were less subtle, using a chemical that was known to be manufactured in Russia, using military officers to carry out the attack, and conveying a hard-hitting warning on what happens to intelligence officials that defect. All the while Russia, especially Vladimir Putin, denied any involvement in attacking their former agents. It seems odd unless we consider the purpose of this kind of influence. It is a warning to others like Skripal to stay in Russia.

The whole purpose behind keeping these operations secret, and denying participation, benefits the ability of a government to credibly say "It wasn't us." They say that with conviction, even knowing the statement is a lie, even one that can be easily identified as such. When the operations fail to maintain that lie, deniability is no longer credible, though that often does not stop countries from continuing their operations while still denying what is obvious. The Russians like to influence their former intelligence agents to stay home after they are done being spies. What they use is a fearful way of influencing them to do that.

Alexander Litvinenko had already been the poster boy for Russian assassination of former-spies-turned-traitors when he was poisoned in 2006 with an unusual substance, polonium 210. A radioactive element not detectable with Geiger counters, it causes a lingering but certain death. The suspects of the poisoning of Litvinenko were Andrie Lugovoi and Dmitri Kontinental, both former Russian intelligence assets. The British were allowed to visit Russia and interview the suspects, and later charged former GRU agent Lugovoi with murder. Shortly after, Lugovoi was elected to the Duma which gave him immunity from prosecution or extradition.[56]

Litvinenko's story has been written over and over in official and press accounts outlining every detail of how the two agents were finally able to poison his tea, after missing several opportunities, flushing the material down their hotel sinks making them the kind of radioactive room that guests would avoid had they known.

But, having failed in the U.K. by denying they were the ones who poisoned Litvinenko, the Russians were about to repeat the process by attempting to kill another former spy. In March 2018, two people, one an older man and a younger woman, were found on a bench in Salisbury, England, suffering from what the local response forces thought was a drug overdose. That mistaken diagnosis may have actually helped to save their lives.

He was in Salisbury because he was caught while spying for MI-6 and was in prison in Russia. He was exchanged after a U.S. operation rounded up ten Russian agents and offered a swap.[57]

They were later identified as Sergei Skripal, 66, and his 33-year-old daughter, Yulia.[58] Skripal was a former intelligence officer for the Main Directorate of the General Staff of the Armed Forces of the Russian Federation, the GRU, the same ones who were there to kill him that day.

A couple of days later, the Porton Down laboratories at Public Health England made a sensational announcement that the two had been poisoned with a nerve agent. It took several more days to identify the exact agent, Novichok, A234. Boris Johnson, who went on to become Britain's Prime Minister, was the first to mention Russia as a suspect.

Within days social media was already starting to mention possible alternatives to Russia doing the deed. Skripal was linked to the "Trump dossier" with the inference that Americans had attempted to kill Skripal because he was embarrassing the U.S. president.[59] Skripal, who was in prison in Russia at the time the dossier was written, must have been surprised that he was linked to it. There was similar speculation that he might have been the target of an internal struggle between the FSB and the GRU, though that would still point to Russia. That would not necessarily point to the leadership of Russia. The British were blamed at one point, as were the U.S. intelligence services, stories which did not have enough credibility to be sustainable.

None of these narratives made as much sense as the likely one: Russia was sending another message to a former spy, to intelligence service personnel who might think about spying, and to the world in general about Putin's leadership style. It was well summarized in a question asked of Putin by Chris Wallace of Fox News, "Why do so many of your enemies end up dead?" Wallace then gave several examples, one of which was Skripal's attempted assassination, the only one Putin mentioned in his response. Putin's said that there were a number of reasons why Skripal may have been attacked in the U.K. and none of them had anything to do with Russia. But he said, "nobody wants to look at those reasons."[60] He was right, of course, since few would accept that attacks on former Russian agents were done by any country other than Russia.

The Role of Cyber
in Influence Campaigns

The U.S. had a damaging network intrusion in December 2020 with the attribution laid on Russia's door by everyone except the two people who would know best, a former Director of National Intelligence in the Trump administration, and the CEO of FireEye which did a large part of the investigation. Both hesitated when asked for attribution, citing instead the Secretary of State who claimed it was Russia.[1] When they were criticized by the incoming president, within a week, they had issued a refined statement that said it was Russia, but the statement was a little soft. The problem is always "What can I say in public about what has happened?" On this kind of case, it is impossible to quickly do accurate attribution in public, using only public sources for the basis of that decision. The type of monitoring required to make that determination is done in places in the intelligence community that do not like to speak in public about much of anything.

> Key government intelligence agencies said Tuesday that the SolarWinds hack is "likely Russian in origin," according to a joint statement from the FBI, NSA, Cybersecurity and Infrastructure Security Agency and Office of the Director of National Intelligence. It's the first time the four agencies have attributed the cyber attack to Russia.[2]

It looks like everyone on the security side had the same problem jumping on the bandwagon of the Secretary of State. They both know what the Russians have been doing to use other countries to mask their activities, so "likely Russian in origin" means it looks like some of those other attacks. They both know what kinds of operations the Chinese have been running, and some of those are very much like this one. We should be sure. It gives any official pause to think who might be responsible and what can be said about it to the public. They hesitated because the investigation is not over and there is much to be discovered. Some government officials want an answer, even if it is not yet proven. Others want an answer that fits a political narrative, even it is wrong. Hesitation is always prudent until all the facts are in.

During the early 2000s, I was the Program manager of a multi-service intrusion detection program called SHADOW. The Navy actually ran the program for all three military services that agreed to participate at some locations. It gave us insight into how hackers were developing, refining and attacking sites from the east coast to the west. Particularly, we found more than one entity outside the U.S. mapping all of the networks in the country, then moving on to other countries.

One day an intrusion analyst found a new attack method and it looked like it came from Russia, but the analyst was not positive of the origin country. We reported what we found but continued the investigation. Because the method was new and the Russians were seen as the culprit, a few other agencies wanted to know what their penetration mechanism was. They pestered our analysts and tried to find others who had seen the same attack. Nobody had. One of the agencies said, "I will shut you down if you don't tell us what you have." They could, but fortunately we were not ready to say definitively and our Director said to wait. He was a 3-star general so we could.

It was a week before the analyst called in the middle of the night and said, "The server is in Rumania. Their vendor ran out of available space and went to their backup site in Russia. They just switched back and I have it." It turned out the developers of this code were secretive and criminals. We turned that case over to law enforcement, but it took weeks, and some patience to get to an accurate attribution. Had we attributed the attack to Russia and reported it, we might never have found the real culprits.

Bradshaw and Howard were undoubtedly right about the number of countries that do influence campaigns well; but they may not be accurate as to which countries are really behind them. To undertake a campaign, a country must have an understanding of how to run a complex operation that does not trace back to itself, and still achieve the results the sponsor expected. Some of the better ones have trouble doing that, even though they have the resources and experience. While many countries may try the same techniques and tools, and therefore look like they have information warfare capabilities, only a handful are good at applying them.[3]

There are similarities between what the Russians are doing in what they call information warfare, what the Iranians do in their cyber influence programs, and what China does to manage its population and influence policies abroad. But what we should be more concerned about is those same techniques are common in political parties in multiple "free world" countries doing—exactly the same kinds of things. Now we find there are commercial companies helping them do it.

The world's protagonists have allies in many places where democracy is the ruling form of government, and where the same techniques are being used by political parties, social media companies, and the press to achieve policy manipulation, even opposing a central government's belief structure.[4] Though many others have interests in influence operations, they do not have the resources or political will to run major campaigns that might be discovered.

Christopher Walker and Jessica Ludwig call this kind of influence "sharp power":

> Authoritarian influence efforts are "sharp" in the sense that they pierce, penetrate, or perforate the political and information environments in the targeted countries. In the ruthless new competition that is under way between autocratic and democratic states, the repressive regimes' sharp power techniques should be seen as the tip of their dagger. These regimes are not necessarily seeking to "win hearts and minds," the common frame of reference for soft power efforts, but they are surely seeking to manipulate their target audiences by distorting the information that reaches them.[5]

The projection of that kind of power is a distortion of our particular view of political warfare. It is not as much about "successful operations" moving a political group to action as it is about disruption of the opposition groups and their ideas. That is why we have so much trouble defining success. The operations do not appear to be working but actually we might be wrong about their target objective.

As much attention as Russian methods have gotten in the last few years, Russia's success has been measured more by wishful thinking on their part than by measurable results. That is not an interpretation favored by everyone. Dr. Fiona Hill, a noted Russian analyst, suggested in congressional testimony that Russia was successful in a disinformation operation, bringing a belief to the U.S. White House that the Ukraine was behind some meddling in the 2016 election.[6] This assertion would imply effectiveness for Russian operations, since it resulted in a change in belief in the U.S. government. As soon as she made that claim, many of the mainstream media in the U.S. repeated it almost verbatim and news outlets carried the story. The context for those remarks were an impeachment hearing attempting to bring charges against the President of the United States, a rare event in U.S. history. Hill was, in effect, saying the president and his intelligence agencies had been duped by Russia.

But, if the Russians were so successful in the 2016 operations in the U.S. election, we must wonder how anyone could know these were Russian operations. The criminal indictments that came out of the Mueller report clearly showed that Russian operations had been monitored by the U.S. for years before Mueller's investigations formally began. If true, the operations in 2016 were discovered long before they ever had a chance to become successful. The usual intelligence operations would attempt to define these attempts and disrupt them or penetrate them for observation, and subsequent indictments in 2020 would indicate that was done. This group was followed electronically for a long time. One has to wonder why they were not disrupted or publicly disclosed long before they came to light.

There are many like Dr. Hill who would argue the success of the Russians is sowing discord in democratic countries. We should wonder about whether it is possible to attribute their alleged success to their actions in several national elections of other countries where they are accused of running operations. We have no measures of their success or failures that can show causation. That is true for both Russia and China.

At the same time, the Russians are getting better, and the club has expanded beyond China, Iran, North Korea and a few others who routinely ventured into the same kind of activities. At times, dissimilar approaches and objectives look very much alike, making it more difficult to attribute them to a specific country.

Infrastructures

Unfortunately, the Chinese drive narratives in a slightly different way, one more difficult to detect and measure. They seem to believe in managing information at its source, rather than manipulating or pushing it out to a destination, though they do some of both. Internet content management lies at the heart of their approach. Very few other countries of the world can control content at this level or manage it on the scale that the Chinese do. It is very resource intensive.

We tend to think of world communication as being an aspect of the Internet, but the Internet is really a small part of communication, albeit an ever-expanding one. As an example, China has 772 million Internet users, with only 38 percent of their people on the net.[7] Yet that's more than twice the population of the United States. We tend to think that managing content for that many users is impossible, and it is; but China does as much as it can, particularly with its own citizens. To manage content on China's population requires some special activities that are unique to China. Nobody *controls content on the Internet*, not even the Chinese—but the Chinese manage content better than any other country because they devote the enormous resources required to do it.

The basic core concepts required to manage content lie in management of websites and networks, extreme censorship, government guidance on what can be published by the press, and "voluntary compliance" by both businesses and individuals. The Russians create programs that amplify differences between people outside their own country and exploit those differences; the Chinese create programs that reduce differences between people inside their country, and influence those outside to conform to the norms set by the Chinese. That is a subtle distinction, but an important one.

Influence programs use social media as their medium of choice. They are cheap and widely used in multiple languages across the whole world. In the days when newspapers dominated information dissemination, it took time to get a story out. We describe that in terms of news cycles, how long it takes to have an issue deemed important enough to take up blocks of print on the page, how long it remains of interest to readers, and how long it takes for that same issue to no longer be important.

Although Internet use is increasing, television remains the leading source of news.[8] The Internet is closing quickly and may soon be the dominant force in news delivery.[9] When discussing social media, Facebook often gets attention as a news outlet because 43 percent of Facebook users get at least some news from Facebook. That statistic is biased in Facebook's favor, and Facebook repeats it whenever they can.

> Facebook is by far the largest social networking site, reaching 67% of U.S. adults. The two-thirds of Facebook users who get news there, then, amount to 44% of the general population. YouTube has the next greatest reach in terms of general usage, at 48% of U.S. adults. But only about a fifth of its users get news there, which amounts to 10% of the adult population.[10]

For things like instructional or entertaining videos, YouTube and other video streaming services are the favorites.[11] Targeting the Internet alone would not be sufficient to get a majority of people to see, let alone act on, a specific narrative. We have to believe those who use social media are actually paying attention to the messages in them and acting on what they read or view. Our own experiences would likely take exception to that idea.

We seem to understand source credibility in social media without having to have training in the subject. It is made up of medium (as in channel) credibility, combined with information credibility.[12]

> Medium credibility refers to the perceived level of credibility that individual users have of a specific medium. Message credibility refers to the perceived credibility of the communicated message itself, such as informational quality, accuracy, or currency. Next, we derive five key factors from the two dimensions; medium credibility and message credibility. Three factors, medium dependency, interactivity, and medium transparency were derived from the medium credibility dimension, two factors, argument strength and information quality were derived from message credibility dimension. Finally, drawing on the persuasion theory, we identify an individual's expertise moderates the effects of those five determinants from medium/message credibility dimension on information credibility.

Li and Suh were studying source credibility on Facebook during one of the more interesting of times for Hong Kong, when demonstrations were at their peak and communications were essential. Individuals chose their media based upon the degree of perceived interactivity and use of that medium platform. Their results show that while argument strength has a significant positive influence on information credibility, information quality has no influence on information credibility.... They conclude, "While the growing popularity of the use of social media platform, especially Facebook, and its potential to propagate misinformation, the ability to judge credible information is becoming more important."[13]

That ability used to be based upon the ability of the user to read and analyze what was written in context with the many other things that came before. We are about to enter an age where that is going to be more difficult, and we have already had an example that shows the consequence of fake content and how easy it is to create and distribute. Benkler, Faris, Roberts and Bourassa describe the categories that are of concern[14]:

- **Algorithmic curation:** Most commonly known as the "filter bubble" concern, algorithms designed by platforms to keep users engaged produce ever-more refined rabbit holes down which users can go in a dynamic of reinforcement learning that leads them to ever-more extreme versions of their beliefs and opinions.
- **Bots:** Improvements in automation allow bots to become ever-more-effective simulations of human participants, thereby permitting propagandists to mount large-scale influence campaigns on social media by simulating larger and harder-to-detect armies of automated accounts.
- **Fake reports and videos**: Improving automated news reporting and manipulation of video and audio may enable the creation of seemingly authentic videos of political actors that will irrevocably harm their reputations and become high-powered vectors for false reporting.
- **Targeted behavioral marketing powered by algorithms and machine-learning:** Here, the concern is that the vast amounts of individually-identifiable data about users will allow ever-improving algorithms to refine the stream of content that individuals receive, so as to manipulate their political opinions and behaviors.

We are about to see a new dimension in deep fakes of both videos and audio messages. There are several definitions of deep fakes, indicating the term is new and inconsistently defined. We should think of deep fakes as intentionally deceptive video or audio messages posted in public to disparage a

person or policy. Deep fakes have been around since governments manufactured official looking fake correspondence on letterhead that appeared
to be authentic. But the ability to fake a document is nowhere near as difficult as the methods being used today to generate video and audio.

Today it is possible to generate an entirely fictional video of a person
saying something they have never really said. A subject is scanned by a neu-
ral network in different lighting patterns and from several angles. Those
scans then become the data from which a new video can be made. The new
video can be made up completely from the stored patterns, making it possible to create a session where the subject says something that person never
said in any of the composite videos.[15] What it also does is give the same
opportunity to any intelligence service that wants to create its own narrative and have a someone appear to support it who never intended to do
so. Since it is very difficult to detect these fakes, it will be some time before
a denial can be made, even if someone reported the video as fake. All the
while, the fake is being repeated though social media trolls and government
media outlets. By the time it is identified, it has already done some damage.
That has already happened.

At the end of November 2020, Chinese Foreign Ministry spokesman
Zhao Lijian posted on Twitter a picture of what appears to be an Australian soldier holding a child's head back while he prepares to kill him. There
is blood on the knife the soldier holds, but it does not look real. The picture
looks staged, and the soldier's nationality might be disputed. The Australian government says the photo is a fake. The Prime Minister of Australia demands an apology and removal of the photo but gets neither. Twitter
refuses to remove the picture, though it has a policy to remove deep fakes.[16]
It did however, some hours later, label the video as sensitive. That is hardly
responsive.

In the background of this posting is a report from the Inspector-
General of the Australian Defence Force that found credible information
that Australian special forces were responsible for the unlawful killing of 39
prisoners, farmers and other civilians, and the cruel treatment of two others, in Afghanistan from 2009 to 2013. The fake photo has a caption: "Don't
be afraid, we are coming to bring you peace!"

This is certainly not diplomacy at its best and it is not intended to be. It
is intended to call attention to the Inspector General's report, in the midst
of a dispute with China over interference in the Australian election. The
objective may be achieved, but the Australians will not forget. Months later,
the Chinese decided to say the actual statement in the photo may have been
misinterpreted.

What the Chinese example brings to the front is how to retaliate
against this kind of fake being delivered through social media. What the

Chinese may not have thought about is the difference between a government office posting this and a citizen posting the same thing. A government spokesman lends some credibility to the authenticity of the photo, and it appears the government officially sanctions the release of it. The Chinese could always renounce the photo and say it was not done with its permission, but they have not done that. Twitter makes a choice in rejecting the statement by the Australian government that the image is a deep fake, something that is not consistent with their policy.

The Australian government can make an effort to delete this photo every place they find it, but the damage has already been done and deleting anything like this is technically difficult. They can take diplomatic action against China, removing the Chinese spokesman, even to remove a few diplomats to go along with him. That would discourage them from using this kind of technique again, but probably not forever. They could reply in kind, submitting deep fakes with images of a popular Chinese official, or they could threaten to ban Twitter in Australia until the fake is removed. These are all political decisions that have to be considered before an action can be taken. But the one thing the Australians cannot do is do nothing. These kinds of fakes will only increase if there is no action taken to stop them.

Social media is one of the great influencers in the world, but it is increasingly clear that about 10 percent of "users" of social media may not be real people. They are bots. Twitter, like other social media outlets, reports the number of suspected bot accounts to the U.S. Security and Exchange Commission—reported figures add up to nearly 48 million.[17] We almost have to look twice at that number. It becomes important when they are used to disseminate misinformation or manufacture support for political issues. When bots represent themselves as human beings commenting on an issue, it is difficult to discover how many of them there are or who manufactured them. We might want to ask Twitter why they are not being removed.

There are a few interesting complaints to the SEC about how those bots are being used. Fake users extol the virtue of certain stocks, like Lukin Coffee, inflating their value. There were thirteen complaints on a Chinese company, GSX Techedu, for inflating its revenue. There were complaints about an increasing number of enterprising "students" who are bots, probably collecting information on exam questions.[18] If there is a way, enterprising bot makers will find a way to monetize it.

Social bots are accounts controlled by software, algorithmically generating content and establishing interactions. Many social bots perform useful functions, such as dissemination of news and publications (Lokot and Diakopoulos 2016; Haustein et al. 2016) and coordination of volunteer activities (Savage, Monroy-Hernandez, and Hollerer 2016). However, there is a growing record of

malicious applications of social bots. Some emulate human behavior to manufacture fake grassroots political support (Ratkiewicz et al. 2011), promote terrorist propaganda and recruitment (Berger and Morgan 2015; Abokhodair, Yoo,
and McDonald 2015; Ferrara et al. 2016c), manipulate the stock market (Ferrara
et al. 2016a), and disseminate rumors and conspiracy theories (Bessi et al. 2015).
A growing body of research is addressing social bot activity, its implications on
the social network, and the detection of these accounts (Lee, Eoff, and Caverlee
2011; Boshmaf et al. 2011; Beutel et al. 2013; Yang et al. 2014; Ferrara et al. 2016a;
Chavoshi, Hamooni, and Mueen 2016). The magnitude of the problem was
underscored by a Twitter bot detection challenge recently organized by DARPA
to study information dissemination mediated by automated accounts and to
detect malicious activities carried out by these bots (Subrahmanian et al. 2016).[19]

While bots are sophisticated entities that require a long time to appear
human, there are other ways to do the same thing without working quite
so hard. For example, algorithms sit behind every search, and they are
biased pieces of code that can be manipulated.[20] While we may search very
carefully for every specific piece of information, Safiya Umoja Nobel says
data discrimination is a real social problem and the combination of private interests in promoting certain sites, along with the monopoly status of
a relatively small number of Internet search engines, leads to a biased set
of search algorithms. This is a hidden bias against collection of information that is invisible to the searcher. Those algorithms can eliminate certain
types of information, sources and content from view.

What Nobel was referring to regarding search engines is that, for the
average user, there are not many search engines to choose from. There are
over 140 engines, but most of them are not widely used.[21] Most users have
only heard of a few of the available ones from Google, Apple Mozilla and
Microsoft. A few of them exist in name only and have not been supported
or widely used for Internet generations. Exclusive agreements dominate
the landscape for the major players in distribution of search engines and
these have become an issue for the courts. Google, Microsoft and Apple
dominate the market, but the concern with the few search engines used is
that Google dominates that small market, even within Apple, which has
Google's engine as an option inside its own browser. The *Wall Street Journal* showed in 2019 that Google manipulates search results more than they
admit, and a lot more than we should be happy with.[22]

The *Journal* claims that they found Google favoring big businesses
over smaller ones, even though they claim not to. Google layers information over searches with "featured snippets" or news results, allowing engineers to make changes or remove data. Google blacklists some sites that
are not illegal, something I was personally affected by. Google manages its
algorithms by having its own employees rank the quality of search results
and adjust them to fit their own beliefs. Google's bias is shown in search

terms to the major participants in the U.S. national election, but not in searches for other politician's names.

> Far from being autonomous computer programs oblivious to outside pressure, Google's algorithms are subject to regular tinkering from executives and engineers who are trying to deliver relevant search results, while also pleasing a wide variety of powerful interests and driving its parent company's more than $30 billion in annual profit. Google is now the most highly trafficked website in the world, surpassing 90% of the market share for all search engines. The market capitalization of its parent, Alphabet Inc., is more than $900 billion.[23]

Eric Goldman holds that search engines give the appearance of being unbiased and free from the intervention of human bias. But he asserts "search engine bias," typically denied by search vendors, occurs when ranking search results.

> Search engines allegedly make manual adjustments of a web publisher's overall ranking, and search engines occasionally modify search results presented in response to particular keyword searches.[24]

Search bias influences what information is returned in a search and how prominent it is. Typically, businesses are interested in their advertising, so much of the research on search results comes from advertising departments. They want their results to appear on the first page of a search, because most people will not search farther than that. Goldman notes search engines are generally "tuned" to support majority interests—defined by the vendor supplying the search engine. This creates a natural bias in displaying search results.[25] Anything further down will never be seen by the casual user.

Search engines are used in social media applications to find posted information. This is used for censorship, but this kind of censoring is necessary—to avoid publishing something that is offensive to young readers or illegal, like child pornography. But it has evolved, at Twitter and Facebook, into something more sinister—censorship of political ideas. This assures that certain political thoughts are prevented from being seen, based solely on the opinion of a type of internal censors who operate almost exactly like Chinese censors. That should not be a surprise to those at Facebook who have Chinese censors employed in their own building. They operate under the heading of Hate Speech Engineering.[26] We should ask ourselves why any U.S. business should look to China to help censor systems which are prohibited in China.

Part of that bias shows up in elections. During the 2020 election a story run by the *New York Post* claimed Hunter Biden had links to communist China through a series of companies paying him consulting fees. They further claimed evidence found on the hard drive of a computer taken in for repair and abandoned at a repair shop. Twitter blocked access to any reference to the story and suspended the account of anyone trying to disseminate it. Facebook was more limited but did some manual censorship. Several news outlets have since criticized the *Post* story and disputed its facts, but the issue was one of disclosure of the story to the public.

Axios said Facebook and Twitter's frantic attempts to stop the spread of the *Post*'s story did not prevent the article from becoming the top story about the election on those platforms.[27] By all appearances, Twitter made a real effort to block the story, and that got congressional attention. It resulted in the CEOs of both Facebook and Twitter being called before congressional investigative committees. Twitter CEO Jack Dorsey admitted the attempt to stop disclosure was a mistake. But to many in the U.S., censorship of the story was too much like Chinese censorship against the cultural ideal of free speech in a democracy.

The Chinese do not even try to hide the fact that they censor political ideas that conflict with those of the Communist Party and their censorship platforms are designed that way, even looking outside their borders. Let the general manager of the Houston Rockets make a pro–Hong Kong statement on his social media account in the U.S. and China finds it. They ban National Basketball Association games from Chinese state television. As a result, businesses have to cope with Chinese efforts to police their speech on different social media channels and with diverse subjects like Tibet, Taiwan, Xinjiang, Hong Kong, recent Chinese history, human rights and Beijing's territorial claims to the South and East China Seas.[28] The list gets longer every day. Businesses self-censor when they have had enough, and that is exactly what the Chinese want. Self-censorship reduces the amount of credible information available to us as decision makers and the Chinese are happy about that.

We often wrongly believe that the truth of information will be "obvious," when it is not.[29] For those outside of Russia or China, especially those who know the press is far from independent, these stories were not so easily accepted. The U.S. had claimed for months that Russia was ferrying troops and weapons across the border area in the south of the Ukraine. The U.S. intelligence community was tracking those movements. Press reports widely supported that view, in spite of denials by the Russians.

> While the interference did not live up to worst fears, numerous examples of it can be found in the kinetic, disinformation, and cyber realms over a period of months. Russia's war with Ukraine and its occupation of parts of Ukraine's territory constitute the most blatant interference, including the disenfranchisement of some 16 percent of the electorate living in Crimea and areas around Donetsk and Luhansk.
>
> Russian interference in the election is part of President Vladimir Putin's regime's larger efforts to impede Ukraine's sovereign right and determination

to remain independent and choose its own future and foreign policy orientation. Russian disinformation and propaganda sought to discredit the election as illegitimate and rigged, and frame Ukraine as a failed state run by fascists and neo–Nazi sympathizers. Kremlin-backed rhetoric argued that Ukraine could not possibly conduct democratic elections—and Ukrainians disproved this line completely.[30]

But the Russians, in 2014 and today, could rely on a low percentage of the world public following anything about Ukraine politics, even fewer, what Russia does there. The Russians only have to influence a minority of those who do pay attention to the details of what they were doing in the Ukraine. Those thought leaders are the ones people turn to when they want to know accurate information about the Ukraine.

During the 2016 election, and the program to change perceptions of Russian doping, the Russians attached the names of real individuals to fake stories that were not written by those people.[31] Why would they do that? It is because they believed these individuals were leaders in some aspect of our society that had influence, either positive of negative, over policymakers. They were not always directly related to the campaign of either political candidate and some of those individuals had no influence on voting. They use the source credibility of these individuals but undermine it with their own fiction. Whether the made-up stories they wrote for these leaders were true or not did not matter. Russia creates a steady stream of stories, both true and untrue that overwhelms the country that is targeted.[32]

But the difficulty is in detecting fakes to begin with. In this case, the fake was identified by a government, but there are some kind of fakes that cannot be so easily detected. The use of synthetic audio can almost be indiscernible from real speech. It can be used in overlays on videos, background voiceovers, or in radio spots. We have practical experience with this type of audio in our own homes. We can tell the difference between synthetic voice and real voice when a spam call comes into our home. The person with such a heavy accent and clipped sentences cannot be working for the U.S. Internal Revenue Service threatening to have us arrested. That lady who wants to verify a credit card number to see if it was stolen has to believe we are not very smart. We can tell it is an artificial voice. But there are improvements in voice quality that make spams more authentic sounding. The accents are gone in some of the messages and it is more difficult to detect the spam and hang up. The increase in the number of applications that generate artificial speech is climbing rapidly and it does not take long for spammers to find and use the better ones.

IBM has a demonstration capability online at https://www.ibm.com/demos/live/tts-demo/self-service/home that shows some of the variables in making speech sound like a real human voice. IBM uses Watson, its artificial intelligence engine, to generate voices from text. It is produced in multiple languages with various dialects. The voice then can have variations belonging to a named pseudonym. Even in this simple demonstration the voices seem to be authentic recordings by a real person.

But, unlike video, audio can be easily altered or inserted into an audio stream with current technology. The Russians and Chinese both have the capability to insert changes in audio or text in a conversation in real time, including encrypted conversations. Security practitioners are very much aware of these kinds of attacks because there are so many uses and variations of them.[33] The most diabolical is the man-in-the-middle attack because it allows for the interception of a conversation and the modification of it while the conversation is going on. A military commander's orders could be changed, a politician's statement could be altered, or private communications between large numbers of people can be modified in different ways depending upon their political orientation. Conversations on certain subjects can be deleted, allowing censorship to occur in real time.

Deep fakes are less than an Internet generation old, with a long way to go. We are only now seeing some of the potential and not liking what we have seen.

Hackers in the Internet Mist

The hackers involved in influence campaigns are not the same as those who steal credentials from banking software on your cell phone. There are different levels of this skill. There are hackers who hack credit cards in a different way by going after the systems that process credit card transactions, and they got good enough that credit card companies had to change to embedded chips to reduce mass collections of card transactions.

These people are as good as the best government hackers, at times better, because they too are going into foreign systems, through some very secure financial institutions' networks and into those transaction aggregators that know they are targets. Those aggregators do things in security that most other businesses would never have to do to keep others out of those computers. They have formidable adversaries, mostly criminals, and only the best can get into hacking at that level.

Government employee hackers, and contractors they hire have different kinds of skills. The difference is also in degree of skill in the areas they hack. We might see 100 men and women that can collect credentials from those cell phones, but only 2 that know enough about the voting tabulation machines or global email systems to repeatedly get into one and not get caught. Hackers do specialize. It is a developed skill that criminals would not often want, unless they get paid more than they can make in credit card schemes.

Microsoft has discovered that prior to the 2020 elections in the U.S.:

… Microsoft has detected cyberattacks targeting people and organizations involved in the upcoming presidential election, including unsuccessful attacks on people associated with both the Trump and Biden campaigns, as detailed below. We have and will continue to defend our democracy against these attacks through notifications of such activity to impacted customers, security features in our products and services, and legal and technical disruptions.…

We have observed that:

- Strontium, operating from Russia, has attacked more than 200 organizations including political campaigns, advocacy groups, parties and political consultants
- Zirconium, operating from China, has attacked high-profile individuals associated with the election, including people associated with the Joe Biden for President campaign and prominent leaders in the international affairs community
- Phosphorus, operating from Iran, has continued to attack the personal accounts of people associated with the Donald J. Trump for President campaign.…

What we've seen is consistent with previous attack patterns that not only target candidates and campaign staffers but also those they consult on key issues.[34]

Imagine what happens when those highly skilled people go up against, e.g., a few makers of tabulation machines certified by the U.S. Election Assistance Commission,[35] vendors in companies that are small, states that have old equipment and no connectivity to other states or national system, tribal systems, territorial systems, private homes, and other polling places we would never imagine would be involved in our system of voting for a candidate. Those systems had substantial attacks directed at them in October 2020.[36]

The range of cyber operations are especially interesting since so many of the operations being run by foreign entities have one cyber element; and in the Russian tampering of the U.S. election of 2016, there were two. They were the same people running operations in Europe, WAPO, and the U.S., and it was obvious they were specialists in election influence campaigns.[37] They were accused of more than hacking: inserting malware in networked computers in hospitals, FedEx partner TNT Express B.V., and a large U.S. pharmaceutical manufacturer, causing damages in excess of one billion dollars. Those are exactly the same kinds of attacks as the ones generated right before the Brexit vote in the U.K.

If we were to look at the maze of information Edward Snowden gave to the public, we can get a good idea of how a really good intelligence service operates. They are smart; they use advanced techniques that others have not thought of; they add some magic and innovation to it. But we wouldn't know anything about what U.S. intelligence was doing if Snowden hadn't defected and told the world what was going on. They would never have been caught. They were not exposed by defenders of systems—at least as far as we know—they were exposed by one of their own.

Occasionally, people who do this kind of work get caught, or they are found in a system where they don't belong. Even the ones who do, are never going to get prosecuted in court, or taken out of the hacking work they were doing. In late September 2020, the U.S. indicted five Chinese hackers targeting pro-democracy politicians and activist in Hong Kong and[38]

> ...more than 100 companies and institutions in the United States and abroad, including social media and video game companies as well as universities and telecommunications providers, officials said Wednesday....

The indictments are part of a broader effort by the Trump administration to call out cybercrimes by China. In July, prosecutors accused hackers of working with the Chinese government to target companies developing vaccines for the coronavirus.[39]

There are groups of people who look for hackers and track their activities, though there should be more people doing this than are right now. From my experience, watching hackers work has an advantage and a disadvantage: The advantage is complicated, though it should be easy to evaluate. We can see progress being made in how the attacks are done—the development processes that went into it—study the code and find out where it might have been made. Eventually, we can even determine what person may have created it, though that is more speculative. Possibly, we can see what was taken from some of the targets. We used to track when updates were being made and tested, not always down to the level of individual developers, but at least to a place, country and a time zone.

That leads to identifying individuals who actually do the work, but their names are generally aliases, like "Lopudlian" or "Gregor II." It is possible to find out how good a programmer this one is and if she is generating original code or copying it from someone else. In a few instances, the indictments showed what those names were. If the hacker generates original code, they need watching. This is someone who will be selling that code or keeping it in-house to be used later by others who aren't quite so smart. Finding and tracking the smart ones is always a priority.

The downside to watching hackers work is knowing they are taking things that are really important. Usually, it is hard to evaluate the information being taken and make a judgment because people who watch hackers don't always know how important some piece of information might be. The trade-off is the value of the information being stolen versus the value of the information about how the stealing was done. In the past, I used the analogy of a sting in law enforcement. We have criminals bringing in things to be sold to a front company run by the police. We see the same criminals coming in, bringing new goods and start to wonder if there is any need to keep allowing (maybe even helping) a criminal enterprise to operate in the neighborhood. At some point, we come to the conclusion that we have all we need to prove a case, the person is arrested (rare though it might be) and the operation is closed down. In hacker cases, there are some differences.

Once in a while, the information they are taking is so sensitive that the theft has to be stopped by warning the people who hold it, or by cutting off the hacker's connection to the data. These examples are both of Chinese hacking.

Two reports have shown what a few Chinese hackers can do: Mandiant's APT 1, exposing one of China's cyber espionage units,[40] and CrowdStrike Intelligence Report, Putter Panda.[41] Both of these reports are about military units in China that spy. Mandiant followed their hackers for almost six years, and CrowdStrike followed theirs for four. That is a long time to wait but from all the evidence collected, not a lot of data was being collected by either one compared to the amount of intelligence material that is collected every day by satellites and other platforms of all types. By volume, neither one got as much as a single Predator drone equipped with an Argus-IS can collect on a good day, six petabytes.[42] But unlike those tracks of ground the Predator got, these officers were focused on specific pieces that focused on positions by individuals. They do not need as much data.

The U.S. Department of Justice documented over 100 companies that were hacked in 2020 and data removed. These companies were not just in the U.S., but in France, South Korea, Japan and Singapore and were hacked by Chinese associated with Chinese intelligence services.[43] From 2016 to 2019 there were 5500 others where data was exposed, or the systems were breached.[44] In April 2015, OPM lost the security clearance data of every person with a U.S. government clearance that lists every place an applicant lived, who they worked for (with points of contact for each supervisor), any medical problems or treatment for mental illness, any crimes committed or arrests and a long list of other things that might have been investigated.[45] It was appalling to those of us who lost data that it was not better protected, and the exact method of penetration was never disclosed. Election infrastructure is not as well protected as any of these others.

Network security plays a significant role in trying to prevent the theft of information, but it has not been very successful in the past. As the Russian WADA hacking showed, even "pretty good security," which few state governments have, is not enough to stop a determined, technically capable hacker from eventually getting in. If a hacker cannot get into the WADA servers directly, he can hack the WIFI accounts and eventually get the information needed to get in. From my own work with them, State governments are terrible at security. Of course, the real problem is what information is on the Internet because it is the Internet that gives foreign hackers a way into world-wide data access. Criminal and government hackers have tried to hack around the world since the 1970s and are only getting better at it.

They have help from an odd source—the U.S. government. From my work in computer security, I had heard "There is no indication that any of the data was stolen ... and if it was stolen, there is no indication it was used for anything that would damage the U.S." more times than most. The victims are usually wrong about both of these things, but nobody knows after an incident, so they are just guessing.

Like the U.K. in the days before the Brexit vote, the U.S. had warned the Russians had increased the activity since May of 2020.[46] From the summaries in the indictments, we can note the Russian agents already had gotten access to vendors of voting machines, state election offices, registration software, voter tabulation equipment and voter registration data in at least some states. They were successful in in Ukraine before they tried in the U.S., so they had plenty of time to look through documentation and decide how to use that kind of information.

At the same time, Election Systems & Software (ES&S), one of the main vendors for election software disclosed it had, from 2000 to 2006 been installing PCAnywhere remote access software in its machines, leaving many to speculate about how much access the Russians already had. Hackers had stolen the source code in 2006 and did not acknowledge it until 2012 when some of the code leaked. Symantec, which distributes the election software, warned users to disable or uninstall it.[47]

PCAnywhere allowed access to upgrade or modify software remotely. A vulnerability analyst described the use of this software like leaving ballots on the square in Moscow.[48] The voting machine vendors and states election authorities all said there is no evidence of penetration of any of these systems. Given the state of these systems over the years, nobody would have been able to discover a penetration since there was a flaw in the systems that did not require passwords until after 2012.[49] The state of security, bad as it was, was facing an adversary that was better than any they ever faced before, with two election cycles and a midterm to practice on.

In October 2020, *Politico* ran a story that began with this[50]:

> The Russian government is behind a recent campaign of cyberattacks on state and local governments and aviation networks that has stolen data from at least two victims, federal officials said Thursday in the latest public alarm about foreign hackers' efforts in the run-up to Election Day....

But while the hackers have "exfiltrated data from at least two victim servers," the agencies said they saw no indication that the intruders had "intentionally disrupted any aviation, education, elections, or government operations."

… "there may be some risk to elections information" because the hackers are targeting state and local networks, the intelligence community has "no evidence … that integrity of elections data has been compromised."

The 2016 indictment gives more details of what the Russians were capable of doing, and none of the "everything is OK" stance of the people who were supposed to be protecting these systems[51]:

It was not OK, in 2016 or 2018, and indications are it was not OK in 2020 either:

In or around June 2016, KOVALEV (KGB officer Anatoliy Sergeyevich Kovalev), and his co-conspirators researched domains used by U.S. state boards of elections, secretaries of state, and other election-related entities for website vulnerabilities. KOVALEV and his co-conspirators also searched for state political party email addresses, including filtered queries for email addresses listed on state Republican Party websites.

In or around July 2016, KOVALEV and his co-conspirators hacked the website of a state board of elections ("SBOE 1") and stole information related to approximately 500,000 voters, including names, addresses, partial social security numbers, dates of birth, and driver's license numbers.

In or around August 2016, KOVALEV and his co-conspirators hacked into the computers of a U.S. vendor ("Vendor 1") that supplied software used to verify voter registration information for the 2016 U.S. elections. KOVALEV and his co-conspirators used some of the same infrastructure to hack into Vendor 1 that they had used to hack into SBOE 1.

In or around August 2016, the Federal Bureau of Investigation issued an alert about the hacking of SBOE 1 and identified some of the infrastructure that was used to conduct the hacking. In response, KOVALEV deleted his search history. KOVALEV and his co-conspirators also deleted records from accounts used in their operations targeting state boards of elections and similar election-related entities.

In or around October 2016, KOVALEV and his co-conspirators further targeted state and county offices responsible for administering the 2016 U.S. elections. For example, on or about October 28, 2016, KOVALEV and his co-conspirators visited the websites of certain counties in Georgia, Iowa, and Florida to identify vulnerabilities.

In or around November 2016 and prior to the 2016 U.S. presidential election, KOVALEV and his co-conspirators used an email account designed to look like a Vendor 1 email address to send over 100 spearphishing emails to organizations and personnel involved in administering elections in numerous Florida counties. The spearphishing emails contained malware that the Conspirators embedded into Word documents bearing Vendor 1's logo.

One has to wonder why the U.S. Intelligence Community thought the Russians were favoring President Trump when the places they were hacking were related to the Republicans, the party of Trump.

These rudimentary attacks were well organized, financed and done over time by patient collectors who know their business. The methods they use are subtle with more sophistication coming between the midterms in 2018 and the election in 2020. Both the Russians and Chinese have focused their more advanced attacks on the supply chain, that stream of products that make the computer networks of the world work. They supply components, service equipment, and build clouds for businesses to use. Supply chain attacks are the real reason for concern with companies like Huawei and ZTE.

In 2018 and 2021 a similar story ran twice claiming Amazon discovered one of those attacks in their own servers (Amazon disputes that they ever discovered it), components of which were made in China. A chip, smaller than a pea, was not supposed to be on the motherboard, but it was.[52] Few companies could have found it.

> "Having a well-done, nation-state-level hardware implant surface would be like witnessing a unicorn jumping over a rainbow," says Joe Grand, a hardware hacker and the founder of *Grand Idea Studio Inc.* "Hardware is just so far off the radar, it's almost treated like black magic."[53]

China makes 90 percent of the world's computer equipment, so we would not have to look far to discover who was behind it. Their willingness to do something like this, knowing what it does to the business reputation of a company when discovered, it is hard to believe. Exposure of the supply chain is harder to detect than the basic types of hacking used to pull data from most computer systems. Hackers do not have to send suspicious looking letters to users hoping they will open them and allow code to flow into their computer systems. Unlike phishing, which is reduced with additional training, hardware penetrations work because users will not see them. The access points are built in.

The methods of a penetration of a system do not matter to the state that sponsors hacking, at least not yet. Supply chain attacks, especially those used in manufacturing, will have a real impact on businesses that are found to have components manipulated to allow someone to bypass security controls and get in. Who would buy a system that was known to be compromised before it was shipped?

Just like the attacks on government in the U.K., just prior to the Brexit vote, while the election campaigning was getting underway in the U.S., the Russians were accused of hacking both the U.S. Treasury and Commerce departments and their contractors, using a similar model though not the same techniques. SolarWinds, a business that supplies network mapping tools, allowed access to their hackers.[54] The Russian embassy said these were "unfounded attempts of the U.S. media to blame Russia," their usual reply. The hack used a method the Chinese have used before: altering software of a company and allowing that company to deliver the modifications to its customers. This kind of attack is also called a supply chain attack, but it is also software manipulation which can allow a trusted vendor to supply software to the target, something they routinely do with updates. The attackers were smart enough to test their penetration method by inserting a change in their code that did not do much of anything. Then, they waited for a time to see if that was discovered (anyone looking to verify the code might have noticed checksums did not match the original code that was prepared). Then, they inserted the access code that gave them a way into any system that installed the next update.[55] These are patient professionals who can wait.

In this case, SolarWinds supplied software to more than just the places the press noted in early reporting. Brian Krebs found that SolarWinds sold to 425 of the U.S. Fortune 500, all ten of the top U.S. telecommunications companies, all five U.S. military branches, the Pentagon, State Department, National Aviation and Space Administration, the National Security Agency, the Postal Service, the Department of Justice and the Office of the President of the United States, all five of the top U.S. accounting firms, and hundreds of universities and colleges.[56] Tampering with this kind of software is difficult but it pays great dividends when it is successful. It starts with a hack of a company and gives potential access to all of that company's customers.

Kevin Mandia, CEO of FireEye, a well-known security company used often by government agencies, said it affected approximately 18,000 entities out of the 300,000 where the code was distributed.

> I think ... it's important to note everybody says this is potentially the biggest intrusion in our history. The reality is the blast radius for this, I kind of explain it with a funnel. It's true that over 300,000 companies use SolarWinds, but you come down from that total number down to about 18,000 or so companies that actually had ... the backdoor or malicious code in a network. And then you come down to the next part. It's probably only about 50 organizations or companies, somewhere in that zone ... that's genuinely impacted by the threat act.... I want to come back to that in a moment, but attribution.... Secretary of State said it's Russia.[57]

We should note that both Mandia and Grenell were hesitant to attribute SolarWinds to the Russians, but both went along with the assessment of the Secretary of State who said it was Russia, based presumably on an assessment inside the U.S. government. Within a week, President Biden was calling for an in-kind response to the attack by Russia.[58] The intelligence community then reiterated its claim that it really was Russia, something that was not yet settled.

There is a tendency to blame the Russians first, and Ambassador Grenell explained the way intelligence analysts work in the U.S. He said the Russian analysts were quick to make an assessment on available information (raw intelligence) and not go through the entire process of analysis that is required. The Chinese analysts were not, being more thoughtful and taking longer to come to a conclusion. This does not make either group more accurate about their conclusions, but it is odd that the analysts follow the conduct of the two country's way of running their own operations.[59] Russia is in a hurry, and China takes its time.

This could turn out to be the largest, and most damaging penetration of U.S. government computer systems in history because so many different parts of the government were involved, and, because of the method used, few of them have actually discovered they have been penetrated. There will be more to come.

The U.S. Justice Department and U.S. Federal Courts, which includes the Supreme Court, announced two weeks later that it can be added to the list.[60] That has a sting to it because all the discussions about why different cases were prosecuted is in the Court computers. Why different cases were declined by the courts, and all the sealed indictments, including unnamed informants and cases yet to be publicly talked about, like Hunter Biden, the president's son. This is all fodder for release to the public. There are quite a few people in Washington, D.C., who all went through the theft of data from the DNC and its subsequent release to the public, wondering when the next shoe would drop.

So, before we retaliate it might be a good idea to be sure of who to retaliate against. Hiding the responsibility for an attack is difficult but it adds additional time to anyone seeking to retaliate for an attack like this. That time creates doubt and allows the attacker to devise more stories to deny the attack.

The Chinese Ministry of State Security has done the same thing with hacks of cloud services in 2019. That was called Cloud Hopper, a massive collector of information with access to clients of cloud services from Fujitsu, Tata Consultancy Services, NTT Data, Dimension Data, Computer Sciences Corp., DXC Technology, Hewlett Packard, and IBM.[61]

This kind of attack is an infrastructure breach which allows time inside a cloud to collect from customers of all of their customer's information. It is very difficult to detect and can go on for some time before it is discovered. Collecting all this data must have a purpose for hackers to spend the time and effort to go to such elaborate means to collect data. That can all be used in influence campaigns, but it has a more business-oriented use too.

The first purpose of this kind of data is to collect proprietary information like production strategies, pricing pending negotiations on deals and trade secrets. Particularly the defense and technology sectors are involved in long lead time product development that can be important to defense strategy or countermeasure development for certain types of weapons. Time-to-market is important to many industries and when products will be available to purchase can be important to an adversary. There are trade secrets and valuable proprietary sourcing agreements that are of interest. Feeding that information back to manufacturers in their own countries is why businesses value hacking of competitors.

The second, which is close behind and closely related, is to make assessments about the intentions of people in business or government. To determine what kinds of actions they intend to take that will influence Russia or China in the conduct of their affairs, especially political and economic matters. Then, they can prepare an influence campaign to change, if necessary, that position. Correspondence, usually email, tells them which people favor the approach they are campaigning against, which favor an approach closer to the one they want to influence, and which are neutral. SolarWinds was preceded by discovery in July 2020 that email accounts at the U.S. Treasury and the Internal Revenue Service were compromised. Microsoft warned of that attack. The emails of the leadership of those organizations were the targets.[62]

What complements that part of influence campaigns is identification of those with influence. Who, for example, communicates with the Secretary of the Treasury about issues relating to what China wants to influence? What are their intentions on various issues? Those people can have more influence than ones who communicate only rarely or only communicate with people at lower echelons. They can then influence some of those people to talk to the secretary on what positions to take. They can even use fake letters sent by e-mails, write papers that were not written by the influencers, and delete emails before they are sent.

Two very limited types of campaigns are required: one for those who oppose a policy the foreign government wants to implement; the other to reinforce those who favor it. That campaign can be to convince a person to change their mind and support a different position or to become neutral on the subject. They can influence directly or indirectly. Directly by providing additional information or having paid trolls to attempt to influence on-line. The Chinese did this with their suppression of news about the COVID-19 in Wuhan, China. They suppressed news of the death of a doctor, Li Wenliang, who had been censored and threatened by the police for spreading rumors about a new disease.

> To stage-manage what appeared on the Chinese internet early this year, the authorities issued strict commands on the content and tone of news coverage, directed paid trolls to inundate social media with party-line blather and deployed security forces to muzzle unsanctioned voices.[63]

All of those social media accounts that the vendors cannot seem to keep out of their systems are put to good use during those campaigns. Indirectly, a government can block the receipt of information from some sources that favor and support their position. The second is to reinforce those who favor a closer policy to the one the government is trying to influence and block information contrary to the Chinese position.

The third is that China is not content to influence only its own citizens. They want to influence everyone they can reach with their view of events. Given the data they have already collected on large populations, that would be a substantial number of individuals.

This narrow view of the influence value of information is a small part of why adversaries hack one another. What is different about this level of attacks is the scale of hacking undermines the security of a country. A country begins to believe it has no secrets. When it starts to behave as if there is no point in trying to protect its own decision-making rationales, it leaks almost everything to justify its own actions. The hacking is so extensive that it adds to that belief for many in other governments.

In previous years, several other major organizations were hacked using a variation of the supply chain attack against security companies: the IRS; Verisign, a crypto-solutions company; USAA, which primarily handles insurance and banking for military people; several locations of Comcast and Computer Sciences Corporation; a few locations of IBM; the U.S. Cert, which handles investigations into computer incidents at the Federal level; FireEye Inc a security company; the Defense Department Network Information Center; Facebook; Fannie May; Freddie Mac (just so we have most of those housing loans covered); Kaiser Foundation Health Care System; McAfee, Inc., the virus people who do nearly all of defense networks; Motorola; Wells Fargo Bank (and Wachovia, now owned by Wells Fargo); MIT; University of Nebraska–Lincoln; University of Pittsburgh; VMWare; the World Bank; and almost every telecommunications company of any size, anywhere in the world, including all the major telecoms in China. So, they were hacking their own telecoms.[64]

Imagine a database of every piece of the collected information from this broad attack. The Chinese know who is in debt, who has missed a house payment, who has diseases which might be disabling but not known to the public, who occupies positions in business and government that may have influence over various kinds of issues, who the IRS is after to pay back taxes, who is getting mental health treatment of any kind, and who among the political candidates might need help in campaign financing. They also know who operates the networks any of these people use and how to get to those networks through a telecommunications vendor who holds their account.

Now apply that breadth of detail to an influence campaign. They have the ability to target vulnerable people who will find it difficult to not cooperate. They have the ability to reward people who already favor their position. That can be done right now but the future allows for even greater amounts of collected data through infrastructure penetration that collects massive amounts.

Countries are rightly concerned about the ability to collect even larger quantities of data from national networks using equipment supplied by other nations. If we consider the volume of material already stolen by hacking and imagine what types of databases could be made with that volume, there is almost nothing a foreign country might know about every person, business, and government entity. And, that data can now be applied in ways we never thought possible.

The ability to influence is helped by artificial intelligence, and not necessarily in the ways we might have anticipated a few years ago. The ability to influence voting behavior came to light with the review of a company involved in the U.S. election of 2016. We now know how data from Facebook was used to influence voters.

> Cambridge Analytica trained an algorithm with a dataset comprising the profiles of Facebook users and friends of Facebook users who had taken a personality quiz. Using profile information such as likes, quiz results, and voting records, the algorithm was able to consider 253 predictions—compare that to a human's ability to process 5–7 pieces of information—to identify political affiliations and people who might be more easily influenced.[65] It then was used to tailor political advertising.

Cambridge Analytica announced in April 2018 that it was closing its doors, its business reputation damaged. Before they did, they left a trail of questions about the potential for influence using social media and simple questions. The problem for them was described by Issie Lapowsky at *Wired*:

> Cambridge Analytica had purchased Facebook data on tens of millions of Americans without their knowledge to build a "psychological warfare tool," which it unleashed on U.S. voters…. Just before the news broke, Facebook banned Wylie, Cambridge Analytica, its parent company SCL, and Aleksandr Kogan, the researcher who collected the data, from the platform…. Immediately, Facebook's stock price fell and boycotts began. Zuckerberg was called to testify before Congress, and a year of contentious international debates about the privacy rights of consumers online commenced.[66]

The initial idea for Cambridge Analytica came from University of Cambridge professor Aleksandr Kogan. He had developed a way to collect data on millions of Facebook users and their friends and parlayed that knowledge into something that could help predict how to influence a person. It also could predict many other things about a person that allowed the users to develop political advertising focused on the profiles.[67] Like the other Russian activities of the election in 2016, there is little research to show how successful these campaigns may have been, but they were a commercial success. The methods will be around long after people have forgotten the company.

The ability to apply AI algorithms to this data produced results that even the inventors of the idea did not particularly find attractive. It made them nervous. They knew they were onto something, but they all had the feeling that the something might be a political hot potato.[68] They were right, as the demise of Cambridge Analytica showed. But however hot that potato may have been, it was not hot enough to stop the application of the same types of techniques to other data that was equally available. The Chinese were already doing just that.

The Chinese have been said to have the best AI in the world because they have the best data to develop algorithms with.[69] It takes data to fine-tune an AI algorithm and make sure it functions properly. As a country they are the most obtrusive in collecting that data—much more than Cambridge Analytica ever thought of collecting—and applying what they learn from it to behavior modification of their own people. When one of their databases is discovered, it is a rarity of note.

In February 2019, a Dutch cybersecurity researcher, Victor Gevers, discovered a database in use in China. It was a compilation of real-time data on more than 2.5 million people in western China, updated constantly with GPS coordinates of their precise whereabouts. Alongside their names, birthdates and places of employment, there were notes on the places that they had most recently visited—mosque, hotels, restaurants. The Chinese can do the same thing to a target country if they can buy or steal location data, most of which is for sale. Gevers discovered the data was constantly updated from facial recognition software that captured faces combining that information with location and personal information already recorded. In case the thought might be that this is a Chinese phenomenon, that same equipment is sold in the U.S. for counter terrorism.[70] If it sounds like George Orwell's *1984*, that's because it is. The Chinese use this kind of data to make a personal rating that can instantly tell those with access to the data, whether a person is suitable to travel outside the country, if a voter voted on election day, gets access to the Internet, or should be arrested at the earliest opportunity.

> Harnessing advances in artificial intelligence and data mining and storage to construct detailed profiles on all citizens, China's communist party-state is developing a "citizen score" to incentivize "good" behavior.... While the expanding Orwellian eye may improve "public safety," it poses a chilling new threat to civil liberties in a country that already has one of the most oppressive and controlling governments in the world.[71]

This is behavior modification on a massive scale. The algorithms have been perfected. The storage requirements refined. The links to enforcement offices completed. That kind of expertise is valuable and can be used for a number of applications that have nothing to do with China's massive population. All they need to do is export the ideas.

If we look at the data stolen by China and apply the same types of principles used by the Chinese government and Cambridge Analytica, we see the ability to influence national thinking in other countries. If we can harness social media and search providers, we can do it even better. The Chinese can buy much of what they would need from U.S. social media vendors.[72] They can then target, or help others target, specific individuals and groups. It does not mean they can control the outcome of an election, but they can certainly influence the vote, which is enough to concern every citizen.

We cannot tolerate this kind of interference in our democracy and must do something about it.

6

A Detailed Look at a Limited Influence Campaign

The real nature of an influence campaign is not easy to see since so much of it is invisible. It is rare that one campaign can be discovered almost in its entirety. To an intelligence service that manages such a campaign, being exposed is embarrassing; and to the government sponsoring it, it is a cause of concern. These kinds of operations are supposed to be state secrets.

An almost obscure campaign that tried to change world sporting officials' opinions about what action to take against Russia for intentionally doping athletes on a broad scale is not significant in a global sense. The techniques used were open to scrutiny by a series of public releases of data regarding aspects of it discovered by different countries. Findings were reported separately, with few countries tying seemingly unrelated activities together.

It began with the release of a German documentary called *Top Secret Doping: How Russia Makes Its Winners*.[1] The film was not an international sensation, but did expose the Russians because it showed details of techniques used to dope athletes at the Sochi Olympics and pointed fingers at Russian government officials who aided in the subterfuge. Most countries would have countered this kind of story with a flurry of news and television articles representing their version of the truth.

But the German documentary was more complicated than that. It called attention to the detailed techniques used to hide and manipulate drug testing results from the World Anti-Doping Agency (WADA), which oversees these athletic events. WADA was saying the Russians did enhance their athletes' abilities to compete by means that were illegal in sports, and the film offered case histories.

WADA announced in November 2015 that Russian track and field athletes were using performance enhancing drugs and blood doping to improve performance and published a detailed report that described how and when these activities took place.[2] The report accused the Director of the Russian Ministry of Sport and other government officials of cooperating with the doping and cover-up. It said the director of the official laboratory in Moscow, Grigori Rodchenkov, was taking cash payments to delay or taint doping results. He later became a leading informant for WADA, exposing many of the methods used. Informants, similar to whistleblowers, have undone many secret influence programs because they are credible eyewitnesses.

In December 2017, the International Olympic Committee Executive Board decided the Russian doping was so egregious, it banned Russian athletes from participating under their own flag, and specific athletes were banned from participation. This was an embarrassment to Russia and its athletes, most of whom did not use drugs.

Vladimir Putin, the former KGB officer, was not happy about the IOC action.[3] That is particularly important because a senior government official is required to begin the process of an influence campaign. As a practical matter, any country that wants to control its influence abroad, or with an extraterritorial body like WADA, is taking a risk that usually can only be accepted by the head of a government. The country needs to have covert commitment of significant amounts of money. The risks of exposure need to be identified, understood, and accepted by a senior official. Conflicts among different government agencies or parts of the intelligence agencies involved have to be identified and resolved. Finally, an end objective and timeline have to be established. Low level officials generally cannot do any of those things.

The Russian campaign's secondary goal appears to be to dissuade the Olympic Committee from banning all Russian athletes from the 2018 Olympics. How did the Russians know that was going to be necessary? They spied on the people who were making the decision on what action would be taken as a result of discovery. They combined the state intelligence functions with the state-controlled press and targeted the organizations that influence decisions. They hoped to influence those decisions before they were made. They were not trying to change world opinion, but only to influence a small group of decision makers who had the authority to decide on the punishment.

To change the narrative, Russia would try to do something novel— infer that doping was a much broader threat to athletic competition throughout the world. Their reasoning, if the rest of the world accepted it, demanded further action beyond Russia in this instance. The evidence suggests this was part of a disinformation campaign to the effect that, "since everybody does it, we should not focus just on the Russians," a strategy with dubious origins or chances of success. It was also partly to save the reputations of Russian athletes through a covert program with a simple objective: save face for Russia by proving that athletes from other nations were doing some of the same things. Logic also says this is not necessarily the best approach to take, because, even if it were to be successful, the Russians were no less guilty of doping.

But there was more going on here than a superficial media influence campaign by a few Russians involved in swinging the opinions of a regulatory body. As with many other influence campaigns, they had help from part of the government intelligence apparatus in Russia.

In the U.S. District Court's Western District of Pennsylvania, seven Russian officers in the Russian Main Intelligence Directorate (GRU), a military intelligence agency of the General Staff of the Armed Forces of the Russian Federation, were indicted for computer hacking, wire fraud, aggravated identity theft, and money laundering.[4] The case involved doping on the Russian Olympic team, which was discredited and banned in the 2014 Sochi Olympics, and criminal offenses committed on foreign soil.

As the indictment shows, the Russians sought to discredit athletes from other countries by showing both real and imagined cases of doping.[5] Although the strategy seemed less than well-thought-out, the Russians obviously believed it would succeed and directed the intelligence collection parts of the GRU to hack into the WADA computers. They initially failed in their attempts to hack those computers but adapted quickly.

The Russians sent a "close access" team to other countries to circumvent WIFI connections and gain access to accounts on the WADA network, which was reasonably secure against other types of attack. WIFI has a relatively short range but is relatively easy to hack if the team is in close proximity.[6] This kind of activity is very high risk for Russia since it requires team members to pretend to be someone other than who they really are and travel to other countries where they might be exposed.

> This investigation had the support of advocates for clean sports, including the United States Anti-Doping Agency (USADA), the Canadian Centre for Ethics in Sport (CCES, Canada's anti-doping agency). Eventually, in some instances only after arbitration rulings by the International Court of Arbitration for Sport (TAS/CAS), approximately 111 Russian athletes were excluded from the 2016 Summer Olympic Games, in Rio de Janeiro, Brazil, by a number of international athletics federations, including track-and-field's International Association of Athletics Federations (IAAF).[7]

This is spying in every meaning of the word. These are Russian intelligence operatives, engaged in covert activities on foreign soil in several different countries. The risks are indicated by the fact that the team was identified, and some members arrested and later expelled from the Netherlands. It could have been worse. The whole effort was exposed, though we actually heard few details of it in the international press, and what was reported on was short lived.

The same team was busy in many places, not just at WADA Headquarters in Canada. Agents hacked meetings of WADA, the International Olympic Committee (IOC), the Fédération Internationale de Football Association ("FIFA") and other locations to find information about ongoing investigations of doping. At the same time, they hacked other organizations of interest to Russia like the Organization for the Prohibition of Chemical Weapons (OPCW).

This was described by the U.S. Justice Department as government intelligence support to the influence campaign, but it is really much more than that.[8] These support activities are critical to any campaign but can be used by any subsequent campaign allowing them to target organizations with information tailored to their intended actions.

At least part of that activity was operating network equipment, proxy servers to hide their identity and location, research on individuals, hacking email systems, affecting "U.S. persons, corporate entities, international organizations, and their respective employees located around the world, based on their strategic interest to the Russian government."

Two years later, the Dutch Ministry of Defense announced the arrest of a 4-man hacking team of Russian GRU agents with wireless hacking equipment in their car. These agents had been trying to hack several networks in the Organization for the Prohibition of Chemical Weapons (OPCW). The U.K. released a statement that identified a number of pseudonyms GRU personnel used in cyberattacks around the world. Additional attempted Russian attacks included spearphishing attacks in March aimed at compromising UK Foreign and Commonwealth Offices, and a similar effort in which GRU agents impersonated Swiss federal authorities to target OPCW officials. "The GRU's actions are reckless and indiscriminate," UK Foreign Secretary Jeremy Hunt said October 4. "This pattern of behavior demonstrates their desire to operate without regard to international law or established norms and to do so with a feeling of impunity and without consequences."[9]

The Russians left a number of traces of their activities. When agents started to go through the captured equipment, they discovered hacking of WADA from Rio de Janeiro (August 2016) and Lausanne (September 2016).

On the particular day they arrived in Lausanne, WADA was holding a meeting on "challenges to the anti-doping system" in the Palace Hotel.[10] The Russians were trying to get ahead of what they knew would be discussions about what to do with their athletes, and add to their work on chemical weapons. They collected intelligence to help shape the influence campaigns. This kind of intelligence helps them discover who supports their policy views, who opposes it, and who shows little interest. This allows them to reinforce those who favor their view, diminish or stifle those who do not, and draw in those who are neutral. Some of that influence comes by releasing information to the public, which in turn can influence the voting members of WADA, if it can be done before those votes take place.

The kind of surveillance the Russians were doing gave them the confidence to suggest that OPCW might help with the investigation of the poisoning of Russian dissident Alexei Navalny with Novichok, a group of seven toxic chemical agents developed by the former Soviet Union in the 1970s and 1980s. These toxins have been used in several assassination attempts by the GRU. They would be able to know persons sympathetic to Russia before extending the invitation, but it never materialized.

The next thing the Russians have to do is influence some of the voters on committees that matter. They did that by releasing some internal emails that would influence the vote. Some of the internal information these hacks were able to collect was released on the Russian Fancy Bear website under the Anonymous hacker banner.[11] This is a Russian intelligence agency releasing stolen information using a hacker group's identity. That information included accusations against such noted athletes as Serena Williams, Simone Biles, Rafael Nadal and over 150 soccer players. Following those releases the same information was transmitted to Russian "troll farms" who repeated the accusations on Twitter.[12]

The problem with such information is, of course, that there is no way to validate the authenticity of the data. Once they collected the information, the Russians could have added some of their own making, modifying some, deleting much of it, or any number of other approaches to influence the content in ways that benefited them. In disparate cases, the Russians used the same techniques in attempts to disrupt campaigns of political candidates in other countries. They used the same techniques in the release of French President Macron's internal correspondence, Hillary Clinton's campaign e-mails, and information stolen from U.S. election officials. They could modify stolen products, selectively release others, and write stories to fit narratives that confused the readers or expressed a view other than what was intended.

The Russian press, principally represented by *RT* and *Sputnik*, used several other news services to support these influence programs by publishing stories of their own which support the Russian position. Although there were many stories, the following are examples:

> In February *RT* published a story about Grigory Rodchenkov, the director of the laboratory in Moscow, that was at the root of claims of Russian doping during the Olympics. This article attempted to undermine his credibility.[13]
> In April 2019, *Sputnik News*, published a story saying the police had opened an investigation of the Russian testing laboratory, accusing

it of overcharging for equipment and tests (but honestly noting it had discovered a 147 percent increase in the number of violations compared to the previous year).[14] It was one small chip at the integrity of the testing laboratory that cooperated in the doping, and the director who cooperated in exposing it.

In April 2018, *RT* published a summary of WADA 2016 test results for athletes under the title "WADA Reveals Worst Doping Cheaters in 2016, Russia Not Even in the Top 5."[15] The title is deceptive because the WADA report included a category of Anti-Doping Rule Violations (ADRVs), which includes hiding or manipulating test results. Russia was first in that category with 176 cases, far surpassing any other country, in any other category. But the Russians occasionally achieve their objective by headlines with thin supporting content.

In the end, the Russian agents succeeded in releasing information on 250 athletes in over 30 countries yet failed to keep themselves from being banned from some events in the 2018 and 2022 Olympics or marching under the Russian flag.[16] The stories they published brought accusations against many top, non–Russian athletes who thought they had long ago resolved their cases with WADA.

In measuring the success of this kind of operation, we must be able to assess whether the objectives were achieved. From an operational perspective, what the campaign against WAPA shows is that covert activities of this kind are less effective if discovered and attributed to the country trying to influence decisions. If we know Russia has stolen and published information, that knowledge degrades the chances that any decision-making authority, like WAPA, will react favorably to the actions the Russians' desire. Fortunately, if the campaign does not influence the decision makers before they make their decisions, a campaign is less effective.

However, each campaign builds on the next. They may not be successful this year, but there is always the next decision cycle to try again. The hacks, the dossiers developed on voting members, the positions of members of the various councils, the use of certain messages targeting specific groups, and the like are all useful to the next campaign. The list of 500,000 persons on voting registers in states considered "swing states" in an election can be important, until they move their voting locations. The Russians are not starting at the beginning when they run their next campaign.

In this instance the Russians had a specific target, ran a small campaign, and had mixed success. Upon appeal to the Court of Arbitration for Sports (CAS), Russia was banned from using its name, flag and anthem at the next two Olympics or at any world championships for the next two years. They are allowed to participate in the Tokyo Games, the 2022 Games in Beijing and the World Cup in Qatar. The Court of Arbitration for Sport's ruling also blocked Russia from bidding to host major sporting events for two years.[17] The CAS did concede one point by allowing "Russia" to appear on uniforms, if "Neutral Athlete" appears in equal-sized text. It was a pointless requirement, because nobody would be reading those country names anyway, unless they were close to the athletes. If this sounds like victory to anyone in Russia, they are deluding themselves.

They were exposed by three governments and their methods identified. Their methods are starting to become known and successfully countered by those who understand them. In France, the Russians were less successful, and although the French are credited with riding out the storm, they may have benefited from Russian mistakes as much as their own countermeasures.

The influence campaign in the French national election was never formally attributed to Russia, though the political party of Macron, En Marche!, did name Russia.[18] We can easily see the similarities with WADA, the U.S. national elections, and other European attempts by Russia. The lack of attribution by the national government is clearly part of a response that is intentional.

President Macron addressed one aspect of the interference in a press conference with President Putin, when he called out *RT* and *Sputnik* for being propaganda agents during the national campaign.[19] This was similar to the way accusations about other athletes appeared in *RT* during the WADA campaign.

The Russian mistake was two-fold: the release of information was too close to the date when information needed to be viewed by the individuals targeted; and some of the documents were so obviously fraudulent they were not credible. Both of these factors reduced the effectiveness of the effort. As a rule, any time email is stolen, there is a risk that it will be selectively released, and those releases will contain content that is developed by the people who stole it.

The French victims avoided attributing the campaign to Russia as a way of deescalating a confrontation with Russia. Germany had the same type of interference in its election in 2017, but also did not attribute the actions to Russia.[20] The problem with attribution is the ability to "prove" that a country actually did what was alleged. That kind of proof is technically available to the kinds of forensic investigators the French, German and U.S. officials have, but it comes at a price. The U.S. issued indictments for criminal activity and intended to go to court to prove its cases. But these covert operations are not suitable for criminal prosecution and there have been no resulting prosecutions.

When it comes to proof in court, we have to expose the methods used to find the evidence that is being presented, and most countries do not want to do that. When Russian oligarch Yevgeniy Viktorovich Prigozhin fought his indictment, the U.S. ultimately dropped its case rather than expose the investigative methods that would to prove his companies guilty. This was worse than never bringing the case at all because Prigozhin can proclaim his innocence and his persecution at the hands of the U.S. Justice Department.

In September 2020, the Department of the Treasury's Office of Foreign Assets Control (OFAC) placed Prigozhin and eight of his associates on the Specially Designated Nationals and Blocked Persons List, based on OFAC's determination that one or more applicable legal criteria were satisfied. All property and interests in property subject to U.S. jurisdiction are blocked, and U.S. persons are generally prohibited from engaging in transactions with Prigozhin.[21]

It is not as if the U.S. does not know what really happened. At least some of those allegations can be proven but exposure of the methods will cause the Russians to change their methods and become more difficult to detect. It could also cause any number of other countries to use the same methods against U.S. assets. It is much better to disrupt these kinds of cases than try to prosecute them in court.

What the U.S. can do is attribute the case to Russia in classified sessions of Congress and never publicly accuse them. The intelligence community and national leadership in the U.S. will know which country is responsible.

7

Elections as a Special Case

Using a different, narrower example of the U.S. election of 2016, Finnish researcher Mika Aaltola took a slightly different slant in identifying the key attributes of election meddling:

> (1) using disinformation to amplify suspicions and divisions; (2) stealing sensitive and leakable data; (3) leaking the stolen data via supposed "hacktivists"; (4) whitewashing the leaked data through the professional media; and (5) secret colluding [between a candidate and a foreign state] in order to synchronize election efforts.[1]

When the Russians were accused of meddling in U.S. elections, very few people in the U.S. Intelligence Community were surprised, except by hearing those charges made in public. Somewhere in the world, there is manipulation of election results going on almost every day, just not always in the same way. Countries that are big enough, and have technical capability, manipulate the perception of events on a regular basis, now mostly through the Internet. They manufacture and distribute news stories, give money to political candidates, support social media campaigns, target specific individuals to weaken or support, pay off corrupt officials, disrupt election result processing, and manipulate or disrupt voting machines to favor an outcome.[2] They occasionally get caught, but not as often as they should.

When they do, they expose a multitude of tactics used in their operations, things the sponsor of a program would not want to see in print. The indictment of Russians via sealed indictment in 2020 shows the step-by-step progress of 11 GRU officers in Unit 26165 in Moscow stealing information in both Russia and the United States.[3] Their pseudonyms online were identified, along with when they sent email to the Clinton Campaign, and how they installed malware on the Clinton servers that let them take information, which ultimately ended up on the Internet. In May of 2016 they were discovered by the DNCC, which hired a private security firm, yet the extractions continued. Anatoliy Sergeyevich Kovalev was a Russian GRU officer who worked for Unit 74455.

GRU officers who knowingly and intentionally conspired with each other ... to hack into the computers of U.S. persons and entities responsible for the administration of 2016 U.S. elections, such as state boards of elections, secretaries of state, and U.S. companies that supplied software and other technology related to the administration of U.S. elections.

One of the difficulties with discovery of their operations was the GRU hackers and their co-conspirators were later charged in October 2020 with computer intrusions and attacks intended to support Russian government efforts to undermine, retaliate against, or otherwise destabilize: (1) Ukraine; (2) Georgia; (3) elections in France; (4) efforts to hold Russia accountable for its use of a weapons-grade nerve agent, Novichok, on foreign soil; and (5) the 2018 PyeongChang Winter Olympic Games after Russian athletes were banned from participating under their nation's flag, as a consequence of Russian government-sponsored doping effort.[4] All the things that the Russian GRU was doing up to that point were being investigated while the 2016 charges were being drawn up. But in 2016, they were still refining their techniques.

Deputy Assistant Attorney General Adam S. Hickey from the U.S. Justice Department laid out the various types of current influence campaigns in October 2018[5]: Almost all of them are related to elections, which tells us what was most on his mind coming into the end of the mid-term elections.

1. ***Cyber operations targeting election infrastructure:*** Such operations could seek to undermine the integrity or availability of election-related data. For example, adversaries could employ cyber-enabled or other means to target election infrastructure, such as voter registration databases and voting machines. Operations aimed at removing otherwise eligible voters from the rolls or attempting to manipulate the results of an election (or even just disinformation suggesting that such manipulation has occurred) could undermine the integrity and legitimacy of elections, as well as public confidence in election results. To our knowledge, no foreign government has succeeded in perpetrating ballot fraud, but raising even the doubt that it has occurred could be damaging.

2. ***Cyber operations targeting political organizations, campaigns, and public officials:*** These operations could seek to compromise the confidentiality of private information of the targeted groups or individuals, as well as its integrity. For example, adversaries could conduct cyber or other operations against U.S. political organizations and campaigns to steal confidential information and use that information, or alterations thereof, to discredit or embarrass candidates, undermine political organizations, or impugn the integrity of public officials.

3. *Covert influence operations to assist or harm political organizations, campaigns, and public officials:* For example, adversaries could conduct covert influence operations to provide assistance that is prohibited from foreign sources to political organizations, campaigns, and government officials. These intelligence operations might involve covert offers of financial, logistical, or other campaign support to, or covert attempts to influence the policies or positions of, unwitting politicians, party leaders, campaign officials, or even the public.

4. *Covert influence operations, including disinformation operations, to influence public opinion and sow division:* Using false U.S. personas, adversaries could covertly create and operate social media pages and other forums designed to attract U.S. audiences and spread disinformation or divisive messages. These messages need not relate directly to campaigns. They may seek to depress voter turnout among particular groups, encourage third-party voting, or convince the public of widespread voter fraud in order to undermine confidence in election results.

5. *Overt influence efforts, such as the use of foreign media outlets or other organizations to influence policymakers and the public:* For example, adversaries could use state-owned or state-influenced media outlets to reach U.S. policymakers or the public. Governments can disguise these outlets as independent, while using them to promote divisive narratives and political objectives.

Attacking election infrastructure is exactly what the Russians did when they went after election equipment vendors. Note that Hickey said: *To our knowledge, no foreign government has succeeded in perpetrating ballot fraud, but raising even the doubt that it has occurred could be damaging.* But that damaging evidence was already published in the Russian indictments, and by others before, and since. Those were clear the GRU hacked vendors of voting machines, state election offices, and registration software, all important to validation of election results. In an unclassified summary of the larger subject of election interference published by the ODNI[6]:

> Cyber actors affiliated with the Russian government scanned state systems extensively throughout the 2016 election cycle. These cyber actors made attempts to access numerous state election systems, and in a small number of cases accessed voter registration databases.
>
> • At least 18 states had election systems targeted by Russian-affiliated cyber actors in some fashion. Elements of the IC have varying levels of confidence about three additional states, for a possible total of at least 21. In addition, other states saw suspicious or malicious behavior the IC has been unable to attribute to Russia.

- Almost all of the states that were targeted observed vulnerability scanning directed at their Secretary of State websites or voter registration infrastructure. Other scans were broader or less specific in their target.
- In at least six states, the Russian-affiliated cyber actors went beyond scanning and conducted malicious access attempts on voting-related websites. In a small number of states, Russian-affiliated cyber actors were able to gain access to restricted elements of election infrastructure. In a small number of states, these cyber actors were in a position to, at a minimum, alter or delete voter registration data; however, they did not appear to be in a position to manipulate individual votes or aggregate vote totals.

The election infrastructure is more complicated than most outsiders realize. There are 10,000 entities running the election. In many municipalities, elections are managed by a clerk, recorder, or registrar, who has other duties in addition to running elections.[7] It is not organized into a national system and there is no effort to do that kind of reorganization. It is a fragmented state system, often using old equipment and managed by election officials who are not very competent with any of the requirements of securely managed systems. Each state is responsible for the part of the infrastructure it builds, including the following:

Voter registration databases: These are used to enter, store, and edit voter registration information, such as servers that host the database and online portals that provide access. Voter registration is an ongoing process to create new records, update existing records, and remove outdated records....[8]

Electronic and paper pollbooks: These contain information on registered voters at polling places and can be used to register voters were permitted by law. Pollbooks must be prepared by transferring information from the voter registration database. Pollbooks are comprised of both technology and processes to view, edit, and modify voter records.

Ballot preparation: This is the process of overlaying political geographies with the contests and candidates specific to each district, and then translating those layouts into unique combinations of ballot data.

Voting machine systems: These consist of the technology and processes used to cast and, in some cases, generate voter ballots of all types (paper-based systems, and electronic-based systems like ballot marking devices and direct-recording electronic machines with or without a voter-verified paper audit trail).

Centralized vote tabulation and aggregation systems: These are used to tally votes shared by sub-jurisdictions such as counties, precincts, and in some cases individual machines or even individual ballots. These systems collect and process data to determine the result of an election contest. Of all the computers used in an election, these are probably the most important.

They are the machines that count the votes. They are not very secure in the way we would hope they would be.

Official websites: Used by election officials to communicate information to the public, including how to register to vote, where to vote (e.g., precinct look-up tools), and to convey election results

Polling places: Including early voting locations, these are locations where individuals cast their votes and may be physically located on public or private property.

Election offices: These are locations where election officials conduct official business, including shared workspaces such as public libraries, municipal buildings, private homes, and public areas for jurisdictions without a dedicated workspace.[9]

In October 2020, DHS and the FBI published a warning on their website under the title Russian State-Sponsored Advanced Persistent Threat Actor Compromises U.S. Government Targets, carrying this detail: Russian state-sponsored advanced persistent threat (APT) actor activity targeting various U.S. state, local, territorial, and tribal (SLTT) government networks, as well as aviation networks. The Russians used common attack techniques using known vulnerabilities.

This is not the kind of hacking the GRU would normally do. These are highly trained agents who specialize in hacking in several countries around the world. That is a scarce resource in any government agency and Russia would not be any different. They are too busy to do work like hacking 10,000 election offices or websites of campaigns. They could find any hacker group wanting to make a little money and have them try to hack every election office in the U.S. Since these computers are not managed as a system, they have a variety of administrators with differing experience in security. No hacker has that kind of experience unless it is acquired over years of work. If we just look at the categories "public libraries, municipal buildings, private homes," we have an understanding of the variety and likelihood of gaining entry. This is not the level of security we would find in a financial institution or classified government computer network.

In or around August 2016, KOVALEV and his co-conspirators hacked into the computers of a U.S. vendor ("Vendor 1") that supplied software used to verify voter registration information for the 2016 U.S. elections. KOVALEV and his co-conspirators used some of the same infrastructure to hack into Vendor 1 that they had used to hack into SBOE 1.

In or around August 2016, the Federal Bureau of Investigation issued an alert about the hacking of SBOE 1 and identified some of the infrastructure that was used to conduct the hacking. In response, KOVALEV deleted his search history. KOVALEV and his co-conspirators also deleted records from accounts used in their operations targeting state boards of elections and similar election-related entities.[10]

What we tend to forget is that this information does not go away when the hacking is done, and Kovalev knew it. That is why he had to clean up when he learned about the hacking that had been detected. If he did his cleanup well enough, it would be difficult to discover if he succeeded in getting into all the places he did hack, and the number of states that were compromised could be higher. The Russians have ways into a number of state election offices and those did not go away because only some of them were discovered.

These offices and equipment are not monitored the way national security systems are. Many do not have any kind of intrusion detection, systems monitoring or cross-platform comparisons of penetration attempts. These are independent operations and not part of a national network of election systems that can be monitored the way it should be. Nor do most states have qualified analysts to make decisions about the success of attacks.

Being hacked is not easy to recover from because the people who do it make changes in the systems they get into to make it easier to get back in if they are discovered. To make that more difficult for anyone tracking them, hackers cover their tracks in the system. Because the FBI had to warn users of voter registration software that they had been hacked, the Russians knew investigators would be looking for evidence of that kind of activity they were up to—what did they take, modify, or delete.

Kovalev began covering his tracks right after the FBI made their announcement. By that time, the Russians had hacked vendors of voting machines, state election offices, registration software, and a number of places we have yet to discover.[11] Because, at the same time they were doing that, they were also collecting information from a number of government offices unrelated to the election.

Only the Russians were accused of election infrastructure hacking, though some recent attempts cannot be attributed to any country, even though they were discovered. The Russians and Chinese have learned over the years and could have holes in every system they got into, to allow them to continue their attacks. The Russians could apply what they learned to the U.S. election in 2016 to subsequent elections. They could wait until the time was right.

In the U.S. elections in 2016, the Russians used a social media campaign to do be more effective at targeting specific issues relating to candidates. They had 500,000 stolen names to run those against and test them before using them on a wider audience. That included hacking of one political party and the release of stolen information to WikiLeaks.[12] Because the campaign was broad and deep, they could direct differently approaches to millions of people seeing and reacting to supporting materials produced by Russian interests. At the same time, they were meddling in the U.S. elections they were conducting similar operations in Europe. They have now been formally charged with those activities, even if it took four years to release some of those charges.

In 2017, before all of these other charges were made, Leonid Reshetnikov, then director of the Russian Institute for Strategic Studies (RISS), visited Bulgaria. Several news outlets say he provided the Socialist Party there with a secret strategy document proposing a road to victory at the ballot box. It contained recommendations to plant fake news and promote exaggerated polling data.[13] He was said to have urged the Socialist Party to adopt a platform that aligned with Kremlin interests, end sanctions on Russia, criticize NATO, and encourage Brexit. None of those things would be surprising to a Russian analyst anywhere in the world, except possibly the move on Brexit.

> Officially, the Russian government asserted its neutrality on the question of the Brexit referendum, but its English-language media outlets RT and Sputnik covered the referendum campaign extensively and offer systematically one-sided coverage supporting a British departure from the European Union and frequently broadcasted statements from UKIP [Independence Party] head [Nigel] Farage.[14]

The British press came to the conclusion there was Russian interference in the Brexit vote more by inference than detection of individual attempts to undermine the vote. The publication of a report, in July 2020, of what the Russians were supposed to have done indicated British intelligence services were never tasked to assess the Russian campaign.[15] The Kremlin has tried to undermine European integration and the EU, sow confusion and undermine confidence in democratic processes. Brexit seemed like a logical place for the Russians to progress, so a logical place for intelligence services to look for Russian activities. Apparently, it was enough that they were never asked to.

The UK's National Cyber Security Centre indicated an increase in direct Russian-based attacks on U.K. government resources from November 2017.[16] Most of the attacks were directed at media outlets, telecommunications and energy sectors.[17] They did not show a link between Brexit and these events but conducting attacks on government sites causes a drain on defensive security, resources that might otherwise have been engaged in research of other election meddling. They have been accused of some similar things in the U.K. with interfering in the Brexit referendum, including promoting exit from the EU in the U.K. and other countries.[18] A leaked report said the results of the Russian interference were "unquantifiable," much like their program in the U.S. national elections.[19]

At the same time, the Russian Internet Research Agency was directing a covert campaign against U.S. presidential candidates, it was also pouring out messaging to Twitter about Brexit. The messages were on both sides of the vote, i.e., some favored staying in the EU, but the majority favored exit from it. But Twitter and Facebook both underestimated the size and scope of the use of their respective social media, just as they did in the U.S. elections.

Twitter said there were only six tweets discovered, all paid for by the Russian news service *RT*, at a cost of less than $1000. Researchers at the University of California and Swansea University in Wales identified 150,000 Twitter accounts with various Russian ties that disseminated messages about Brexit before the referendum.[20] Researchers at Oxford University found among the main social media outlets like Facebook, Twitter and Instagram, "leave" messaging positions were five to seven times greater on those media.[21] The final vote (52 percent to 48 percent) was much closer than these numbers would predict.

In a statement before the U.S. Senate Select Committee on Intelligence, Dr. Constanza Stelzenmueller described the Russian efforts to influence the German national election this way:

> The impact of Kremlin interference, if we're honest here, is also hit and miss, often miss. In many ways, its meddling in European elections over the past year has produced the exact opposite of what was intended. It has produced stable, democratic, and non-populist governments that are pro–European Union and indeed pro–NATO and pro–American. The populists have lost out almost everywhere and NATO and the E.U., I'm happy to say, are experiencing a renaissance of purpose.[22]

This was undoubtedly not the outcome the Russians were expecting or desired. Yet that has not deterred them from continuing this type of interference, nor did those observations seem to convince them to stop.

The Senate Intelligence Committee reported on accusations of Russian interference during the 2017 election in Germany, an account that sounds familiar to anyone examining the Russian tactics used in the United States.[23] Italy complained of Russian interference blaming the EU for immigration policies that were not favored.[24] France indicates its institutions successfully negated a similar attempt during the French election in 2017.[25] Even before they used an array of means to influence elections in the Ukraine, the Russians were perfecting methods of influence in a number of Eastern European countries, especially those in NATO. As much as they deny any such activity, the preponderance of evidence suggests they are engaged in these kinds of covert activities, and they are successful in stirring up trouble in democratic countries where they are able to apply their techniques. They are not necessarily achieving their political objectives, but they are learning how to be more successful.

Posing as U.S. citizens, the GRU sponsored political events on both political sides of the elections, hid its association with the Russian government and used real or fictitious companies and locations to make themselves more difficult to discover. In the French election, some of the first anti–Macron websites were in the U.S. and run by alt-right groups who suddenly appeared within a month of each other.[26] By all indications, this was a covert, deniable program with hidden leadership, financing, and participants. The program generated social media sites that were supported with program-generated artwork and technical teams.

> The ORGANIZATION [GRU and associated commercial interests] sought, in part, to conduct what it called "information warfare" against the United States of America through fictitious U.S. personas on social media platforms and other Internet-based media.[27]

It would be a mistake, however, to characterize information warfare by the standards the Russians set in this one case. It is much more than the manipulation of people's perceptions about political candidates and the process of electing them. They were feeding organizations and attacking ideas that are basic to the core values of people in various countries. It is the manipulation of perceptions of a broad group of policies and changing people's attitudes to more closely align with the internal positions of government leaders in the sponsoring country, Russia. Information war has a broader application than elections including such things as electronic warfare, intelligence integration and offensive hacker operations to counter some types of attacks. That is more difficult than messaging in any single campaign. For all their effort, the Russians cannot claim success, at least not in 2016 and 2018. We still do not know enough about what they did in 2020 to make an assessment.

In international operations today, we seldom will publicly know which country actually sponsored a covert program. They are careful to not use domestic electronic networks to launch their attacks. These networks are easily traced by other governments. They use "false flags" to imply that certain types of campaigns originate in other countries, such as those used to indicate the Ukraine stole Hillary Clinton's emails and released them to the public, when the U.S. intelligence community indicated it was the Russians.[28] They have cover stories for assets used in their own country. They make it harder to discover the origins of any campaign. The Russians were very *ineffective* in their U.S. operation, which began in 2014, before anyone knew who the candidates would be. The measure of their lack of success can be found in the details discovered and published by the U.S. government which attributed these operations to the Russians. They were too easily discovered to be called successful.

In the Russian campaign of 2016, there were at least seven named companies, first among them being the Internet Research Agency (IRA). Also named were Internet Research LLC, MediaSintez LLC, GlavSet LLC, MixInfo LLC, Azimut LLC, and NovInfo LLC. There were 12 individuals named in the indictment, with Yevgeniy Viktorovich Prigozhin at the center of the investigation. Prigozhin is an oligarch and financial backer of the troll farm known as the Internet Research Agency, according to Russian media. He is a caterer who has been nicknamed "Putin's chef" because of his proximity to the Russian president.[29] Prigozhin owned or controlled two other participating companies, Concord Management and Consulting LLC, and Concord Catering.

Employees of these companies and the Russian government were accused of most of the operations associated with the U.S. election campaign. They stole identities of real people, masqueraded as fictitious U.S. nationals, penetrated computer systems in the U.S. and launched their attacks from them to hide the real source of their communications. Finally, "Defendants, together with others known and unknown to the Grand Jury, knowingly and intentionally conspired to defraud the United States by impairing, obstructing, and defeating the lawful functions of the Federal Election Commission, the U.S. Department of Justice, and the U.S. Department of State in administering federal requirements for disclosure of foreign involvement in certain domestic activities."[30]

Several peripheral activities were created and funded covertly: "a graphics department; a data analysis department; a search-engine optimization ('SEO') department; an information-technology ('IT') department to maintain the digital infrastructure used in the ... operations; and a finance department to budget and allocate funding."[31]

We might know where these operations were carried out, even what was done, but countries want to cover up their participation in them. The U.S. was able to determine that Project Lakhta was broader in scope than just the U.S. operations. According to the indictment, Project Lakhta was funded through fourteen bank accounts all related to Concord Catering.[32] The accounts were supposed to be monies transferred for software and software development. These programs would have been more sensitive to the Russians than those addressed by the indictment. For the Russian leaders of Project Lakhta, the inability to prosecute by the Justice Department must have been a relief.

It is possible that the Russians are telling the U.S. that they can attack us with impunity and the U.S. will do nothing. I was involved in one investigation where Russian hackers told the investigators they would not stop illegal hacking and the person speaking even chuckled slightly when he replied. He knew there was not much we could do about it, but he invited retaliation by laughing at our leadership. He may have been used to being investigated and have the investigation fade away over time, but some organizations have a long reach, and they will not give up on anyone.

Iran acted the same way when they issued public denials of any involvement in missile and drone attacks on facilities in Saudi Arabia in September 2019, blaming them on Houthi rebels in Yemen. The Yemeni forces publicly accepted the claim that it was them; Iran still denies being involved. The attacks threatened the world's oil supplies without the loss of life that usually accompanies such broad attacks, without putting the Saudis and Iranians in direct conflict.

A lesser-known attack on the same oil processing facility was in late 2004 and was done with the encouragement of Osama bin Laden.[33] Terrorist groups looking for notoriety are more likely to claim attribution even if they are not responsible. Although the U.S. blamed Iran for the latest attacks, many other governments did not take the same stand. Attribution of the missile and drone strikes is still being debated, complicating a response. There was no doubt the missiles were Iranian, but the launch points were disputed. It is difficult for any government to manage non-attribution programs, but impossible when their denial is clearly not supportable by technical surveillance.

This leads security analysts to describe attribution in the same terms used by the intelligence communities to describe confidence in an assessment, with high, medium or low confidence that a summation is accurate. The assignment is largely arbitrary. Levels of confidence in assessments allow for consideration of several alternative interpretations without rejecting any of the alternatives.[34] So, when the Intelligence Community Assessment of Russian Activities and Intentions in Recent U.S. Elections says:

> We also assess Putin and the Russian Government aspired to help President-elect Trump's election chances when possible by discrediting Secretary Clinton and publicly contrasting her unfavorably to him. All three agencies agree with this judgment. CIA and FBI have high confidence in this judgment; NSA has moderate confidence.[35]

—this allows for a disagreement to be stated without much impact on the final assessment. We may be curious about why the National Security Agency would not have the same level of confidence that the CIA and FBI did, but we will also likely never find out because those decisions are classified national security information. Information declassified in October 2020 disclosed that "former CIA Director John Brennan briefed former President Obama on Hillary Clinton's purported 'plan' to tie then-candidate Donald Trump to Russia as 'a means of distracting the public from her use of a private email server' ahead of the 2016 presidential election."[36] The Russians seemed to be able to capitalize on attempts by both parties to discredit one another.

In the United States, public perception often underestimates the scope and effectiveness of the last few years of Russian activities. Only about 60 percent of Americans believe the Russians interfered with the election in 2016.[37] The Republicans, who won the presidential election, still were believers in the Russian influence, but only half the time. Most public evidence has not said whether Russian disinformation campaigns actually persuaded voters to vote in a particular way. It is unlikely any agency knows if they did. That may not have been the intent, but if it were it was not very successful. What is more likely is what the U.S. Director of National Intelligence said in October 2018:

> We are concerned about ongoing campaigns by Russia, China and other foreign actors, including Iran, to undermine confidence in democratic institutions and influence public sentiment and government policies. These activities also may seek to influence voter perceptions and decision making in the 2018 [mid-term elections] and 2020 U.S. elections.[38]

Notably, this attribution does not say which candidates were favored and which not, as the first two assessments did. It makes sense if they real intent was to undermine institutions rather than elect a particular individual. Disrupting foundational democratic institutions would be more important than any political party or candidate.

In July 2020, FBI Director Christopher Wray gave a speech at the Hudson Institute outlining some of the known actions taken by China that concerned the administration. In addition to the previously referenced commentary on theft of intellectual property and attaining leadership in certain areas of technology, he added:

> The second thing the American people need to understand is that China uses a diverse range of sophisticated techniques—everything from cyber intrusions to corrupting trusted insiders. They've even engaged in outright physical theft. And they've pioneered an expansive approach to stealing innovation through a wide range of actors—including not just Chinese intelligence services but state-owned enterprises, ostensibly private companies, certain kinds of graduate students and researchers, and a whole variety of other actors working on their behalf.

He mentioned that the Chinese used bribery and illegal business and education relationships to manipulate individuals who favor Chinese political positions. Perhaps one of the more controversial education relationships is that of the Confucius Institutes, which began in the U.S. in 2004. Universities allowed the formation of ninety of these institutes, which are supposed to be education centers, with Mandarin language classes, cultural programs, and outreach to K-12 and "other communities." Ten of these institutes have already closed after criticism that they used teachers from China, imposed censorship, and lacked academic freedom.[39] But the wider range of techniques gives the Chinese good results without a high level of risk.

What we fail to realize is the length of time the Chinese have been doing this kind of infiltration into our society. I had personal experience with Chinese students at a major university when I did Industrial Security inspections at corporate and educational institutions in the 1980s. At two of the universities I inspected, Chinese national students were employed by laboratories operated on behalf of the U.S. government. These contracts with the universities stated specifically that they were to allow only U.S. citizens to work in these labs, yet Chinese nationals were still working there. The U.S. has recently been investigating Chinese researchers in the U.S. who have ties to companies and government agencies in China, but their penetration of U.S. institutions has been going on for many years. The participants travel back and forth to these companies and educational institutions and share information. The U.S. has started to question these individuals where their visas were obtained under fraudulent circumstances or were overstayed. The *Global Times* in China has said China may retaliate by detaining U.S. citizens in China.[40]

But the Chinese go further in many other areas, as pointed out in 2018 by the Hoover Institute.

> United Front organizations in China have been surprisingly aggressive and transparent in their public tasking of Chinese Americans to carry out activities that support the PRC policies. One example occurred after the 19th Party Congress in October 2017. The state-owned *Fujian Daily* reported on November 24, 2017, that representatives of local Chinese community associations based in the United States, Australia, the Philippines, and Europe had gathered in Fujian and received letters of appointment from local provincial and city United Front agencies in China to serve officially as "overseas propaganda agents" on their return to their home countries. These commissions obliged them to accept responsibility for promoting the decisions of the Party's recent national congress in their home countries.[41]

In June of 2020, ASIO and Australian law enforcement raided the home of Shaoquett Moselmane (Labor Party), who had previously praised Xi Jinping for his response to the coronavirus outbreak. This was part of an inquiry into a campaign by the Chinese to influence politics by donations, pressure and promises to politicians.[42] The Australian police also raided the homes of four journalists working for Chinese state media, seized their electronic devices and allowed them to return to China.[43] At the same time, Australia warned journalists in China to return home, which they did.[44] The Australian government has seen the same types of interference in politics that the U.S. is just starting to explore for the 2020 election.

In Australia, these methods have included monetary inducements to politicians to change their stance on key issues; support for research institutes that carry a pro–Beijing line; threats to mobilize Chinese Australian voters to punish political parties who do not support Beijing's policy preferences; "astroturfing" local grassroots organizations to give the appearance of broad support for Beijing and its policies within the Chinese Australian community; coopting Chinese-language media and local civic organizations to promote narratives and individuals who are friendly to Beijing; and a variety of efforts to drown out or silence critics. These efforts are designed to remain hidden from public view, often arranged indirectly through proxies, in order to create a layer of plausible deniability that makes it more difficult to nail down precisely the degree of interference and the scope of the problem.[45]

We will not soon know if the Russians attempted to limit what they did to promoting candidate Donald Trump, nor denigrating Hillary Clinton and Joseph Biden. In 2016, the Russian operations run against the U.S. were diverse, supporting both Bernie Sanders and candidate for President, Donald Trump, while disparaging Hillary Clinton, Ted Cruz, Jeb Bush, and Marco Rubio. The latter three were Trump's opponents in the primary elections that selected who would run for President. At the same time, the Russians ran voter suppression campaigns and operational support for third-party candidates.[46] They were undoubtedly spread thin trying to devote resources to some many different kinds of activities, many of questionable benefit.

The release of internal Democratic National Committee emails to WikiLeaks constituted stories, of a sort, as selected persons in Hillary Clinton's campaign leadership were saying to one another about the electorate, the other candidates from both parties, and disclosure of a question to be asked of candidates during a debate. The information that was released was "negative" in the sense that it showed the Democratic leadership in a negative light. But the Russians were not running ads the way politicians do and were spending small amounts of money. In two battleground states, Wisconsin and Pennsylvania, the Russians spent less than $2000, and $300, respectively.[47]

Perhaps the Russians, who are very good at human perception and behavior modification research, were not as good at applying that knowledge to the audience of people in the United States. A few disciplines, like advertising and political campaigning, have a real interest in behavior modification of adults and none of them are usually successful over long periods of time. In advertising, for example, the goal is to sell goods and services to a consumer who had a choice in what product to buy. The behavior to be modified is consumption, not necessarily feeling better about it, knowing what the product name is (fortifying a brand), nor going to a sponsored event where the product is demonstrated. Some of those activities might be helpful in motivating a person to buy a specific product, but they are not successful unless "enough" people actually buy it. To measure what is enough, the advertiser must analyze increased sales based on the cost and effectiveness of different types of advertising. In other words, we must know how much sales went up for a given amount of advertising and whether the profitability of those additional sales justifies the expense.[48]

So, to evaluate a campaign to influence voters in the U.S., the Russians would have to know how many voters actually voted for a candidate because of something they saw in the Russian information campaign. They can see the bigger result—who actually won the election—but will they ever know if they had any influence on how voters responded? Not likely.

In order to determine cost effectiveness, the Russians would have to know that it was their influence that caused voters to vote for Donald Trump and be able to discern if that vote was because of some operation their intelligence agency performed, or in spite of it. The calculus is to the benefit versus the amount of money it will cost in the time allotted. A campaign to change the minds of voters has a fixed date. We have to work backwards from election day to determine whether the campaign will reach voters before they go to the polls. Those fixed dates tend to raise the price of the operation, sometimes to the point when it might not be worth doing, or we may have difficulty determining if the resources can be allocated effectively in the time remaining.

The Russians can know how many people saw their promotional material in the different social media channels involved (the U.S. investigation of their activities actually helped them determine that); they can know what their costs were for running the campaign; they can see some of the results, like the number of people who showed up at several "flash mob" events to photograph themselves with a person pretending to be an incarcerated Hillary Clinton. But, without exit polling that would ask about what kinds of stimulus resulted in them voting a particular way, they will never know why U.S. voters voted as they did. Even then, what people say in exit polls is always suspect.

> "Exit polls are garbage," said Lee Drutman, a political scientist and senior fellow at New America. "Any smart person at this point knows not to make any judgments about the electorate from exit polls, because the sampling methodology is just totally off."[49]

Before the Russians celebrate their winning strategy, they need more information than is available to them to determine the effect. They have that in the 2020 election.

We have to wonder if the Russians a have a reason for conducting operations that are so easily detected and attributed to them, yet deny the operations are theirs. This approach is almost counter-productive to them and makes it more difficult to conduct similar operations in the future.

The Russian activities were covert, but from an intelligence perspective, clumsy enough to easily identify the perpetrators. Were the Russians telling us they could interfere with our elections anytime they wanted, and that we should stay out of theirs, or was there more to it than that simple message? The Director of U.S. National Intelligence said the Russians likely saw their efforts as successful because they created interest and were read by many people.[50] But, that is hardly the characterization of a successful influence program. To be successful, the program must actually influence the course of action it is intended to affect. We do not know if the outcome of the election was the result of Russian actions or that those programs had any effect at all. Second, it is not the first time the Russians ran similar operations that did not succeed as well as they had hoped.

Special Counsel Robert Mueller's report and his filing of indictments against those who carried out the campaigns, document details of covert operations that the Russians must have been surprised to see in print, and available to the public. To the Russians, they stand as evidence that the operations were not successful at their main goal: plausible deniability, the mainstay of covert operations. When we know which country actually did a covert operation, it is easier to defend against the next one of a similar nature, and perhaps the U.S. did as well as France in that. Either the Russians are clumsy in the way they protected their operations, or their intent was disruption without regard to the election outcome. In that context, the Russians did not care who won the election, as long as the parties were disrupted. In that they may have been more successful.

8

Economic Aspects
of a Campaign

China uses economic warfare prominently in modern influence campaigns. The Chinese have the second largest economy in the world and use it for leverage in almost every aspect of their competition with the U.S., Europe, Asia and Australia. They used to be subtle about it, but in recent years have become more direct, even using in-your-face tactics like flagged carriers to deliver coal, which violated U.N. sanctions on North Korea.[1]

China has improved its influence campaigns by taking a longer view of success and dominating in technology areas that benefit their intelligence services, which support all aspects of government including economic matters. China influences through its leverage over businesses and institutions, with its main focus being its strength—economic and political warfare leverage used to persuade different audiences. They have created a number of very successful programs to convince leaders they are no threat the U.S. As just one example, the U.S. has recently stopped allowing its congressional staffers to take trips to China paid for by the Communist Party. Those were directly trying to get them to come to China where the intelligence services could promote China and influence the leadership and staff of Congressional committees, businesses, and educators. Of course, while there, they were subject to the usual intelligence activities run against any important visitor.[2]

One might ask who thought it was a good idea to allow these kinds of visits? These all-expense-paid junkets were part of the Mutual Educational and Cultural Exchange Act (MECEA) that have been going on since 1961. The Director of National Intelligence said this was part of a "massive influence campaign" targeting several dozen members of Congress and congressional aides.[3] That campaign coincidentally became known when a member of the U.S. House of Representatives Intelligence Committee was identified as the beneficiary of campaign organizing by a Chinese spy. The focus on the Intelligence Committee is not a coincidence, since some of the most sensitive U.S. program information is passed through that committee.

In both cases, it was not until the FBI notified the congressional office that either knew of the Chinese spies in their midst. This does not speak well for the vetting of employees of Congress but does show that the Chinese get influence by helping out in fundraising and getting close to places where they listen to conversations between influencers and members of Congress. But, while dramatic and movie-inspiring, spying is not the most common way the Chinese influence policy.

When there is conflict between China and another country, influence is applied specifically by withholding trade, until they win. In that respect, the Chinese are more like a boa constrictor in how they influence. They squeeze until there is no more will to carry on. Furthermore, the U.S. Director of National Intelligence said, "There are no moral or ethical boundaries to their pursuit of power."[4] It would have been helpful to know more about that statement, but he did not elaborate.

Australia and China have come to diplomatic blows over the perception that China is interfering in Australia's internal affairs. It was the first country to demand an independent investigation into the corona virus origins. After that, China raised import taxes on barley, wine, beef and seafood.[5] So, if a country questions the official position of the Chinese Communist Party, it gets an almost immediate slap in the form of trade restrictions. For smaller countries, the impact is greater because it does not take many trade restraints to influence a country heavily dependent on trade, but, even for larger countries, the longer these disputes go on the worse China's actions become.

In November 2020, the Chinese stopped trade to Australia in wheat, worth $394 million, adding to bans on sugar and copper ore. Ports have blocked up to $4 billion in goods for various reasons. Timber was suspect because of a beetle infestation the Chinese claimed to find. Lobsters from Australia came under scrutiny because the Chinese took an interest in them, and for no other reason. China's steel mills were told to stop importing coal from Australia, yet no official announcement was made.[6] When the Chinese later suffered coal shortages and unprecedented blackouts, it had only itself to blame. In what might be seen as justice, there were 50 Australian ships loaded with coal prohibited from docking.[7] Wine made in Australia is the most recent target for China.[8] China claims dumping.

There is a practical limit to how much leverage the Chinese have in these matters. Reciprocity is a key ingredient to international trade and both countries can play the same game. The Australians are far from the only country to question the origins of COVID-19 and Chinese actions to refuse to allow foreign investigators into Wuhan, the halt on publishing research on the virus, the failure to hand over physical virus samples rather than genome sequences all show the party is tightly controlling access to information about the virus. The EU wants to have an independent evaluation of the lessons learned. The Australian prime minister has spoken to the U.S., France, Germany, Britain, and other members of the World Health Organization to organize a response that will probably not be one China is anxious to see.[9] To make matters worse some of the members have spoken about Taiwan being allowed to attend the meeting as an observer. China warned New Zealand about supporting that view. It is proof that China does not have unchecked leverage on the actions of other countries.

One of Chairman Xi's policies is to encourage overseas Chinese to get involved in domestic politics of the countries they live in. Three New Zealand Members of Parliament are ethnic Chinese and in the 2014 election, seventy-five percent of them voted for the National Party.[10] Chinese gave money to both parties, but more to the Nationals which suffered a significant defeat in 2020 to the Labour Party.[11]

What Anne-Marie Brady cited was a string of business relationships between Chinese who held positions in China and in New Zealand at the same time. These individuals had business relationships with political figures in New Zealand and held fund raising events and gave substantial donations to them.

> [A similar pattern] was shown in a 1997 report by Canada RCMP-SIS identified a pattern of foreigners with high-level political contacts being placed in high profile roles in over 200 Chinese companies or Chinese-funded entities in Canada. Examples of this can also be found in New Zealand. Concerns have repeatedly been raised about these relationships in the New Zealand media and in parliament.[12]

Even in the U.S., the same kinds of things are going on with our Congress. One would think a member of the U.S. Congress on an Intelligence committee would know even more about how the Chinese work and be less likely to fall victim to their techniques, but in fact two of them have had Chinese spies working for them. Former Chair of the House Intelligence Committee Diane Feinstein had a spy working as her driver for her for 20 years.[13] Not only was this not news, Silicon Valley has known for many years that the Chinese spent money for intelligence collection and influence buying in the home of technology innovation. They spied on the technology companies and the U.S. Congress at the same time.[14]

Most recently, Fang Fang, a Chinese spy, was discovered helping U.S. Congressman Eric Swalwell with his financing, and placing an intern inside Swalwell's office.[15]

Hamilton and Ohlberg documented several cases of Chinese leaders' involvement with the leadership of U.S. financial institutions.[16] These are incestuous business relationships that benefit specific companies by providing jobs and favors to the leaders of Chinese institutions or, in many cases, their children. From their examples, we can conclude this is a favorite way of influence in China for more than the finance sector. But these companies are seldom prosecuted because they would require a great deal of investigation that China does not afford the SEC. The companies will not volunteer information unless there is a good reason, like exposure to an investigation. The SEC mentioned that the companies hired children who were "unqualified for the positions on their own merit." J.P. Morgan was one that resulted in substantial settlement fees.

J.P. Morgan agreed to pay $105,507,668 in disgorgement, plus $25,083,737 in interest, to settle the SEC's case. The SEC considered the company's remedial acts and its cooperation with the investigation when determining the settlement.[17]

Perhaps surprisingly, New Zealand was center stage in a scandal revealed in the exposure of a Panamanian law firm, Mossack Fonseca. By Brady's account, in 2016, New Zealand was described as being "at the heart" of global money laundering. There was really no connection to Chinese money laundering until someone stole and published the internal documents used to set up shell corporations around the world. The so-called Panama papers were tied to a number of well-known political leaders, but specifically Xi Jinping and three of the seven members of the Chinese Communist Party Standing Committee. The *New York Times* exposed the references to family members in boards and governance bodies for many of the shell companies that were formed, so in recognition for their work, China blocked the English language version of the *Times*.[18]

Mossack Fonseca has more offices in China than any other country, indicating there may be even more Chinese with their noses under the tent of shell companies.[19] When it comes to protection of personal wealth, China's leadership seems to be no different than other nations.

China is going to have a problem if it decides it wants to try to manage a response to every issue they object to, especially when they originate from some of the most powerful countries in the world. It certainly cannot apply sanctions to every country that asks for an independent review of the Covid-19 virus or criticizes China's way of handling demonstrations in Hong Kong. This is only one indication that China has begun to see some limits in its strategy to force its views using economic sanctions. It has tried too hard to limit any criticism.

Where China has seen the most resistance is in its Belt and Road initiatives, which largely use Chinese labor. There have been clashes between Chinese laborers or management in Kenya, Nepal, Indonesia, Sri Lanka, Zambia, and anti–Chinese street protests in Kazakhstan.[20] The laborers are taking jobs that would otherwise go to locals, which is not very popular in the pandemic years where jobs have been even more scarce. There is more trouble in Kazakhstan related to the 1100–mile border with China, in the same region where internment camps are filled with Muslims that include some ethnic Kazakhs.[21]

Kazakhstan is probably the best example of where China's economic leverage meets the reality of its attempts to manage world public opinion about its internal policies. No issue has had more influence on how China is viewed globally than its roundup of Uighurs in Xinjiang, except their oppressive monitoring of the people there. Muslims notice when other Muslims are confined, without trial, and put into prisons. The rest of the non–Muslim world disapproves on humanitarian grounds that go beyond religion. The BBC ran a series of articles that showed the growth of these camps which the Chinese describe as "reeducation camps." No matter how often they use that phrase, there are always dissenting views. BBC used Google Earth to show the dramatic expansion of camps over the period 2015–2018.[22] The camps do not look like schools—watchtowers surround them. Guards follow every visitor and keep them far enough away to avoid close encounters.

In the latest complication for China, the U.S. Commerce Department has added 11 companies to a list of those using forced labor in the Xinjiang Uighur Autonomous Region. Among them was Nanchang O-film Tech, a supplier to companies like Apple, where it makes the iPad mini, Amazon, and Microsoft.[23] The issue for these companies is twofold: first, they are benefiting from forced labor China conducted in the Autonomous Region camps which are slowly taking over in the prison system there. The shift benefits the Chinese who claim these facilities are retraining centers where the inhabitants learn new skills. A German researcher claims part of that new skill set is picking cotton.

Adrian Zenz has injected himself into this matter by publishing a report for the Center for Global Policy that claims 517,000 people have been forced to pick cotton in the Xinjian area.[24] Zenz has been almost immediately attacked by the Chinese press any time he publishes a new report. The *Chinese Global Times*, which splashed a story with the headline, "Xinjiang Think Tank Unveils Adrian Zenz as Swindler Under Academic Disguise," and a more blunt critique by the China Global Television Network (CGTN), "Six Lies in Adrian Zenz's Xinjiang Report of 'Genocide.'"[25]

The second reason for the Commerce Department's action is the taking of DNA from men and boys across much of China, including the Autonomous Region. Authorities leveraged genetic data from all Xinjiang residents between the ages of 12 and 65, which according to Human Rights Watch had been collected since 2017 under the guise of a public health program.[26]

This will complicate life for O-Film because restrictions go with their placement on the list of those using forced labor. Commerce restricts the export, re-export, and transfer (in-country) of items subject to the Export Administration Regulations (EAR) to persons (individuals, organizations, companies) involved. Sanctions are great counters to this kind of influence. But this is a very small part of a much larger institutional problem. China is trying to dominate world markets in technology areas that give them access to large parts of the communications between people all over the world. They use influence campaigns to do that.

The critical part of this campaign is resistance to Chinese incursions into the U.S. and global networks effected by advances in technology. These are described by General Keith Alexander, the former National Security Agency Director, who said we are in a cyber-enabled war with China in these areas of technology:

> telecommunications, advanced computing, robotics, energy generation, resource extraction, aerospace, and the medical sciences, to name just a few. We are currently facing off with China on 5G technology, machine learning, quantum computing, nuclear and solar power, satellites, rare earth metals, biotechnology, and pharmaceuticals.[27]

What he is describing is the future global telecommunications networks that allow us to communicate. China can influence communications by limiting the flow of data between countries, blocking certain military communications, selectively filtering data, storing it for its intelligence services, and modifying content while it is being processed. Second, the areas where China has the most leverage by dominating the market in critical technologies the rest of the world cannot do without, like rare earth minerals. These are leverage areas that allow China to influence by withholding or selling goods to countries that follow their policy positions.

In October 2020, the Standing Committee of the National People's Congress enacted new legislation called the Export Control Law, which is going to tighten controls on the very items Alexander described in his comments. It is going to create a class of products that are military-related, or dual use in the defense and civil sectors.[28] Almost immediately, the price of rare earth metals went up. Neodymium, a rare earth metal used in making magnets, rose 27 percent in one month.

What this law has given them is a huge list of items that allows the Chinese to claim "national security" for almost anything they export. Importers are taking notice and looking for other sources.

What China did to Australia in an influence campaign related to the corona virus independent investigation is an indicator of what China could do with this new law. It turns international trade on its head and makes China less of a reliable trading partner. Another aspect of that is the way Chinese businesses are dragged into the businesses of enforcing policy decisions made in the tight Communist Party leadership circles involves spying and sanctions violations. China uses its state-influenced businesses to do both. It runs a different kind of influence campaign that gives its own businesses a head start in competition by ignoring norms of behavior among international businesses.

China pretends its businesses are good international partners, no different than any others in the world. It incorporates its businesses, gives them boards of directors, issues publicly traded stock, and enacts internal policies that look the same as any other company's. Only they operate more as extensions of the Chinese Communist Party rather than as independent companies.

As an example, I was speaking in an unclassified conference to a group of business and government employees about China and a business representative told us a story that illustrated a point I had been speaking about. He had a communications server that was widely known around the world. His company was building a version of that server for China, in China. The operating system of the Chinese server was different than the one they used within the company which had the U.S. version that was not exportable. The Chinese repeatedly asked that they move all the equipment hosted in their own facility into space controlled by the People's Liberation Army (PLA). They prevented that from happening by ignoring the request for over a year. One of the other participants said that was not so easy to do now.

They were met with some variation of the request every week. Finally, they were forced to move the equipment by a ruse that caused them to believe their existing space was being taken from them. Within a week, the U.S. version of the operating system was stolen, but some of the company employees observed that being done and reported it to the internal security of the company. I asked him what they did when it was discovered since it is not a simple task to take on the PLA in China. He surprised everyone when he said, "We re-wrote the entire operating system. It was a lot of work, but we did it." Perhaps they learned a lesson about bringing a new version of an operating system to China.

This is not the kind of behavior one should expect of a business partner, but China is not the average partner. The partnerships are forced by Chinese laws, and they will steal technology when it cannot be obtained other ways. They are brutally open about it with their internal companies, but publicly deny they do any such thing.

China has had legislation for many years forcing joint ventures and partnerships with Chinese majority ownership. They recently changed that policy for some U.S. financial institutions already doing business in China, allowing them to hold majority ownership (51 percent).[29] They have not done this for all financial institutions nor extended the principle to other types of businesses, like manufacturing.

But in the battle for control of global networks, two Chinese companies stand out. In what must seem an endless battle with the U.S. and partner governments, Huawei and ZTE, the two largest Chinese telecommunications companies, are seemingly attacked from all sides for trying to do business outside of China. This may have very little to do with the theft of data from other competing businesses and more about what the intelligence communities already know about them.

In 2019, Huawei and its U.S. subsidiary, Futurewei Inc., were indicted in a New York federal case for trying to steal trade secrets from six U.S. technology companies, lying about its business in North Korea, and helping Iran track protesters during the 2009 anti-government demonstrations in that country.[30] Huawei assisted the government of Iran by installing surveillance equipment, including surveillance equipment to monitor, identify, and detain protesters during the anti-government demonstrations.

> U.S. national-security adviser Robert O'Brien this week asserted that Huawei can secretly tap into communications through the networking equipment it sells globally. The company disputes that, saying it "has never and will never covertly access telecom networks, nor do we have the capability to do so."[31]

In 2020, new charges for racketeering conspiracy and conspiracy to steal trade secrets were added accusing Huawei and Huawei Device Co., Ltd. (Huawei Device), Huawei Device USA, Inc. (Huawei USA), Futurewei Technologies, Inc. (Futurewei) and Skycom Tech Co., Ltd. (Skycom)—as well as Huawei's Chief Financial Officer Wanzhou Meng. The new superseding indictment also contains the charges from the prior superseding indictment, which was unsealed in January 2019.[32]

The 2020 indictment charges Huawei with:

> Huawei and its subsidiaries' involvement in business and technology projects in countries subject to U.S., E.U. and/or U.N. sanctions, such as Iran and North Korea—as well as the company's efforts to conceal the full scope of that involvement. The defendants' activities, which included arranging for shipment of Huawei goods and services to end users in sanctioned countries, were typically conducted through local affiliates in the sanctioned countries.[33]

The U.S. companies mentioned by the *Wall Street Journal* as victims were Cisco Technology, T-Mobile U.S. Inc., Motorola Inc., and others.

The Chinese are better at the technical side of information war than most other countries. They are good at manipulation of software and hardware platforms that we use to communicate. Those, in turn, can be used to capture information from around the world, and can be focused on particular individuals or large companies. The Great Cannon, China's concept for a series of devices that can manipulate data at several levels of granularity creating misinformation and disinformation in everything they touch.

Chinese businesses are bound by rules that make them subservient to Chinese intelligence services, without publishing all of those rules. Not publishing them gives deniability if they are discovered.

The U.S. DNI has been much more direct in describing his frustration with the Chinese, their spying and theft of intellectual property:

> Listen, they're a dangerous adversary. I don't mean to minimize them, but you made the point correctly about economically, Russia can't compete the way China can. The largest economy in the world is the United States. The second largest is China. Russia's not in the top ten. Italy, Brazil, and the state of Texas have a larger economy than Russia. So, as dangerous as Russia can be, they cannot compete with us the way China is, and China has a very specific plan to do that. And one of the ways that China has made their way to the top is they understand that information is the key to their dominance. So, they're going to get there any way they possibly can. That's what subsidizing Huawei and ZTE is all about. Those are Chinese companies that are run by the Chinese government. They know that they can steal more information if they run the telecommunications networks over which our information travels. That's one of the ways that China has gotten so good in terms of getting into our networks and into our information society.[34]

So, when the United States government said that Chinese companies, Huawei and ZTE Corporation (ZTEC), and three of China's telecommunications companies are national security threats, it was also speaking to a fear of Chinese incursions into their networks, and other networks around the world. The fear is that China is using their communications devices to collect information about the users in countries where they sell their technology. They are doing much more than that.

Since 2007, the United States has, for good reasons, taken more than a casual interest in what was happening with these two. Both were undermining sanctions imposed on several countries, including Iran, Cuba, North Korea, and almost any country sanctioned by the United Nations, by selling them banned goods. It is almost like China chooses to undermine any sanctions that are agreed to in the U.N. and we would have to wonder why, since they voted for those sanctions.

> ZTEC's most senior managers constructed an elaborate scheme to evade detection by U.S. authorities. The company, along with its co-conspirators, including ZTE Parsian, Beijing 8 Star, Chinese Company A, Iran Company A, and Iran Company B, purchased U.S.–origin parts and then transshipped, exported, or reexported those parts, either as a component of a larger system or separately, from China to Iran without a license from the Department of Treasury's Office of Foreign Assets Control ("OFAC"). During the course of the conspiracy, ZTE Parsian and Beijing 8 Star acted as alter egos of ZTEC.[35]

ZTE was originally sanctioned after pleading guilty to these charges. A plea agreement was entered into with details on what conditions were attached to the arrangement between the U.S. Government and ZTE "ZTEC and the Department agree that a $286,992,532 criminal fine [with additional penalties for a total of $1.1 billion] and a period of three years of corporate probation (more fully described in paragraph 7) is an appropriate sentence and should be imposed by the Court in connection with ZTEC's guilty plea to the Information…."

"Paragraph 7, referenced above, adds requirements for an independent compliance monitor, the disclosure of violations and information pertaining to those violations, and a little-known requirement to terminate four specific employees ('ZTEC agrees that the four employees identified as having signed the document described in paragraphs 40–41 of the Factual Resume have resigned or will resign or will be terminated, along with any and all payment obligations owed to them. ZTEC further agrees that it will accomplish this within six months of signing this Plea Agreement and that it shall provide the Department corroborating documentation of these actions')."[36]

Within a year, ZTE was back in the fire over these same charges because they had not taken the actions in the plea agreement. The response by the U.S. Government was to stop ZTE from buying American goods, which as it turns out, included software used in much of its "equipment."[37] It had a crippling effect on ZTE, but within a few weeks, the matter was revisited after President Xi telephoned President Trump.[38] ZTE ended up paying a fine, taking some of the actions described in the plea agreement, but continued using U.S.-made products. The U.S. President was criticized by supporters and detractors for his manner of dealing with ZTE, but ZTE fared better than Huawei.

In December of 2018, the CFA of Huawei, Meng Wanzhou, was arrested in Canada based upon a warrant issued in August at the request of the U.S. Justice Department. The Canadian prosecutors said the charges involved Huawei's attempts to hide trade with Iran which violated international sanctions agreements, but there was more to the story than that.[39] The *Wall Street Journal* reported the details this way: Ms. Meng made a presentation to HSBC, later used against her in court, to explain a relationship with SkyCom Tech and Iranian businesses. Ms. Meng had been a board member on SkyCom and said she resigned. *Reuters* exposed SkyCom's relationship with Iranian companies in 2013, so it was known in 2018. HSBC was slow to ask about it, but they did ask. The article closes with this:

> U.S. authorities now allege Ms. Meng misrepresented the ties to Skycom so that Huawei could keep moving money out of countries … banks cleared hundreds of millions of dollars of transactions for Huawei that may have violated sanctions, exposing the firms to "serious harm."[40]

The arrest of such a high-ranking corporate officer seemed to come out of the blue, but it had been a long time coming. It was no surprise to those following the deteriorating trade negotiations with China, but Huawei had already been watched for many years by then.

In 2007, the *New York Times* reported the National Security Agency (NSA) had begun an operation to penetrate the networks of Huawei to find out if they were connected to the People's Liberation Army.[41] At that time there were questions about what exactly Huawei was doing, if anything, to collect intelligence on networks where it was supplying equipment.

Since that time, if we judge by the publications and briefings given to Congress that warn about Huawei being a national security threat, we can only conclude that Huawei is doing something that is a threat to the U.S. National Security. But no government agency, until 2019, has publicly said what that is. Huawei denies doing anything they have been accused of. Of course, NSA gives no comment when asked what it has done to find out about Huawei, nor what it found out. But we should not misunderstand the U.S. on the matter of Huawei. If what the *New York Times* said was true, they are not guessing what Huawei does in the furtherance of China's international objectives—they know.

Sometimes, the inability to see a story in the intended context is because it is very complicated and obtuse to the casual reader. What is unique about this story is the basis for it to be classified as a Chinese state secret, and the efforts to expose Huawei has many elements that are U.S. state secrets. In spite of that, both continue to make elements of these classified matters public.

In May of 2019, President Trump signed an Executive Order, widely described in the press as a ban on Huawei equipment in the U.S. infrastructure. In fact, the EO does not mention Huawei at all:

> I further find that the unrestricted acquisition or use in the United States of information and communications technology or services designed, developed, manufactured, or supplied by persons owned by, controlled by, or subject to the jurisdiction or direction of foreign adversaries augments the ability of foreign adversaries to create and exploit vulnerabilities in information and communications technology or services, with potentially catastrophic effects, and thereby constitutes an unusual and extraordinary threat to the national security, foreign policy, and economy of the United States. This threat exists both in the case of individual acquisitions or uses of such technology or services, and when acquisitions or uses of such technologies are considered as a class.[42]

For over 10 years, the U.S. Government has restricted access to Huawei in the U.S., especially in technology areas it was trying to purchase (see *The Chinese Information War*). Those restrictions have been gradually ratcheted up, even while Huawei denies spying for the Chinese central government. What makes the U.S. suspect that Huawei was involved in intelligence collection? General Michael Hayden, former director of the National Security

Agency and the Central Intelligence Agency:

> I stand back in awe at the breadth, depth, sophistication and persistence of the Chinese espionage campaign against the West…. God did not make enough briefing slides on Huawei to convince me that having them involved in our critical communications infrastructure was going to be okay. This is not blind prejudice on my part. This was my considered view based on a four-decade career as an intelligence officer.[43]

Most of the information needed to make an assertion that Huawei is acting for the Chinese government is in the public domain. Certainly, people like Hayden, who have had access to some of the most sensitive secrets known about China, are only one aspect of the belief structure surrounding Huawei. One such piece was David Sanger's article in the *New York Times*, written after Edward Snowden disclosed the existence of a U.S. program to find out if Huawei was working for the People's Liberation Army.[44] So, some might wonder if Huawei was doing that. NSA is not saying, but they know.

Since that time, more and more countries are looking more closely at Huawei's telecommunications equipment, especially 5G, where it is being used in the most sensitive parts of their networks. Australia, Bahrain, Telecom Italia, British Telecom, parts of the EU, France (phase-out of equipment by 2028) are part of a growing list that partially ban Huawei. But for every country or company that bans Huawei and/or ZTE, there are several others that are debating whether to use other vendors of 5G equipment.[45] For the two companies, it will be a long time before either of them can be trusted.

At the end of January 2019, the U.S. Justice Department issued an indictment against Huawei for wire fraud and theft of trade secrets from T-Mobile USA. It is notable that the FBI Director announced the indictment, when the details had been known for some time.[46] The T-Mobile case is unusual because the Chinese were warned several times about trying to collect information from the T-Mobile testing lab in Seattle. After the first few times, employees of Huawei got nervous enough to tell their management that there were too many questions being asked about what the Chinese were doing in the lab. The Huawei employees thought they should stop trying to get any more information. Instead, Huawei flew in an engineer from China. Shortly after that, T-Mobile restricted access to the testing laboratory and allowed only one employee from Huawei. A couple of weeks later, that employee stole the parts they had been seeking.[47]

To try to counter some of the accusations made against them, in February of 2019, Huawei launched its own influence campaign, which included television appearances by some of its officials in the U.S. and a lawsuit against the U.S. Government. In November 2019, the U.S. Federal Communications Commission (FCC) voted to stop cellular carriers from using federal subsidies to buy equipment from Huawei and ZTE. In the process of defending themselves, Huawei sued the FCC. As part of their case, Huawei hired Zhong Lun, a Chinese law firm, submitted its case to the U.S. Federal Communications Commission in May.[48] The suit claimed Huawei had a "constitutional right"—citing the U.S. Constitution—to sell goods and services in the United States. A federal judge disagreed and rejected the case.[49] Huawei claims it is being discriminated against, and its past discretions are in the past. Huawei's Director of Security in the U.S. was on various television news shows explaining, among other things, that Huawei had never been prosecuted for stealing technology from another company.

Since that time, the FCC has issued an order to carriers to "rip and replace" equipment provided by China Telecom and Huawei. Most of the equipment involved is in small, rural carriers but it will require almost a billion dollars to remove and replace it.[50] We still have to see if that money will be appropriated by Congress.

So, if Huawei is not connected to the Chinese intelligence services, it must have been embarrassed to find out that one of its employees was. Poland's counterintelligence agency arrested Weijing Wang, the local sales director of Huawei. But he was not the only person arrested, and the whole saga deserves more attention than it gets in a short news cycle because the circumstances are more like an intelligence operation than a sales activity. The spokesman for Poland's counterintelligence agency was quick to point out that the arrests do not necessarily reflect on Huawei, a statement that is curious given the facts as they came out.

A Polish individual, Piotr Durbajlo, was an instructor at a school, Military University of Technology, that provided graduates who mostly worked for the Polish government. But, more than that, the school had a relationship with Huawei though program called "Seeds of the Future" where students could write essays and qualify for an all-expense paid trip to China to visit the headquarters.[51] In espionage circles, this is a classic form of recruitment.

The rules of this kind of influence campaign are to establish relationships with various people in a country and find the potential for those who would work for a particular company, or for the Chinese intelligence services directly. It is similar to the one that invited U.S. Congressmen to China. The counterintelligence service in Poland could be making the distinction between Huawei and the intelligence services of China when it says it may not be Huawei per se. It could have been any company under the influence of Chinese intelligence. But it looks like recruitment of potential spies no matter who they were working for, and Huawei facilitated those activities, as they would be required to do under the Intelligence law published formally in 2017.[52]

A few U.S. IT firms operating in China have expressed concerns about the wide-ranging obligations the new law might place on them to provide technical support to security officials for intelligence-gathering or other activities. The Intelligence Law itself grants officials general authority to demand "assistance" from private organizations and access or use their "communications" facilities…. But companies could face even more serious burdens if the law is applied in concert with the new Cybersecurity Law, which accords officials far more specific authority to access and regulate many features of corporate networks that might be useful for intelligence-gathering. These include key business and personal data (which must be stored in China), proprietary codes, and other intellectual property. And like the Intelligence Law, the Cybersecurity Law broadly requires network operators to cooperate with public security and state security officials.[53]

Nothing involved in this kind of intelligence collection is unusual, except that it was made public. Governments have sanctioned intelligence collection on commercial businesses for decades, but there is a difference in how those work products are used. President Obama recalled his discussions with China about this:

I raised once again our very serious concerns about growing cyber-threats to American companies and American citizens. I indicated that it has to stop. The United States government does not engage in cyber economic espionage for commercial gain. And today, I can announce that our two countries have reached a common understanding on the way forward. We've agreed that neither the U.S. or the Chinese government will conduct or knowingly support cyber-enabled theft of intellectual property, including trade secrets or other confidential business information for commercial advantage.[54]

From that warning, the Chinese already knew that their agreement with President Obama was an agreement that was backed up with the threat of further action if their behavior did not stop. It did not stop, but the White House did not respond.

Neither the U.S. nor China, however, agreed to stop collecting intelligence on the other. That agreement worked against the U.S. In the U.S., spying done by the government is not passed along to businesses. China is willing to plow intelligence back into its business base. NSA may have been spying on Huawei, but it was not for the commercial gain of U.S. companies. It is more than regrettable that intelligence could not be used for that purpose. The U.S. telecom industry would love to know where Huawei intends to expand and what pricing structures they will use, but they do not get to find that out from the snooping that NSA was said to have done. Does NSA know more about the intentions of Huawei than it is willing to talk about in public? Of course. But, keeping those secrets about what it knows is just as important as getting the facts it needs to discover the intentions of Chinese leadership.

In the prior year, China Telecom has been accused of hijacking U.S. telecommunications to mainland China before sending them on to their intended recipients. The claim is China Telecom diverted huge swaths of communications from the U.S. by manipulating border gateway protocols that route traffic from 2015 to 2017, and European sites in 2019.[55] This is a little like grabbing all the telephone traffic from cell towers, copying it, and listening to voice traffic when the thieves have time. These are tests of denial-of-service attacks, or collection of data which could be used in the future, unless they are stopped.

Over a year ago, the Chinese made a new rule that restricts outside contractors from selling components in China. The percentage of contracts allowed to be made with foreign suppliers starts at 70 percent but goes down steadily each year, for three years, until it reaches zero. These contracts will only be let to Chinese domestic industries.[56] When the same is done by the U.S., China cries foul and discrimination in commerce.

Most countries do not want foreign investment in their telecommunications infrastructure for reasons that are not hard to understand, but are less than obvious. Two countries that are allies can disagree about the risk, as the U.K. and U.S. did over the use of Huawei equipment in sensitive telecommunications. The U.K. decided to use Huawei's 5G technology over the objections of the U.S. which shares very highly classified information over networks that interconnect the two countries. The rationale and mitigation were published by the GCHQ's National Cyber Security Centre (NCSC). The U.K. thought that the use of Huawei equipment could be mitigated by oversight.

Since 2010, the NCSC actually has an oversight board, with membership from the U.K. government and Huawei, exclusively focused on security issues. The most recent annual report shows "'**Further significant technical issues have been identified in Huawei's engineering processes,** leading to new risks in the U.K. telecommunications networks,' which were mitigated with procedures developed between the participants in the oversight board."[57]

These issues were centered around the inability of Huawei to show that "various equipment build-related issues, it is hard to be confident that different deployments of similar Huawei equipment are broadly equivalently secure." The simple explanation is that configuration management across tested platforms could not be verified throughout the development process. That kind of work was called "sloppy" by some U.K. engineers.[58]

Few countries have ever put any vendor through this level of scrutiny at such a low level of detail, but the reasons for it lie in servicing equipment that is purchased. In spite of the belief that they can control Huawei equipment, the U.K. recently decided to remove all Huawei 5G equipment by 2027, and to stop buying new equipment after December 2020.[59] When both the U.S. and U.K. stop buying Huawei equipment and plan the expensive removal of what is already installed, we have to infer there is something seriously wrong with that equipment, *and* it is something that cannot be mitigated. It is more than just sloppy manufacturing.

Buying telecommunications equipment is not done without a service contract for the support to that equipment. The company makes software changes to its hardware and that software has to be put into the equipment. We could allow the vendor to do that directly, but would we want to have a Chinese company installing software remotely? That is a risk that would have to be mitigated, either by maintaining the software or by checking it against a baseline before allowing it to be inserted. Neither of those is easy or quickly done, but the mitigation by the U.K. is obviously considering this risk and many others like it. Do we want to allow Chinese technicians to repair hardware that fails? Do we want to allow components to be made in other countries other than China and the U.K.? Can we trust component changes sent by Chinese companies? Do we care about identification of vulnerabilities in any component that are identified by global security vendors? Vendors seem to do so every day but without much thought to the security risks.

But the real risks can also involve influence campaigns. These platforms can generate large quantities of data that can be turned into information useful in pinpointing where people work and live, go to church, and eat out. The networks their equipment is on can be monitored even if they promise not to do so. When foreign companies supply components to the infrastructure of any country, they have potential access to every commercial carrier, internet service provider, backbone provider, military network, business network, social media infrastructure and the most sensitive of encrypted networks. We have to trust them to not do it because they say they will not. The vendor making that equipment could selectively reroute or block network traffic, analyze the traffic patterns of these streams, selectively filter areas of the country or specific types of businesses. When a country accepts the risk of allowing components from a potential adversary like China, risks are difficult to mitigate. These Chinese carriers are transmitting communications outside the U.S. without oversight over how that will be done. They can study it as long as they want.

China has been dealing with state governments selling office equipment to a number of them with the same kind of oversight—none. This equipment has, for example, state police data, health information, and during the pandemic, non-public information about disease spread, deficiencies in distribution of vaccines, and hospital shortages.

A sample of publicly-available contracts negotiated between state governments and Chinese technology vendors shows that information transmitted on the vendors' equipment is now subject to collection, transfer, processing and inspection by the vendor, and could be transferred to any country where the vendor does business and to any entity with whom it works. For example, one U.S. sales agreement with technology manufacturer Lenovo states that data can collected on devices can be transferred to any country where Lenovo does business. In any event, China's 2017 National Intelligence Law compels this.

The National Association of State Procurement Officers (NASPO) frequently negotiates contracts on behalf of its members. However, security is not a parameter of NASPO's evaluations.[60]

China has operated in the U.S. telecommunications infrastructure since 1999 and we have to ask why. Only recently has that access been challenged. The Federal Communications Commission (FCC) has responsibility for oversight of these carriers but has not had the resources to do so adequately. As a result, President Trump signed Executive Order 13913, which formalized the Executive Order (EO) Telecom Committee, set deadlines by which the committee must complete reviews, and provided for input from other Executive Branch agencies, including the intelligence community.[61] (It is described later in a press release from the Homeland Security & Government Affairs Permanent Subcommittee on Investigations as an "informal committee," which generally means unfunded.) In April 2020, the committee made its first consequential decision—to revoke and terminate China Telecom's license because it had failed to comply with the terms of an existing agreement with the Justice Department.[62] We can see how long that revocation will last in the Biden administration.

There is an almost endless list of considerations for reviews of multiple pieces of network equipment, control systems, and service procedures and this is where countries can disagree about how far the reviews need to go. At some point it becomes too difficult to keep up with the mitigation strategies required to deal with all of the risks, assuming that the risks are all known. That is why some countries say this cannot be mitigated without excessive cost and reduction in the capability of network components. That can be just another way of saying it is too much trouble to do all the things necessary. China, the U.S., and a number of other countries have done that in banning equipment made by third parties in their critical core infrastructures. And, since there is no common definition of core infrastructure, the decision of what that is falls to the communications regulators in each country. Regulators can ban other countries from supplying core components, especially those made in another country. Core components are not just 5G, the next generation of cell technology, but because core components are so critical, other technology elements like encryption, fiber optics, supercomputers, chip technologies, and the like are also monitored and restricted.[63] At the same time, China has designs on network controls at a much larger level and they use some clever methods to influence standards bodies to make their products seem more attractive.

> Although the Chinese government may publicly state that it is opening the tele-communications market, foreign companies are subject to burdensome regulatory requirements; required to enter into joint ventures majority owned by Chinese parties; and often forced to transfer both technology and know-how to Chinese counterparts.[64]
>
> But, at the same time China restricts foreign companies from operating in China, it encourages its carriers to expand into foreign markets. [three cited in the announcement are operating in the U.S.: China Telecom Americas, China Unicom Americas, and ComNet USA] At least one Chinese carrier, is publicly alleged to have hijacked and rerouted communications data through China several times since 2010. This allows Chinese actors to access sensitive communications, regardless of whether the data is encrypted.[65, 66]

China's telecommunications companies took its direction seriously and, since 2000, branched out into Europe, Latin America and the U.S. But this is more than just the sale of equipment made in China. China seeks to influence the policy making bodies that surround network communications and make standards that other countries will follow. Those standards are then woven into contracts and international agreements. Those policies will fit China's technical equipment specifications and integrate with the Belt and Road Initiative, so that technical standards are written into agreements between China and its signatories.[67] These same standards are used internally in China to discourage and limit foreign participation in manufacturing and medical devices. China requires its participating members to vote as block in international standards bodies, regardless of the technical merits of proposed standards.[68] Because it has put so many Chinese members into these committees, the Chinese vote can carry many decisions that are not technically sound, but which benefit Chinese industries and network control standards.

In March 2020, Huawei proposed an alternative standard for the Internet Protocol, which allows an internet service provider to have complete oversight and control over every device connected to the Internet through their service, allowing for top-down control of information flows within a country's networks.[69] This is the model China uses now. But China has gone further by claiming extraterritorial jurisdiction over data and internet activity outside of China.

> China's draft Data Security Law, released July 2020, grants Chinese law enforcement power to access data and regulate, investigate, and prosecute data controllers located outside of China that harm "the national security, the public interest, or the law interests of [Chinese] citizens or organizations." "National security" is undefined in the law, but Chinese authorities may interpret it

expansively in application. Notably the law applies equally to Hong Kong and Macau, further eroding Hong Kong's separate legal system. China's Anti-Terrorism Law, enacted in 2015, similarly requires internet service providers and platforms to provide surveillance access to any and all data concerning Chinese nationals, even if they are located outside of the country.[70]

This is a new law that is difficult to assess until it plays out in actual policy implementation. It opens the door to pressure on holders of data outside China to make that data available to Chinese authorities if they claim a national security interest. That will be a bridge too far for most countries because it infringes on sovereignty over data, the same issue the EU has introduced with the General Data Protection Regulation (GDPR), which defines *personal data* as "any information relating to an identified or identifiable natural person."[71] But, we should consider that protection of privacy data is not just about protection of individuals.

> Authorities in a growing number of countries are weighing measures to control the flow of data in and out of their national borders. Cyber norms promoted by China and Russia are expanding to countries such as Brazil, India, and Turkey, where legislators had been debating data localization provisions.... If passed, these measures will facilitate the collection of sensitive data by government agencies, enabling a further crackdown on free expression, privacy, and a range of human rights. This splintering of the internet will also embolden more governments to pursue a model of cyber sovereignty, with grave implications for the future of internet freedom.[72]

The control of data has become increasingly important to influence campaigns and a major issue for countries trying to balance privacy and national security. Control is important to those who claim the data as theirs because it tells an adversary where an individual is located and who he communicates with. Countries running influence operations want the data for the same reason, but to help target those individuals who are influencers. From a sovereignty point of view, more countries will want to deny information to countries who might run operations against them.

We can see why control of data is so important to China in the public release of a database of two million Chinese Communist Party members to Internet 2.0, an Australian security company. According to their own estimates, this is less than 2.1 percent of the total number of CCP members.[73] Considering the paranoia in China over the internal security of its data, the release of this information will be cause for even more concern. According to Internet 2.0, it passed through chat groups "frequented by activists from a range of backgrounds including Hong Kong, Taiwan, and the Falun Gong." The data show several billionaires and persons who work for Five Eyes governments.[74] (Five Eyes is an intelligence-sharing alliance consisting of the U.S., U.K., Australia, Canada and New Zealand.) But the concerns of business and government are magnified more through a lens of spying and influence, which may or may not be associated with CCP membership. For the Chinese, it is another reason to seek control over data on its own people.

That means more isolation of infrastructure from foreign actors who can observe data inside a sovereign country, and more restrictions on network equipment manufactured in potentially hostile countries. This equipment can be made to facilitate surreptitious entry to networks that cannot be detected by normal security procedures. The world's networks are linked in ways that have never been accurately described, though many have tried. There are hundreds of millions of networks, each administered to different standards by people who are fallible. Many security practitioners have found networks connected to the Internet that were supposed to be isolated. They have found connections to networks that were never approved by anyone. Databases that were state secrets connected to the Internet or with no access controls. At the same time, there are hackers looking for just such things that can be exploited. Sooner or later, they find mistakes and take advantage of them.

As the Chinese and Russians tighten controls on their own networks, it becomes more difficult to steal information from them. Each country applies its own professionals who collect data, and they must work harder to overcome the new controls. This raises the level of play on both sides of the data protection and data extraction businesses.

Last, we need to have in our schools and in our personal enlightenment better crap detectors and less acceptance of crap that is disseminated. We facilitate social media censorship and dissemination of disinformation disguised as free speech. Those rules for dissemination follow China's way of censoring. That cannot be a coincidence.

Investigation of China's methods will sort out some of the similarities in finance, information control, and personal manipulation of leaders of our countries. There are not investigations conducted by U.S. leadership that has tried to discover and document the methods being used in other countries, like those the Chinese used in Australia and New Zealand. The leaders who benefit are the ones who fight this kind of investigation. It is about time we find out who benefits, how those leaders prevent investigations of China's influence campaigns, and make recommendations to stop them to allow those investigations to be carried out.

9

A Failed Response
Against Campaigns

In 2018, the Hoover Institute put together a working group on what to do about Chinese influence in the United States.[1] In it, they address some of the most important things that needed to be done to reduce the impact of Chinese intrusions. Their focus was guided by three main principles which are important to getting back to normalized relations with China:

> Throughout the report, the Working Group articulates three principles to guide the response of government and various sectors to China's influence activities. These principles are shaped by the core values, norms, and laws of the United States. They include commitments to transparency, integrity in maintaining the independence of American institutions, and reciprocity in pursuit of a productive relationship between China and the United States....

- Congress should perform its constitutional role by continuing to investigate, report on, and recommend appropriate action concerning Chinese influence activities in the United States. It should update relevant laws and regulations regarding foreign influence, and adopt new ones, to strengthen transparency in foreign efforts to exert influence.
- Executive branch agencies should similarly investigate and publicize, when appropriate, findings concerning these activities, with a view to promoting healthy and responsible vigilance among American governmental and nongovernmental actors.
- The U.S. media should undertake careful, fact-based investigative reporting of Chinese influence activities, and it should enhance its knowledge base for undertaking responsible reporting.
- Faculty governance is the key to preserving academic freedom in American universities. All gifts, grants, endowments, and cooperative programs, including Confucius Institutes, should be subjected to the usual procedures of faculty oversight.

- U.S. governmental and nongovernmental sectors should disclose financial and other relationships that may be subject to foreign influence.

Some progress was made in every one of these areas except those most glaring lack of congressional or media-based investigations of Chinese influence campaigns. It seems the working group had confidence in the institutions of the U.S. to (1) recognize the need to reduce Chinese influence in the U.S. (2) see the things that are needed within those institutions, (3) see the benefits of taking action to reduce that influence and (4) organizing and funding responses. Perhaps we should all be more optimistic about the capacity to realize what we are faced with and take action against it. The U.S. is not alone there. Many countries fail to run the kinds of operations required to stop foreign countries from being successful in influence campaigns. Instead, they seem to want to emulate them. As individuals, we have to think about whether that is what we want.

Making recommendations on this kind of complex campaigns is not as easy as a focus on cyber or finance. These are very complex programs, and they deserve more explanation in why certain types of recommendations are being made.

Finance

The U.S. Treasury Department, through the Committee on Foreign Investment in the United States (CFIUS) and the Financial Crimes Enforcement Network (FinCEN) have the resources to identify and expose illegal foreign investment in U.S. industries and to U.S. individuals. We need to know where and how China invests in U.S. institutions and people so it can promote people with ideas favorable to China and discourage those with contrary ideas. For that to happen, we must have studies focused on which institutions are targeted, how they get money from China, and the results of these campaigns.

There was, in 2018, $4.4 trillion of Direct Investment in the United States from other countries.[2] We already know that is too much money for any commission to examine, and they rely on industries to self-report, for the most part. That is a failing strategy that needs to be corrected. They need to combine resources and computing power to look more closely at those investments and report on those types that need further examination for their ability to apply foreign influence campaigns to U.S. businesses or individuals.

Unfortunately, too much time is required for them for form cases that are easily understood and timely enough to take action before the damage is done. In my first book, *The Chinese Information War*, I described several cases where the technology the U.S. was trying to protect has been siphoned off before the case was ever exposed and actions taken to mitigate the influence. It is pointless to thrash around trying to stop the theft of U.S. technology if the actions cannot preempt those thefts. Treasury needs to change their procedures to do that. If they identify the funding sources and the targets, they have a head start on where individuals are being supported and what benefit does China get from those investments. But, it cannot be a reactionary agenda. They need to look more closely at those institutions and individuals who receive money and identify what causes are being favored. Those need to be exposed.

The U.S. Government thought it had done that when in 2020 CFIUS oversight capability was improved through a change in regulations applying to the Foreign Investment Risk Review Modernization Act of 2019 (FIRRMA). The final FIRRMA regulations created a mandatory filing requirement for certain transactions and expanded the kinds of technologies and types of transactions subject to review. Under the new regulations, CFIUS may review noncontrolling investments into U.S. critical technologies and infrastructure, or into companies collecting sensitive data on U.S. citizens.[3] Those are changes that occurred, only two years ago, are matched against $4.4 trillion transactions that are carefully invested. Even legitimate transactioners seek to operate with minimum of exposure to press and other businesses, so secrecy is natural to them.

CFIUS is not a government organization; it is a committee within the U.S. Treasury Department, and not a very big committee, with just nine permanent members. Anyone who has ever been on one of these government committees knows they do not work very well. Participants are reluctant to share all they know about a company being investigated. Some companies do not cooperate in an investigation, even hiding what they are doing. Once identified, discovery is layered in the same kinds of hidden agreements between the participants so carefully protected from exposure. If CFIUS is going to be able to accomplish objectives with its new role in foreign influence, it needs to have an expanded permanent staff with researchers and policy experts to supplement its membership.

A controversial decision by the U.S. Supreme Court in January 2010 changes U.S. foreign investment policy in ways that have potentially large economy-wide implications and affects CFIUS response to those. The Citizens United ruling tossed out the corporate and union ban on making independent expenditures and financing electioneering communications. It gave corporations and unions the green light to spend unlimited sums on ads and other political tools, calling for the election or defeat of individual candidates.[4] More money entered the stream going to those candidates as a result. The dollar amounts spent in U.S. elections are reflected in that change. We have lost control of any oversight of campaign financing as a result.

CFIUS needs to be expanded just to keep up with the new levels of authorized investment. It can barely keep up with this new role, although Congress has noted it has increased its cases.[5] It is nowhere near what needs to be examined. There are also constraints in the court system.

There are some objections to any changes as a reaction to the D.C. Circuit Court opinion in *Ralls Corp. v. Committee on Foreign Investment*.[6] The decision says that courts have jurisdiction to review the process used by the president to investigate cases and prohibits foreign investment transactions that threaten national security. This causes conflicts between private equity investment and national security. There is adequate law to encourage compliance with the Foreign Corrupt Practices Act (FCPA) through the Securities and Exchange Commission, as the case of J.P. Morgan shows. What is missing is the reviews allowing identification, and examiners to review the details. There are far too many to do either, and those companies become victims of foreign ownership and influence.

At the same time, we have too many companies that just want the money and will take it without reporting. They occasionally get caught, but it is a constant strain on resources to do discovery and bring an action, especially when those actions are in foreign countries that block any investigation. In 2019, CFIUS increased its enforcement actions on companies who do not report:

- It forced Beijing Kunlun Tech Co., Ltd. to divest its 2016 acquisition of the dating app company Grindr, LLC, apparently based on concerns about the Chinese government's potential exploitation of sensitive data relating to U.S. citizens.
- It required iCarbonX—another Chinese investor—to divest its majority stake in PatientsLikeMe, Inc., an online network for discussing health conditions, likely due to similar concerns about sensitive personal data.
- It reissued a partially Russian-backed investment fund, Pamplona Capital Management, to divest its minority stake in a U.S. cybersecurity firm.
- It imposed the first-ever civil penalty—$1 million—for repeated violations of a 2016 CFIUS mitigation agreement requiring the parties to a transaction to establish security policies and provide periodic compliance reports to CFIUS.[7] Enforcement is difficult when countries and businesses do not honor the agreements, then make it difficult to investigate those transgressions.

These were all done under the final FIRRMA regulations. It is important that governments increase their oversight of investments in their own countries in a more aggressive way or they will find purchases are increasingly not in their national interest.

We should consider also that the Commerce Department Bureau of Industry and Security (BIS) plays a bigger role in identifying and sanctioning companies that violate licensing requirements for controlled goods or treaties with the U.S. For example, it changed its rules closing a loophole that allowed Huawei to buy U.S. technologies through non–U.S. companies outside the U.S.

This whole program is a black hole because it involves thousands of products, some with severe penalties, like the Missile Control Regime, and millions of transactions that mask the important ones. The whole export-import control system needs to be reexamined to simplify and speed up purchases between countries, and should be focused on one set of categories instead of five. They are constantly swamped in detail and should be streamlined.

Foreign influence on business is always a concern that cannot be completely controlled and is difficult to measure. For companies with security clearances (companies and individuals can hold clearances in much the same way), the Defense Investigative Service (DIS) has a National Industrial Security Program (NISP) to evaluate and mitigate that influence though the issue is much more complicated than the NISP rules. For the most part, that program fails to identify and influence companies before they report to CFIUS, so it does not do what is intended. Companies do have foreign nationals working in them, as we have seen—even Chinese members of the Communist Party in our defense industries. The role of DIS is to prevent them from getting access to U.S. classified information and to minimize their participation as board members and principal officers. The DIS role limitations are exactly the reason they have very little enforcement actions. DIS should do much more to have an effective role against foreign influence but they are constrained by being under the Defense Department. Their foreign ownership role should be managed by the Treasury Department.

Altogether, only five investments were blocked though all of these various groups, all through CFIUS, although a few proposed transactions may have been withdrawn by the firms involved in lieu of having a transaction blocked. President Obama used the FINSA authority in 2012 to block Ralls Corporation, an American firm owned by Chinese nationals, from acquiring a U.S. wind farm energy firm located near a Department of Defense facility, and in 2016 to block a Chinese investment firm from acquiring Aixtron, a Germany-based firm with assets in the United States.[8] Both of these acquisitions were national security related.

In 2017, President Trump blocked the acquisition of Lattice Semiconductor Corp. by the Chinese investment firm Canyon Bridge Capital Partners; in 2018, he blocked the acquisition of Qualcomm by Broadcom; and in 2019, the Committee raised concerns over Beijing Kunlun Company's investment in Grindr over concerns of foreign access to personally identifiable information of U.S. citizens. After the challenge, the Chinese firm divested itself of Grindr. As a part of the noted emphasis on collectors of private information, CFIUS ordered the Shenzhen-based iCarbonX to divest its majority stake in PatientsLikeMe. In 2017, PatientsLikeMe raised $100 million and sold a majority stake to iCarbonX, which was started by genomic scientist Jun Wang. About 700,000 people use the PatientsLikeMe website to report their experiences with medical conditions. China's ENN Ecological Holdings Co. recently announced it had withdrawn its offer for Toshiba's U.S. liquefied natural gas business because of failure to win approval from CFIUS and shareholders by a specified closing date. Toshiba attributed the delay to the U.S. government shutdown in early 2019.

The U.S. has stepped up its efforts to block China's intelligence collection in networks through applications and foreign investment in U.S. networks. There were executive orders against two popular Chinese communications applications, TikTok and WeChat.[9] The scope of their ability to influence is found in the numbers of U.S. users on their platforms and the ability to track users on both of them (100 million U.S. users on TikTok[10] and 3.3 million U.S. users on WeChat).[11] We have almost 288 million Internet users in the U.S. and more than a third of those are using one of these Chinese platforms. These users have the same censorship rules and limitations on subjects that China has. Facebook and Twitter are banned in China. If this does not make sense to many who use the Internet, you are certainly not alone in the world.

According to the orders, both are accused of allowing access to location data and personal information on smartphones. Australia also had the same adventure with WeChat. WeChat, with over a billion users world-wide, was accused of monitoring individuals, censoring speech, punishing people who take dissenting views.[12] Both companies have won delays in the enforcement, which will mean a new U.S. president will be making a decision on whether these restrictions will continue. The importance lies in location data, which as China has shown is valuable in identifying where an individual goes and what places they visit. That location data is important to China to maintain the kinds of databases that track individuals. It is difficult to run any kind of operation if China knows where we are all the time.

These types of actions have a minimal effect on influence campaigns, though they do reduce ability to extract personal information about large

numbers of people in the U.S. and reduce the impact of foreign influence on U.S. businesses, especially those in critical technologies. Though
the numbers of cases are small, they are not unimportant when viewed
together. If there was more of an effort to focus all government agencies
involved in oversight of financial transactions and foreign operations in
the U.S., there might be some synergy developed for dealing with influence
campaigns.

We are desperate to stop the current level of foreign influence, so I
suggest a model used in the U.S. Ballistic Missile Defense Organization
(BMDO), formed to counter a specific foreign threat for a limited time. As
an independent organization, BMDO managed programs the military services ran and controlled funding for them, until the mission was completed
and the U.S. had missile interceptors in the ground.

In this case, the financial services parts of any organizations that investigate foreign influence would be directed by the U.S. Treasury. The other
agencies in that role would get their money and oversight from the Treasury. BMDO worked from 1974 until the original threat was met, then the
organization became a management organization within the Department
of Defense. The president decides when that activity has run long enough
to achieve its objective.

But, where government action is most required is in two areas, money
laundering and campaign financing. Money laundering is the mother's milk
of foreign campaign financing rule violations. Political parties seem reluctant to stop or limit this kind of financing of political campaigns because
both major parties probably have some money filtered through this complex system.

The World Bank said the U.S. has ten times the number of shell companies than the next forty-three tax haven jurisdictions combined.[13] This
particular type of tax shelter was addressed in legislation at the end of the
Trump administration. It requires disclosure of the beneficial owner of
anonymous shell companies. But tax shelters are hardly the only reason for
some of these accounts. They are used for drug transactions, political contributions and, in the case of Chinese leadership, hiding wealth from the
public. Edward Luce says "America is the largest dirty money haven in the
world. Its illicit money flows dwarf that of any other territory.... The U.S.
Treasury estimates that $300bn is laundered annually in America."[14] This
figure shows the potential for influence campaigns and political influence
from foreign sources, yet that part does not seem to have been addressed in
this legislation. We seem reluctant to do much about expanding investigations into this kind of influence.

The Association of Certified Anti-Money Laundering Specialists
calls these kinds of transactions "conduit contributions" and they are well

known. In the U.S. Code, Section § 110.6, Earmarked contributions 52 U.S.C. 30116(a)(8) are defined:

> (a) General. All contributions by a person made on behalf of or to a candidate, including contributions which are in any way earmarked or otherwise directed to the candidate through an intermediary or conduit, are contributions from the person to the candidate.
>
> (b) Definitions
>
> (1) For purposes of this section, earmarked means a designation, instruction, or encumbrance, whether direct or indirect, express or implied, oral or written, which results in all or any part of a contribution or expenditure being made to, or expended on behalf of, a clearly identified candidate or a candidate's authorized committee.
>
> (2) For purposes of this section, conduit or intermediary means any person who receives and forwards an earmarked contribution to a candidate or a candidate's authorized committee, except as provided in paragraph (b)(2)(i) of this section.

The banking community is most responsible for discovering and alerting law enforcement to financial crimes, but not conduit contributions that violate the Federal Election Campaign Act. That needs to change. The Federal Election Commission investigates those reports when the Treasury should be the investigator; the FEC is not a law enforcement agency and largely handles cases of little import.[15] We can derive that from looking at cases over the last few years on the FEC website. They are almost exclusively cases at the local and state campaign level. The bulk are campaign funds violations. Mostly they do not involve foreign money, or they do not involve money that was identified as foreign. The FEC can refer cases, but often cases are already in the courts before they do. It is too slow to react to be useful.

Streamlining and investigating conduit contributions should be a priority to simplify overlapping responsibilities. FinCEN should have a bigger role in influence campaigns because their main role is working with banks to discover money laundering. In the past few months, FinCEN has focused on wallets of cryptocurrency which are a complication that adds to the difficulty of identifying the owner of wallets transferring money to political campaigns.[16] It is difficult enough to identify and deal with these kinds of cases, which have drastically changed by modern drug dealers, and focus on election-related money laundering.

In 2017, the U.S. Justice Department made a decision to tighten registration under the Foreign Agents Registration Act of 1938 (FARA) partly because Russian and Chinese propaganda outlets were being used to influence U.S. elections. It did not go far enough. In 2020, FARA identified the same thing happening with Chinese news sources, though by that time the influence measures had been going on for more than 10 years. More than that, the Justice Department has a "China Initiative" which is described this way:

> Under the Initiative, the Department educates American colleges and universities about potential threats to academic freedom and open discourse from covert Chinese malign influence efforts, raises awareness among the business community that acting as an agent of the Chinese government could trigger obligations to register under FARA, and continues to evaluate whether foreign media organizations [such as state-controlled television network CGTN] operating under the editorial direction or control of a foreign government are complying with FARA.[17]

FARA is weak. While it is widely believed that FARA prohibits companies from engaging in activities that are representing foreign interests in the U.S., that is not what it does. Originally set down during the infusing of many propagandists from Nazi Germany prior to World War II, it did not prohibit their activities, but required businesses to register as agents and report their expenditures on these activities. In changes made in 1966, the focus was changed to economic matters and "prohibited contingent fee contracts, broadened exemptions to ensure legitimate commercial activities were not burdened, strengthened provisions for the disclosure and labeling of propaganda, and required the Department of Justice to issue regulations on the act (28 C.F.R. §5.1 et seq.)."[18] It requires disclosure of all contracts with the foreign entity.

How is it that we can allow a foreign government to dispense propaganda from a U.S. platform in the name of free speech? How can we allow Chinese companies to buy campaign advertising in the U.S. when our own businesses cannot? A small example of the application of these policies should be enough for Congress to see the reason for changing it.

After being sued in 2019, the Justice Department filed a civil counterclaim against RM Broadcasting, a Florida company, when Justice required RM to register as a foreign agent of the "Federal State Unitary Enterprise Rossiya Segodnya International Information Agency (Rossiya Segodnya), a Russian state-owned media enterprise created by Vladimir Putin to advance Russian interests abroad." RM Broadcasting had a service contract to provide unedited broadcasts of stories from Rossiya Segodnya's "Sputnik" radio programs on AM radio channel 1390 WZHF in the Washington, D.C., region. As the services agreement established Rossiya Segodnya's direction and control over RM Broadcasting, the FARA unit of the National Security Division informed RM Broadcasting that it was acting as a publicity agent and an information-service employee of Rossiya Segodnya, and was required to register as an agent of a foreign principal.[19] Following that decision, in January 2020 Sputnik started to air Russian propaganda on three radio stations in the Kansas City area via stations controlled by Alpine Broadcasting Corporation of Liberty, Missouri. The owner of Alpine sees this as a commercial venture and has the right to take money from Russian news agencies associated with the Russian government.

> ... Public disclosure forms show that the Russian government is paying more than $2 million over three years, starting in December 2017, for the Washington broadcasts. In Kansas City, the fee is $324,000 for three years, or $49.27 per hour, according to RM Broadcasting's Foreign Agents Registration Act filing. Mr. Schartel said he gets $27.50 of that hourly rate.[20]

What the case demonstrates is that companies doing business with foreign entities are allowed to participate in influence campaigns as long as they register as agents of a foreign entity. It does not prevent them from operating their propaganda outlets through U.S. entities but does require the disclosure of those activities. Registration may be seen by some companies as restrictive, embarrassing, even unconstitutional. The court said that view was not justified.

Cyber

Deterrence against China and Russia is not very successful and hundreds of companies and government agencies have noted for the past 10 years. This is partly because deterrence is not working; there is no coherent strategy to address these complex influence programs with the same level of effort those countries have applied to us. There are two problems with the way we are trying to solve this.

We have a business community that acts like it does not believe security of computer networks is very important. There are not as many businesses like that as there used to be but judging from the numbers and breath of hacking events in the last three years, there are still quite a few. I heard one businessman say in a meeting of his peers, "We can out-innovate them." Many of those companies have offices and manufacturing in China, where their ideas are stolen right off the manufacturing floor, yet they believe we can stay ahead of China though our own innovation. That is naïve.

Second, the problem of attribution is greater when we cannot even identify that a country has attacked us. Most countries use their intelligence services to make a determination of which countries made an attack. It is a limiting factor in what specifically can be done to counter these types of operations. There are more steps than jumping to conclusions and retaliation. That is the response of those who apply reciprocity or retribution as deterrence in Cyberspace. They almost never work. President Biden threatened to respond "in kind" to Russia before we can say for sure that it is Russia that is responsible.[21] Responding in kind is not the correct strategy, and the first time the government gets it wrong, they will discover how important it is to wait a bit before launching a strike.

This strategy flies in the face of the purpose of a response. The purpose is deterrence which used to be the best response. Michael J. Mazarr, senior political scientist at the RAND Corporation:

> Deterrence is the practice of discouraging or restraining someone—in world politics, usually a nation-state—from taking unwanted actions, such as an armed attack. It involves an effort to stop or prevent an action, as opposed to the closely related but distinct concept of "compellence," which is an effort to force an actor to do something.... The classic literature distinguishes between two fundamental approaches to deterrence. Deterrence by denial strategies seek to deter an action by making it infeasible or unlikely to succeed, thus denying a potential aggressor confidence in attaining its objectives—deploying sufficient local military forces to defeat an invasion, for example.[22]

There seems to be no indication that any kind of deterrence has been tried in any of the influence campaigns we have witnessed. We know that in cases of foreign hacking in the U.S., the FBI brings criminal charges, and that will lead so some arrests, but not enough to match the amounts of money involved in crime. Criminals are not so easily deterred.

The Obama Administration decided warnings were a good idea to deter the Russians, and the 2016 elections debacle resulted. It was not enough to deter the Russians and it would not come close to deterring the Chinese.

Influence campaigns are not going to be deterred by traditional means because the countries that are good at them are not deterred by anyone anymore. They are successful, and that success makes deterrence impossible. That forces a different approach, one that most governments are not willing to take. We need to shift the strategy from detection to disruption, which in itself is deterrence. It requires the exposure of secrets. Not the exposure in long congressional hearings or investigations that take years and have a political purpose. These kinds of operations have to be disrupted while they are going on. That requires a constant application of force itself not politically influenced.

Our focus on these campaigns has been to limit Chinese and Russian influence in infrastructure in the U.S. by placing more restrictions on foreign ownership, control, and influence (FOCI) which is more strategic than tactical. The fact is, not very many countries can say they do well at countering the kinds of influence campaigns we are seeing today because the traditional institutional response does not work. The traditional response is retaliation, usually retaliation in kind. This is the traditional "do something" government response, which almost always fails in its objective. We should take a longer view like the Chinese do.

What we have not done well is define these campaigns for what they are: foreign government attempts to undermine our belief systems and institutions. They are campaigns approved at the highest levels of government, and an affront to the leadership of one country by another. Those affected have a right to respond in a way proportional to the damage done, but also in a way that provides some deterrence against future actions. Deterrence is one of the most difficult areas to address because of attribution. These campaigns are not like dropping an atomic bomb on an adversary. We can deter that by making it possible to retaliate in kind. Responding "in kind" to an influence campaign with another influence campaign is useless.

What is necessary is an offensive attack against the influence campaign, destroying and exposing the financial relationships supporting it, and its political aims. It requires the identification of the individuals, businesses and government agencies involved, without necessarily prosecuting them in a court of law. The FBI does something like this when it warns a congressman they are being targeted by a Chinese spy. It requires the exposure of intelligence sources and methods used by the country of origin, without the requirement to expose those of the country countering that operation. There will be no court rooms needed, at least not often. It just requires the affected countries to get the information to the publics of the world, without compromising their own operations.

It requires disruption of the electronic communications of the participants. Why do we allow millions of accounts on Facebook and Twitter that are owned by foreign trolls, and rely on social media companies to get rid of them? We need to disrupt the operational elements making those accounts. Get Facebook and Twitter out of the whack-a-mole business of trying to keep up with an automated system that manufactures accounts faster than they can delete them. Go after the Internet Research Agencies of the world and undermine their capability to make new accounts and pay people to use them. We need our own Great Cannon to accomplish this.

The Great Cannon is not a thing, it is an idea that China has that we do not. But not-invented-here has killed many new ideas that work. It can be implemented with different type of servers that are multipurpose—this is not using it the way the Chinese do when they disrupt news and information that is contrary to the CCP's policies and publication guidance.

Citizen Lab did its own analysis of the Great Cannon which validated many of the least understood methods used by China.[23] China was attacking some servers outside its country with denial of service attacks (DDOS). It is an offensive weapon, that denies users access to those servers and the information they contain. The servers that were doing the attack belonged to Baidu, a Chinese internet services company, but they denied being attacked, or having any role in the Great Cannon. Given the technical abilities of the devices involved, that might be true, but Chinese law would not allow Baidu to refuse to do it. U.S. law would.

The Great Firewall is China's eavesdropping computer system. It actually assembles each transmission that users make and looks for banned content being sent to a destination. The Great Cannon, which was developed later, can go further by injecting or suppressing traffic, but it does so to a smaller subset of the total amount of traffic. In the Baidu case, 98 percent of traffic was passed without action being taken on it. Most users would not even notice that a few of their transactions were not passed to a server, unless they frequently fell into the 2 percent that was being intercepted.[24] Usually, those people know they are being watched, and they know why.

> The Great Cannon is not simply an extension of the Great Firewall, but a distinct attack tool that hijacks traffic to (or presumably from) individual IP addresses, and can *arbitrarily replace unencrypted content as a man-in-the-middle* [emphasis in original].
>
> The operational deployment of the Great Cannon represents a significant escalation in state-level information control: the normalization of widespread use of an attack tool to enforce censorship by weaponizing users. Specifically, the Cannon manipulates the traffic of "bystander" systems outside China, silently programming their browsers to create a massive DDoS attack. While employed for a highly visible attack in this case, the Great Cannon clearly has the capability for use in a manner similar to the NSA's QUANTUM system, affording China the opportunity to deliver exploits targeting any foreign computer that communicates with any China-based website not fully utilizing HTTPS.[25]

The same technology can be used for good. We should be applying our technical capabilities to disrupt the troll makers, their account making systems, and keeping them suppressed. The Great Cannon has a number of variations, blocking certain types of transactions, accepting and recording other types so the messages can be traced or blocked, or actually interfering with certain known offenders. There is no reason to not have such a system operating against countries that are trying to influence the U.S. Weaver, et al., suggested the National Security Agency has such a system already to use in counter-terrorism operations.[26]

It must be done independently. Politicians of almost every advanced country are deathly afraid of exposing influencing campaigns. Exposure of political figures is the main reason they are shy around discussions of the effectiveness of influence campaigns. They never know where all of those political contributions are coming from, and often do not want to know.

If that woman who ran my political campaign financing turns out to be a Chinese spy, it will not help that I did not know where she got that money going into the campaign fund. The public exposure of the facts will be enough to cause trouble for anyone. Foreign money in a U.S. election is illegal, as with many other countries. Exposure of that kind of risk is inherent in every politician's fund raising. Still, that does not mean it does not need to be identified and the money removed.

Financing Counter-Influence

We have to match resources being applied to campaigns. The operations required to suppress influence campaigns are expensive and budgets will be built on what is required to fund a defense against these programs. The criminal indictment of the Internet Research Agency says it had a monthly budget of $1.25 million per month leading up to the 2016 election in the U.S.[27] Since the Chinese and Iranian efforts were never investigated, we have no figures for their activities. If we can estimate an amount equal to what the Russians were spending, there was at least $30 million spent on disrupting the 2016 election, most likely a low estimate. It always costs more to defend against multiples of threats.

To fund an organization to develop budget estimates, appropriate money, oversee a budget, and coordinate activities requires more than $30 million a year and the political will to establish and maintain that capability. For about $200 million a year it could be started. It is an idea that may be a little naïve because getting that much money appropriated will not be easy, given the shyness of those who have to make money available. We still have to raise these issues and develop congressional support.

Executive Responsibility

When Malcolm Turnbull introduced legislation to counter influence campaigns in Australia, he made comments worth noting. They raise the need for executive action to fight these kinds of campaigns:

> First, we are focused on the activities of foreign states and their agents in Australia and not the loyalties of Australians who happen to be from a foreign country. There is no place for racism or xenophobia in our country. Our diaspora communities are part of the solution, not the problem. To think otherwise would be not only wrong and divisive but also folly—in a nation where most of us come from migrant families and one in four of us was born overseas.
>
> Second, interference is unacceptable from any country whether you might

think of it as friend, foe or ally. Nations and their representatives will be judged by their behaviour in Australia, not who they are.

Third, we will not tolerate foreign influence activities that are in any way covert, coercive or corrupt. That is the line that separates legitimate influence from unacceptable interference.

We are not concerned with "soft power," as the term is properly understood, as an attractive force. If another nation has cultural or economic gravitational pull, then it suggests they are doing something right and we would all benefit from being involved.

We will always assert our national interests, and we expect other countries to do the same. But we do insist that all players engage openly and within the rules.

Finally, and most importantly, our rejection of covert, coercive or corrupting behaviour leads naturally to a counter-foreign-interference strategy that is built upon the four pillars of sunlight, enforcement, deterrence and capability.[28]

He is saying we need a balance of approach that protects people who came to our countries as immigrants and those who live as citizens today to avoid the transference of government leaders who run influence campaigns and the citizens who they are directed towards. It is important for us to distinguish the kinds of activities run by intelligence agents and the people of those countries.

As the prosecutions of agents involved in these activities have shown, influence campaigns are products of foreign intelligence officers, or their proxies, running government-sponsored campaigns. We have to stop thinking about them as criminals who have to be prosecuted in court, or groups of individuals who are just communicating with one another about social issues. That view is what drives law enforcement, particularly the FBI, to lead investigations into influence campaigns. They are not just those things, and they need to be addressed by intelligence services.

That change would allow for two things (1) the methods of collecting information about the activities are not bound by law enforcement rules, and (2) operations that counter influence campaigns would not have to be disclosed to the world in open court.

The significance of this kind of shift is the reliance on law enforcement to manage the investigations and defenses against this kind of campaign. Right now, it is law enforcement trying to investigate operations against the intelligence services running the campaigns. It is not a fair fight, nor one that we need. Intelligence services are much larger, and better funded than any law enforcement agency. In the U.S., the FBI, the chief law enforcement agency, is part of the Intelligence Community (IC) but not a very big part, nor have they been doing intelligence work very long. The FBI cannot lead this kind of effort.

There is a place for law enforcement, but not as the leader of anti-influence campaigns. The intelligence services should be the leads for offensive and defensive operations against influence campaigns. In the countries that run them, they are managed by intelligence services. Countering these kinds of campaigns should fall to intelligence services mostly because they are covert. Law enforcement runs some covert but mostly clandestine programs. There would be more accountability if the President had to approve each one of these operations.

Only law enforcement can prosecute crimes that are identified in these operations, but the equities between intelligence and law enforcement should be considered before any prosecutions are contemplated. Equities are those conflicts that arise between the exposure of intelligence sources and methods and the need to deter future conduct by prosecuting an individual. Those equities need to be resolved by the Director of National Intelligence with the Central Intelligence Agency the lead for operations.

The disruption of influence campaigns should be covert.

> Unlike covert action, clandestine activities do not require a presidential finding, but they may require notification of Congress. This definition differentiates clandestine from covert, using clandestine to signify the tactical concealment of the activity. By comparison, covert activities can be characterized as the strategic concealment of the United States' sponsorship of activities that aim to effect change in the political, economic, military, or diplomatic behavior of an overseas target.[29]

We should not be talking about what we are doing to activate programs to defend a country against influence campaigns because those actions are subject to the response against them. Bringing criminal cases on each one tells our adversaries what we know and some of how we found out. It is not in our national interest. It allows our enemies to see and influence every step we take. Planning and execution should be done as any other covert program. That means very few participating industry leaders unless they can qualify for a government security clearance. Congressional hearings, especially budget hearings should be closed. It is true that all of this may be happening unbeknownst to any of us right now, but we do not know.

Every country has its own representatives collecting intelligence. They operate satellites, they listen to telephone conversations and watch public media broadcasts; they intercept business correspondence and meetings. At the far extreme, they manage spies who are on the ground inside other countries. We rarely consider prosecuting these people for the jobs they do, though there will be consequences for those who get caught inside another country committing illegal acts; they know those risks and accept them as a part of their job.

At the same time, every government has a counterintelligence function which tries to identify potential adversaries and prevent them from stealing information, planting spies and disrupting national operations. Although counterintelligence has a role to play in defending against influence campaigns, it is not a traditional role and not defined. Those assets need to be brought in to counter these kinds of operations. There has been no call for counterintelligence services to be used in a counter influence role. But, if a foreign adversary is trying to influence vote counts in our country by manipulating voting machines, the counterintelligence functions would be better suited to dealing with that than CISA, which is less capable.

Law enforcement is overwhelmed by the scope of this kind of activity and few people in law enforcement have security clearances at the levels required for international operations. This was the reason for developing new methods of response to terrorist events after September 11, 2001. The traditional ways of stopping terrorist events, by inference, did not work. We should be able to understand why. Law Enforcement did not have the resources, but part of that is the prioritization of what it did have.

In a speech in July 2020, FBI Director Christopher Wray said his agents open a new case on Chinese operatives every 20 hours.[30] But the FBI's interest in counterintelligence is mostly the theft of intellectual property from business, leaving few resources to influence campaigns. Wray said he had 5000 active cases and fewer than 900 agents, who have other work to do besides these cases.[31] They are also spread all over the country and legal attaches outside the U.S. These cases have raised the interest among the public particularly with respect to thefts of U.S. technology by Chinese business interests, but did little to address the Chinese influence campaigns against the U.S. They spent all their time on the Russians.

Second, the FBI had resources to pursue these kinds of cases but broke up that group and scattered them around the organization. The law enforcement aspect of the Bureau should have remained to pursue these campaigns. The FBI should support anti-influence through the CIA.

Free Speech

Who has the right to free speech in the democracies of the world? Does a paid troll on the Internet have a right to repeat the position of government censors as their own? Do they have a right to pretend to be someone they are not and publish the same ideas for multiple pseudonyms using free speech as the justification? Foreign language newspapers published on-line are frequently free and viewable by millions, so content of those publications is not the issue with free speech. We easily read some of them knowing they are government controlled with restricted and biased content, so that too is not the issue. We do that with a clear understanding of what we are dealing with. Registration and disclosure of those activities are not enough. We need to disrupt those operations and reject the arguments for free speech when the person is a bot, or represents another government.

But the most difficult issue is not being addressed by registration and disclosure. How do we define the difference between free speech and influence campaigns? When it pertains to government sponsored content in influence campaigns, especially content presented as something else, or prepared by someone other than the person actually writing it, is it free speech? As an example, suppose a government creates an article about a political party in its own country. The article accuses the party of caucusing in secret to discuss overthrowing the existing government without force of arms. A plan was proposed and actions to be taken were identified. The article is sent to every major press outlet in the country. Simultaneously, trolls begin to recount a closed-door meeting of the party that had members talking about plans of some sort to take over power. Articles appear that were allegedly written by prominent businessmen who have evidence of the same meeting haven taken place. One businessman complains he did not write such an article. A reporter tries to contact one of the writers and finds the person does not exist. The latter two incidents are not widely reported and those articles are no longer found on the Internet. The methodology is simple; the objective is simple. It is a repeatable process repeated often.

The same kind of issues arise when foreign press outlets controlled by China and Russia impose rules on their own reporters working overseas. China began to restrict foreign journalists, particularly those from the U.S., in March 2020. But China and Russia do not have free speech, as its journalists and the former demonstrators in Hong Kong know.

They are told what stories can be run and what cannot, and they expect foreign journalists in China to adhere to the same instructions issued every day. For the past several years, China has started to shorten visas and permits for foreigners to less than six months, and attempts to have news organizations self-censor the same way their own press outlets comply with censorship rules.[32] The influence is broader in this case. Those that do comply longer visas, up to a year. But they were motivated by U.S. restrictions limiting numbers of foreign reporters on Chinese controlled press outlets. When China takes these kinds of actions, there should be reciprocity from any other country dealing with them.

But what the social media giants also can do is remove some accounts associated with intelligence services that are engaged in influence campaigns. In the post-election reaction to Russian meddling in 2016, Facebook and Twitter started to announce the removal of accounts, many of which were identified as part of the Russian programs in 2016. Those trolls already had their influence by then. None of the social media companies have done very much at removing the total number of accounts managed by the countries involved. When the Russians said they were disseminating content to social media, nobody at the time really knew how big a dissemination they were making, nor how they created this dissemination mechanism.

Twitter acknowledged the removal of 10,000 accounts that were used to depress voter participation among Democrats. However, Twitter later removed "millions of accounts" without specifying how many were used by Russian interests.[33] As fast as they were removed, new ones sprung up with different usernames and affiliations, but it is difficult to see the real scope of the Russian effort. The process of creating accounts was automated and outpaced efforts to quantify the number, or true ownership of them.

From October 2018 to March 2019, Facebook found and removed over *three billion* accounts, which it said were "automated attacks by bad actors who attempt to create large volumes of accounts at one time...."[34] That is a staggering number. What made this removal significant was that it reflected total numbers that exceeded the number of active users of Facebook. Facebook tried to give this number some perspective by saying it represented 5 percent of monthly active users, but this is not indicative of the total number of fake accounts capable of producing information for other Facebook users, if needed. They are ignoring the problem and should be required to cooperate in removing accounts identified as intelligence sponsored. Much more has to be done.

Why would any social media company use the Chinese to censor in the U.S.? Those censors are representatives of a foreign interest and should be registered. We should know what they are doing and what their relationship is to U.S. censorship in social media.

It takes so long to identify the stories and accounts as a government-sponsored activities, the trolls to be identified, or faked content sourced that the effects are felt before they can be corrected. Foreign governments are stealing source credibility from others who are legitimate influencers when they publish stories in their name, yet there is no emphasis by social media companies on identifying and deleting those kinds of accounts. They undermine our basic core values by undermining our democratic thought leaders. They control the dialog and subject matter first. Yes, social media companies delete accounts, but they need to be replaced as the disrupters of that kind of bogus account making. I do not get to see material created in my name, nor even know how to identify who has opened an account on a system in my name. I could not find one if it were to be made. I at least need a way to determine if anyone uses accounts in my name. So, take that problem out of the hands of social media and have them notify me any time an account is made in my name.

We can also consider what information has been filtered out by social media censors. China has an army of individuals who filter content, but so do social media in the U.S. Both, to some extent, rely on "self-censorship" to filter thoughts from our view. Jillian York, director for international freedom of expression at the Electronic Frontier Foundation, says publishers should consider what this means for them. "The rules under which they're publishing are no longer law," says York. "They're proprietary terms of service."[35] Congress should change that. When Amazon, Google, and Twitter ban the President of the United States and close down an application (Parler) running on servers on Amazon's webhosting service, there is no longer dialog on any side of an issue. That is censorship, but more importantly it is undemocratic censorship. It is only the social media owners that have a say. That is an abuse of the terms of service under which social media is allowed to operate.

The campaigns by both Russia and China are becoming more varied with a wider number of targets. The amounts that are required to sustain these widely varied campaigns indicate how both countries feel about the success of their operations. Ignoring either of them is suicide. Yet, the political parties seem set on ignoring the biggest offenders' interference. Do they have so much self-interest that they cannot put aside their own for a focused approach to fending off these disruptions?

In the past, we have been able to focus on external attacks by organizing our defenses in ways to counter the activities of our enemies. In that sense, it is focused on America to engage our allies to defend our friends who pursue the same objectives. This situation is a little different. The disruptors are attacking us pretending to be human beings.

We have at least two countries attacking a fundamental set of core values of our democracies and those democracies need to do more things together to fight them. Creating awareness of what we are fighting against is the first step. We need to have more sharing on what the Chinese and Russians are doing but keep it in the intelligence agencies and cooperate in disrupting it. How do we allow the beneficiaries of influence campaigns to not be identified? Bringing those who benefit to the front and publicizing their sources of income can be done even if the campaigns are covert. Exposure of these sources will illuminate the beneficiaries and allow governments to determine what actions to take.

Lastly, we owe it to ourselves to be more skeptical of each other's claims, particularly those of the press. When we hear the same word choices being used to describe an action there is something suspect about that. In the U.S. elections anyone challenging the claim that there was no election interference by any country sees the word "baseless" describing the claim. By definition there was no voter fraud, no election interference, but no investigations of either the Chinese or Iranian influence campaigns. That cannot be a logical conclusion. We do have enough information to say it is baseless, yet we allow the press to be the arbiter of truth.

Appendix

Foreign Threats to the 2020
U.S. Federal Elections

DECLASSIFIED by DNI [Director National Intelligence] Haines on 15 March 2021
SECURITY NATIONAL INTELLIGENCE COUNCIL
INTELLIGENCE COMMUNITY ASSESSMENT 10 March 2021
Foreign Threats to the 2020 U.S. Federal Elections
ICA2020–00078D
UNCLASSIFIED

This document is a declassified version of a classified report. The analytic judgments outlined here are identical to those in the classified version, but this declassified document does not include the full supporting information and does not discuss specific intelligence reports, sources, or methods.

This Intelligence Community Assessment was prepared by the National Intelligence Council under the auspices of the National Intelligence Officer (NIO) for Cyber. It was drafted by the National Intelligence Council and CIA, DHS, FBI, INR, and NSA, and coordinated with CIA, DHS, FBI, INR, Treasury, and NSA.

Background

This document is a declassified version of a classified report that the Intelligence Community provided to the President, senior Executive Branch officials, and Congressional leadership and intelligence oversight committees on 07 January 2021. The Intelligence Community rarely can publicly reveal the full extent of its knowledge or the specific information on which it bases its analytic conclusions, as doing so could endanger sensitive sources and methods and imperil the Intelligence Community's ability to collect critical foreign intelligence. The analytic judgments outlined below are identical to those in the classified version, but this declassified document does not include the full supporting information and does not discuss specific intelligence reports, sources, or methods.

Scope Note

This Intelligence Community Assessment (ICA), as required by Executive Order (EO) 13848(1)(a), addresses key foreign actors' intentions and efforts to influence or interfere with the 2020 US federal elections or to undermine public confidence in the US election process. It builds on analysis published throughout the election cycle and provided to Executive Branch and Congressional leaders. This ICA does not include an assessment of the impact foreign malign influence and interference activities may have had on the outcome of the 2020 election. The US Intelligence Community is charged with monitoring and assessing the intentions, capabilities, and actions of foreign actors; it does not analyze US political processes or actors, election administration or vote tabulation processes, or public opinion.

- Pursuant to EO 13848(1)(b), after receiving this assessment, the Attorney General and the Secretary of Homeland Security, in consultation with the heads of any other appropriate Federal, State, or local agencies, will evaluate the impact of any foreign efforts on the security or integrity of election infrastructure or infrastructure pertaining to a political organization, campaign, or candidate in a 2020 US federal election, and document the evaluation in a report.
- Pursuant to EO 13848(3)(a), after reviewing this assessment and the report required by EO 13848(1)(b), the Secretary of the Treasury, in consultation with the Secretary of State, the Attorney General, and the Secretary of Homeland Security, will impose appropriate sanctions for activities determined to constitute foreign interference in a US election.

Definitions

For the purpose of this assessment, election influence includes overt and covert efforts by foreign governments or actors acting as agents of, or on behalf of, foreign governments intended to affect directly or indirectly a U.S. election including candidates, political parties, voters or their preferences, or political processes. Election interference is a subset of election influence activities targeted at the technical aspects of the election, including voter registration, casting and counting ballots, or reporting results.

Sources of Information

In drafting this ICA, we considered intelligence reporting and other information made available to the Intelligence Community as of 31 December 2020.

Key Judgment 1: **We have no indications that any foreign actor attempted to alter any technical aspect of the voting process in the 2020 U.S. elections, including voter registration, casting ballots, vote tabulation, or reporting results.** We assess that it would be difficult for a foreign actor to manipulate election processes at scale without detection by intelligence collection on the actors themselves, through physical and cyber security monitoring around voting systems across the country, or in post-election audits. The IC identified some successful compromises of state and local government networks prior to Election Day—as well as a higher volume of unsuccessful attempts—that we assess were not directed at altering election processes. Some foreign actors, such as Iran and Russia, spread false or inflated claims about alleged compromises of voting systems to undermine public confidence in election processes and results.

Key Judgment 2: **We assess that Russian President Putin authorized, and arrange [sic] of Russian government organizations conducted, influence operations aimed at denigrating President Biden's candidacy and the Democratic Party, supporting former President Trump, undermining public confidence in the electoral process, and exacerbating socio-political divisions in the U.S. Unlike in 2016, we did not see persistent Russian cyber efforts to gain access to election infrastructure.** We have high confidence in our assessment; Russian state and proxy actors who all serve the Kremlin's interests worked to affect U.S. public perceptions in a consistent manner. **A key element of Moscow's strategy this election cycle was its use of proxies linked to Russian intelligence to push influence narratives—including misleading or unsubstantiated allegations against President Biden—U.S. media organizations, U.S. officials, and prominent U.S. individuals, including some close to former President Trump and his administration.**

Key Judgment 3: **We assess that Iran carried out a multi-pronged covert influence campaign intended to undercut former President Trump's reelection prospects—though without directly promoting his rivals—undermine public confidence in the electoral process and U.S. institutions, and sow division and exacerbate societal tensions in the U.S.** We have high confidence in this assessment. We assess that Supreme Leader Khamenei authorized the campaign and Iran's military and intelligence services implemented it using overt and covert messaging and cyber operations.

Key Judgment 4: **We assess that China did not deploy interference efforts and considered but did not deploy influence efforts intended to change the outcome of the U.S. Presidential election.** We have high confidence in this judgment. China sought stability in its relationship with the United States, did not view either election outcome as being advantageous enough for China to risk getting caught meddling, and assessed its traditional influence tools primarily targeted economic measures and lobbying—would be sufficient to meet its goal of shaping U.S. China policy regardless of the winner. The NIO for Cyber assesses, however, that China did take some steps to try to undermine former President Trump's reelection.

Key Judgment 5: **We assess that a range of additional foreign actors— including Lebanese Hizballah, Cuba, and Venezuela some steps to attempt to influence the election.** In general, we assess that they were smaller in scale than the influence efforts conducted by other actors this election cycle. Cybercriminals disrupted some election preparations; we judge their activities probably were driven by financial motivations.

Please also see DNI memorandum: Views on Intelligence Community Election Security Analysis, dated January 7, 2021.

Discussion

Foreign governments or other foreign actors often try to influence the politics and policies of other countries. They may, for example, advocate for and try to shape other countries' foreign policies in ways that benefit their political, economic, and military interests. These efforts range along a spectrum from public statements and foreign assistance efforts, to sanctions and other economic pressure such as boycotts, to covert or clandestine efforts such as covert messaging and recruiting agents of influence . When such activities are intended to directly or indirectly affect an election including candidates, political parties, voters or their preferences, or political processes—the IC characterizes it as **election influence.** If a foreign government, as part of its election influence efforts, attempts or takes actions to target the technical aspects of elections—including voter registration, casting and counting of ballots, and reporting of results, the IC characterizes it as **election interference.**

In 2020, the IC tracked a broader array of foreign actors taking steps to influence U.S. elections than in past election cycles, a development that may be explained by several factors. First, increased IC focus on this issue may have uncovered a higher percentage of efforts. Second, more actors may view influence operations as important tools for projecting power abroad. The growth of internet and social media use means foreign actors are more able to reach U.S. audiences directly, while the tools for doing so are becoming more accessible. Third, some foreign actors may perceive influence activities around U.S. elections as continuations of broad, ongoing efforts rather than specially demarcated campaigns. They may also perceive that such a continuum makes it more difficult for the U.S. to single out and respond to specifically election-focused influence efforts. Finally, as more foreign actors seek to exert influence over U.S. elections, additional actors may increasingly see election-focused influence efforts as an acceptable norm of international behavior.

Greater public and media awareness of influence operations in 2020 compared to past election cycles probably helped counter them to some degree. U.S. Government public messaging as well as Government and private sector actions probably also disrupted some activities. For example, proactive information sharing with social media companies facilitated the expeditious review, and in many cases removal, of social media accounts covertly operated by Russia and Iran.

Additionally, public disclosure of Russian and Iranian efforts and U.S. Government sanctions on some of the responsible actors probably hindered their ability to operate deniably.

Election Interference

We have no indications that any foreign actor attempted to interfere in the 2020 U.S. elections by altering any technical aspect of the voting process, including voter registration, ballot casting, vote tabulation, or reporting results. We assess that it would be difficult for a foreign actor to manipulate election processes at scale without detection by intelligence collection on the actors themselves, through physical and cyber security monitoring around voting systems across the country, or in post-election audits of electronic results and paper backups. We identified some successful compromises of state and local government networks prior to Election Day. We assess these intrusions were parts of broader campaigns targeting U.S. networks and not directed at the election. Some foreign actors, such as Iran and Russia, spread false or inflated claims about alleged compromises of voting systems to try to undermine public confidence in election processes and results.

Over the course of the election cycle, the IC, other U.S. agencies, and state and local officials also identified thousands of reconnaissance or low-level, unsuccessful attempts to gain access to county or state government networks. Such efforts are common and we have no indications they were aimed at interfering in the election.

- Some of these government networks hosted, among a variety of other government processes, election-related elements like voter registration databases or state election results reporting websites. We have no indications that these activities altered any election processes or data.
- Defensive measures such as firewalls, up-to-date patching, cybersecurity training for government personnel, and separation of election-specific systems from other computer networks probably helped to thwart thousands of compromise attempts. Such measures probably also would have helped prevent the network intrusions we detected.

Russia's Efforts to Influence 2020 Election, Exacerbate Divisions in U.S.

We assess that President Putin and the Russian state authorized and conducted influence operations against the 2020 U.S. presidential election aimed at denigrating President Biden and the Democratic Party, supporting former President Trump, undermining public confidence in the electoral process, and exacerbating sociopolitical divisions in the US. Unlike in 2016, we did not see persistent Russian cyber efforts to gain access to election infrastructure. We have high confidence in these judgments because a range of Russian state and proxy actors who all serve the Kremlin's interests worked to affect U.S. public perceptions. We also have high confidence because of the consistency of themes in Russia's influence efforts across the various influence actors and throughout the campaign, as well as in Russian leaders' assessments of the candidates. **A key element of Moscow's strategy this election cycle was its use of people linked to Russian intelligence to launder influence narratives, including misleading or unsubstantiated allegations against President Biden, through U.S. media organizations, U.S. officials, and prominent U.S. individuals, some of whom were close to former President Trump and his administration.**

Kremlin Direction of Influence Activity

We assess that President Putin and other senior Russian officials were aware of and probably directed Russia's influence operations against the 2020 U.S. presidential election. For example, we assess that Putin had purview over the activities of Andriy Derkach, a Ukrainian legislator who played a prominent role in Russia's election influence activities. Derkach has ties to Russian officials as well as Russia's intelligence services.

- Other senior officials also participated in Russia's election influence efforts—including senior national security and intelligence officials who we assess would not act without receiving at least Putin's tacit approval.

Actors, Methods, and Operations

We assess that Russia's intelligence services, Ukraine-linked individuals with ties to Russian intelligence and their networks, and Russian state media, trolls, and online proxies engaged in activities targeting the 2020 U.S. presidential election. The primary effort the IC uncovered revolved around a narrative that Russian actors began spreading as early as 2014 alleging corrupt ties between President Biden, his family, and other U.S. officials and Ukraine. Russian intelligence services relied on Ukraine-linked proxies and these proxies' networks—including their U.S. contacts—to spread this narrative to give Moscow plausible deniability of their involvement. We assess that the goals of this effort went beyond the U.S. presidential campaign to include reducing the Trump administration's support for Ukraine. As the U.S. presidential election neared, Moscow placed increasing emphasis on undermining the candidate it saw as most detrimental to its global interests. We have no evidence suggesting the Ukrainian Government was involved in any of these efforts.

- A network of Ukraine-linked individuals including Russian influence agent Konstantin Kilimnik who were also connected to the Russian Federal Security Service (FSB) took steps throughout the election cycle to damage U.S. ties to Ukraine, denigrate President Biden and his candidacy, and benefit former President Trump's prospects for reelection. We assess this network also sought to discredit the Obama administration by emphasizing accusations of corruption by U.S. officials, and to falsely blame Ukraine for interfering in the 2016 U.S. presidential election.
- Derkach, Kilimnik, and their associates sought to use prominent U.S. persons and media conduits to launder their narratives to U.S. officials and audiences. These Russian proxies met with and provided materials to Trump administration–linked U.S. persons to advocate for formal investigations; hired a U.S. firm to petition U.S. officials; and attempted to make contact with several senior U.S. officials. They also made contact with established U.S. media figures and helped produce a documentary that aired on a U.S. television network in late January 2020.
- As part of his plan to secure the reelection of former President Trump, Derkach publicly released audio recordings four times in 2020 in attempts to implicate President Biden and other current or former U.S. Government officials in allegedly corrupt activities related to Ukraine. Derkach also worked to initiate legal proceedings in Ukraine and the U.S. related to these allegations. Former Ukrainian officials associated with Derkach sought to promote similar claims throughout late 2019 and 2020, including through direct outreach to senior U.S. Government officials.

We assess that Russia's cyber units gathered information to inform Kremlin decision-making about the election and Moscow's broader foreign policy interests. Through these operations, Russia probably gathered at least some information it could have released in influence operations. We assess Russia did not make persistent efforts to access election infrastructure, such as those made by Russian intelligence during the last U.S. presidential election.

- For example, shortly after the 2018 midterm elections, Russian intelligence cyber actors attempted to hack organizations primarily affiliated with the Democratic Party. Separately, the GRU unsuccessfully targeted U.S. political actors in 2019 and 2020; this activity aligned with the tactics of a larger intelligence-gathering campaign.

- In late 2019, GRU cyber actors conducted a phishing campaign against subsidiaries of Burisma holdings, likely in an attempt to gather information related to President Biden's family and Burisma.
- We judge that Russian cyber operations that targeted and compromised U.S. state and local government networks in 2020—including exfiltrating some voter data that were probably not election-focused and instead part of a broader campaign targeting dozens of U.S. and global entities.

Throughout the election cycle, Russia's online influence actors sought to affect U.S. public perceptions of the candidates, as well as advance Moscow's longstanding goals of undermining confidence in U.S. election processes and increasing sociopolitical divisions among the American people. During the presidential primaries and dating back to 2019, these actors backed candidates from both major U.S. political parties that Moscow viewed as outsiders, while later claiming that election fraud helped what they called "establishment" candidates. Throughout the election, Russia's online influence actors sought to amplify mistrust in the electoral process by denigrating mail-in ballots, highlighting alleged irregularities, and accusing the Democratic Party of voter fraud.

- The Kremlin-linked influence organization Project Lakhta and its Lakhta Internet Research (LIR) troll farm—commonly referred to by its former moniker Internet Research Agency (IRA)—amplified controversial domestic issues. LIR used social media personas, news websites, and U.S. persons to deliver tailored content to subsets of the U.S. population. LIR established short-lived troll farms that used unwitting third-country nationals in Ghana, Mexico, and Nigeria to propagate these US-focused narratives, probably in response to efforts by U.S. companies and law enforcement to shut down UR-associated personas.
- Russian state media, trolls, and online proxies, including those directed by Russian intelligence, published disparaging content about President Biden, his family, and the Democratic Party, and heavily amplified related content circulating in U.S. media, including stories centered on his son. These influence actors frequently sought out US contributors to increase their reach into U.S. audiences. In addition to election-related content, these online influence actors also promoted conspiratorial narratives about the COVID-19 pandemic, made allegations of social media censorship, and highlighted U.S. divisions surrounding protests about racial justice.
- Russian online influence actors generally promoted former President Trump and his commentary, including repeating his political messaging on the election results; the presidential campaign; debates; the impeachment inquiry; and, as the election neared, U.S. domestic crises. Influence actors sometimes sought to discourage U.S. left-leaning audiences from voting by suggesting that neither candidate was a preferable option. At the same time, Russian actors criticized former President Trump or his administration when they pursued foreign

policies—such as the targeted killing of Iranian General Qasem Soleimani in January 2020—at odds with Russia's preferences.

- LIR, which probably receives tasking and strategic direction from the Kremlin, pushed stories supporting former President Trump and denigrating President Biden after he became the presumptive nominee in April.

Evaluating Moscow's Calculus on the 2020 Election

We assess that Russian leaders viewed President Biden's potential election as disadvantageous to Russian interests and that this drove their efforts to undermine his candidacy. We have high confidence in this assessment.

- Russian officials and state media frequently attacked President Biden for his leading role in the Obama administration's Ukraine policy and his support for the anti-Putin opposition in Russia, suggesting the Kremlin views him as part of a reflexively anti-Russia U.S. foreign policy establishment. Putin probably also considers President Biden more apt to echo the idea of American "exceptionalism," which he and other Kremlin leaders have often publicly criticized as problematic and dangerous.
- Moscow's range of influence actors uniformly worked to denigrate President Biden after his entrance into the race. Throughout the primaries and general election campaign, Russian influence agents repeatedly spread unsubstantiated or misleading claims about President Biden and his family's alleged wrongdoing related to Ukraine. By contrast, during the Democratic primaries Russian online influence actors promoted candidates that Moscow viewed as outside what it perceives to be an anti-Russia political establishment.
- Even after the election, Russian online influence actors continued to promote narratives questioning the election results and disparaging President Biden and the Democratic Party. These efforts parallel plans Moscow had in place in 2016 to discredit a potential incoming Clinton administration, but which it scrapped after former President Trump's victory.

We assess Russian leaders preferred that former President Trump win reelection despite perceiving some of his administration's policies as anti-Russia. We have high confidence in this assessment based in part on the Kremlin's public comments about him and the consistency and volume of anti-Biden messaging we detected from Russian online influence actors.

As the election neared, Kremlin officials took some steps to prepare for a Biden administration, probably because they believed former President Trump's prospects for re-election had diminished.

- Putin—while praising former President Trump personally during an interview in October—noted that President Biden appeared willing to extend the New START Treaty (NST) or negotiate a new strategic offensive reduction treaty. The comments were consistent with Russian officials' view that a potential Biden administration would be more open to arms control negotiations.

Moscow almost certainly views meddling in U.S. elections as an equitable response to perceived actions by Washington and an opportunity to both undermine U.S. global standing and influence U.S. decision-making. We assess that Moscow will continue election influence efforts to further its longstanding goal of weakening Washington because the Kremlin has long deemed that a weakened United States would be less likely to pursue assertive foreign and security policies abroad and more open to geopolitical bargains with Russia.

- Russian officials are probably willing to accept some risk in conducting influence operations targeting the U.S.—including against U.S. elections—because they believe Washington meddles similarly in Russia and other countries and that such efforts are endemic to geostrategic competition.
- Russian officials probably also assess that continued influence operations against the United States pose a manageable risk to Russia's image in Washington because U.S.-Russia relations are already extremely poor.

Iran's Influence Campaign Designed to Undercut Former President Trump's Reelection, Sow Discord

We assess with high confidence that Iran carried out an influence campaign during the 2020 U.S. election season intended to undercut the reelection prospects of former President Trump and to further its longstanding objectives of exacerbating divisions in the U.S., creating confusion, and undermining the legitimacy of U.S. elections and institutions. We did not identify Iran engaging in any election interference activities, as defined in this assessment. Tehran's efforts were aimed at denigrating former President Trump, not actively promoting his rivals. We assess that Tehran designed its campaign to attempt to influence U.S. policy toward Iran, distract U.S. leaders with domestic issues, and to amplify messages sympathetic to the Iranian regime. Iran's efforts in 2020, especially its emails to individual U.S. voters and efforts to spread allegations of voter fraud, were more aggressive than in past election cycles.

- We assess that Tehran's efforts to attempt to influence the outcome of the 2020 U.S. election and Iranian officials' preference that former President Trump is not reelected were driven in part by a perception that the regime faced acute threats from the US.
- Iran's election influence efforts were primarily focused on sowing discord in the United States and exacerbating societal tensions—including by creating or amplifying social media content that criticized former President Trump—probably because they believed that this advanced Iran's longstanding objectives and undercut the prospects for the former President's reelection without provoking retaliation.

Actors, Methods, and Operations

We assess that Supreme Leader Ali Khamenei probably authorized Iran's influence campaign and that it was a whole of government effort, judging from the involvement of multiple Iranian Government elements. We have high confidence in this assessment.

- Iran focused its social media and propaganda on perceived vulnerabilities in the United States, including the response to the COVID-19 pandemic, economic recession, and civil unrest.

During this election cycle Iran increased the volume and aggressiveness of its cyber-enabled influence efforts against the United States compared to past election influence efforts. This included efforts to send threatening e-mails to American citizens and to amplify concerns about voter fraud in the election.

- In a highly targeted operation, Iranian cyber actors sent threatening, spoofed emails purporting to be from the Proud Boys group to Democratic voters in multiple U.S. states, demanding that the individuals change their party affiliation and vote to reelect former President Trump. The same actors also produced and disseminated a video intending to demonstrate alleged voter fraud.
- Since early 2020, Iranian actors created social media accounts that targeted the United States and published over 1,000 pieces of online content on the United States, though U.S. social media companies subsequently removed many. Tehran expanded the number of its inauthentic social media accounts to at least several thousand and boosted the activity of existing accounts, some of which dated back to 2012.

Post-Election Activity

We assess that Iran continues to use influence operations in attempts to inflame domestic tensions in the U.S. For example, in mid-December 2020, Iranian cyber actors were almost certainly responsible for the creation of a website containing death threats against U.S. election officials.

- We assess Iran is also seeking to exploit the post-election environment to collect intelligence.

We assess that Iranian actors did not attempt to manipulate or attack any election infrastructure.

- In early 2020 Iranian cyber actors exploited a known vulnerability to compromise U.S. entities associated with election infrastructure as a part of a broad targeting effort across multiple sectors worldwide. Given the breadth and number of the targets, we judge that Iran did not specifically intend to use the results of this effort as part of its election influence campaign.

We assess that Iran primarily relied on cyber tools and methods to conduct its covert operations because they are low cost, deniable, scalable, and do not depend on physical access to the United States. Iranian cyber actors who focused on influence operations targeting the election adapted their activities and content based on political developments and blended cyber intrusions with online influence operations.

- As part of their influence operations, Iranian cyber actors sought to exploit vulnerabilities on U.S. states' election websites, as well as news website content management systems.

- Iranian cyber actors sent spearphishing emails to current and former senior officials and members of political campaigns, almost certainly with the intent to gain derogatory information or accesses for follow-on operations.

China Did Not Attempt to Influence Presidential Election Outcome

We assess that China did not deploy interference efforts and considered but did not deploy influence efforts intended to change the outcome of the U.S. presidential election. We have high confidence in this judgment China sought stability in its relationship with the United States and did not view either election outcome as being advantageous enough for China to risk blowback if caught. Beijing probably believed that its traditional influence tools, primarily targeted economic measures and lobbying key individuals and interest groups, would be sufficient to achieve its goal of shaping U.S. policy regardless of who won the election. **We did not identify China attempting to interfere with election infrastructure or provide funding to any candidates or parties.**

- The IC assesses that Chinese state media criticism of the Trump administration's policies related to China and its response to the COVID-19 pandemic remained consistent in the lead-up to the election and was aimed at shaping perceptions of U.S. policies and bolstering China's global position rather than to affect the 2020 U.S. election. The coverage of the U.S. election, in particular, was limited compared to other topics measured in total volume of content.
- China has long sought to influence U.S. politics by shaping political and social environments to press U.S. officials to support China's positions and perspectives. We did not, however, see these capabilities deployed for the purpose of shaping the electoral outcome.

Beijing probably judged risk of interference was <u>not worth the reward</u>.
We assess that Beijing's risk calculus against influencing the election was informed by China's preference for stability in the bilateral relationship, their probable judgment that attempting to influence the election could do lasting damage to U.S.–China ties, and belief that the election of either candidate would present opportunities and challenges for China.

- We judge that Chinese officials would work with former President Trump if he won a second term. Beijing since at least 2019 has stressed the need to improve bilateral ties after the election regardless of who won.
- In addition, China was probably concerned the United States would use accusations of election interference to scapegoat China. This may, in part, account for Beijing waiting until 13 November to congratulate President Biden.

We assess that Beijing also believes there is a bipartisan consensus against China in the United States that leaves no prospect for a pro-China administration regardless of the election outcome.

China probably expected that relations would suffer under a second term for former President Trump because he and his administration would press for further economic decoupling and challenge China's rise. It probably also believed that China in this scenario could increase its international clout because it perceived that some of the Trump administration's policies would alienate U.S. partners.

- Beijing probably expected that President Biden would be more predictable and eager to initially deescalate bilateral tensions but would pose a greater challenge over the long run because he would be more successful in mobilizing a global alliance against China and criticizing China's human rights record.
- Beijing probably judged that Russia's efforts to interfere in the 2016 election significantly damaged Moscow's position and relationship with the United States and may have worried that Washington would uncover a Chinese attempt to deploy similar measures to influence or interfere in the election and punish Beijing.

Beijing probably continued to collect intelligence on election-related targets and topics.

China probably also continued longstanding efforts to gather information on U.S. voters and public opinion; political parties, candidates and their staffs; and senior government officials. We assess Beijing probably sought to use this information to predict electoral outcomes and to inform its efforts to influence U.S. policy toward China under either election outcome, as it has during all election cycles since at least 2008 and considers an acceptable tool of statecraft.

- We assess Beijing did not interfere with election infrastructure, including vote tabulation or the transmission of election results.

Minority View

The National Intelligence Officer for Cyber assesses that China took at least some steps to undermine former President Trump's reelection chances, primarily through social media and official public statements and media. The NIO agrees with the IC's view that Beijing was primarily focused on countering anti-China policies, but assesses that some of Beijing's influence efforts were intended to at least indirectly affect U.S. candidates, political processes, and voter preferences, meeting the definition for election influence used in this report. The NIO agrees that we have no information suggesting China tried to interfere with election processes. The NIO has moderate confidence in these judgments.

This view differs from the IC assessment because it gives more weight to indications that Beijing preferred former President Trump's defeat and the election of a more predictable member of the establishment instead, and that Beijing implemented some and later increased election influence efforts, especially over the summer of 2020. The NIO assesses these indications are more persuasive than other information indicating that China decided not to intervene. The NIO further assesses that Beijing calibrated its influence efforts to avoid blow back.

Other Actors

A range of additional foreign actors took some steps to attempt to influence the election. In general, we assess that they were smaller in scale than those conducted by Russia and Iran.

We assess that Hizballah Secretary General Hassan Nasrallah supported efforts to undermine former President Trump in the 2020 U.S. election. Nasrallah probably saw this as a low-cost means to mitigate the risk of a regional conflict while Lebanon faces political, financial, and public health crises.

We assess Cuba sought to undermine former President Trump's electoral prospects by pushing anti-Republican and pro-Democrat narratives to the Latin American community. Cuban intelligence probably conducted some low-level activities in support of this effort.

The Venezuelan regime of Nicolas Maduro had an adversarial relationship with the Trump administration and we assess that Maduro had the intent, though probably not the capability, to try to influence public opinion in the U.S. against the former President. We have no information suggesting that the current or former Venezuelan regimes were involved in attempts to compromise U.S. election infrastructure.

Foreign Cybercriminals Disrupted Some Election Preparation

Profit-motivated cybercriminals disrupted election preparations in some U.S. states with ransomware attacks intended to generate profit. We have no indications that these actors sought to use these attacks to alter election functions or data, nor do we have indications that they were acting on behalf of any government.

- In October, a hacker briefly defaced a presidential campaign website after gaining access probably using administrative credentials.
- For example, in late October, probably foreign ransomware actors demanded payment from a New York county after encrypting 300 computers and 22 servers on the network with Ragnarok malware that prevented it from connecting to a statewide voter registration system. County officials directed voters who had applied via email for an absentee ballot to call and verify their ballot application had been received and processed.
- We do not know whether cybercriminals specifically targeted election-related networks with profit-making schemes or whether their activity reflected a general targeting of state and local government networks that also happen to host election-related processes.
- We assess foreign cybercriminals probably did not work to interfere or influence the U.S. elections on behalf of or at the direction of a nation state. We have low confidence in this assessment. We assess that some cybercrime groups probably operate with at least the tacit approval of their nation-state hosts.

Foreign Hacktivists

The IC tracked a handful of unsuccessful hacktivist attempts to influence or interfere in the 2020 U.S. elections.

- In October, a hacker briefly defaced a presidential campaign website after gaining access probably using administrative credentials.
- In November, hackers promoting Turkish nationalist themes breached and defaced a website previously established for a candidate in the U.S. presidential campaign, according to U.S. cybersecurity press.

Estimative Language

Estimative language consists of two elements: judgment about the likelihood of developments or events occurring and levels of confidence in the sources and analytic reasoning supporting the judgments. Judgments are not intended to imply that we have proof that shows something to be a fact. Assessments are based on collected information, which is often incomplete or fragmentary, as well as logic, argumentation, and precedents.

Judgments of Likelihood

The chart below approximates how judgments of likelihood correlate with percentages. Unless otherwise stated, the Intelligence Community's judgments are not derived via statistical analysis. Phrases such as "we judge" and "we assess" and terms such as "probably" and "likely" convey analytical assessments.

Almost no Chance.	Very Unlikely	Unlikely	Roughly Even Chance		Very Likely	Almost Certainty
0	20	40		60	80	100
Remote	Highly Improbable	Improbable	Roughly Even	Probable	Highly Probable	Near Certainty

Confidence in Our Judgments

Confidence levels provide assessments of timeliness, consistency, and extent of intelligence and open-source reporting that supports judgements. They also take into account the analytic argumentation, the depth of relevant expertise, the degree to which assumptions underlie analysis, and the scope of information gaps.

We ascribe high, moderate, or low confidence to assessments:

- **High confidence** generally indicates that judgments are based on sound analytic argumentation and high quality consistent reporting from multiple sources, including clandestinely obtained documents, clandestine and open source reporting, and in-depth expertise; it also indicates that we have few intelligence gaps, have few assumptions underlying the analytic line, have found potential for deception to be low, and have examined long-standing analytic judgements held by the IC and considered alternatives. For most intelligence topics, it will not be appropriate to claim high confidence for judgements that forecast out a number of years. High confidence in a judgment does not imply that the assessment is a fact or a certainty; such judgments might be wrong even though we have a higher degree of certainty that they are accurate.

- **Moderate confidence** generally means that the information is credibly sourced and plausible but not of sufficient quality or corroborated sufficiently to warrant a higher level of confidence. There may, for example, be information that cuts in a different direction. We have in-depth expertise on the topic, but we may acknowledge assumptions that underlie our analysis and some information gaps; there may be minor analytic differences within the IC, as well as moderate potential for deception.

- **Low confidence** generally means that the information's credibility and / or plausibility is uncertain; that the information is fragmented, dated, or poorly corroborated; or that reliability of the sources is questionable. There may be analytic differences within the IC, several significant information gaps, high potential for deception or numerous assumptions that must be made to draw analytic conclusions. In the case of low confidence, we are forced to use current data to project out in time, making a higher level of confidence impossible.

Chapter Notes

Preface

1. Summary, "Election 2020: How Trump and Biden Compare on the Key Issues," *Wall Street Journal*, November 2, 2020.

2. Dimock, Michael, and Richard Wike, *America Is Exceptional in the Nature of Its Political Divide*, Pew Research Center, November 13, 2020. https://www.pewresearch.org/fact-tank/2020/11/13/america-is-exceptional-in-the-nature-of-its-political-divide/.

3. *Ibid.*

4. Romm, Tony, and Elizabeth Dwoskin, "Twitter Purged More than 70,000 Accounts Affiliated with QAnon Following Capitol Riot," *Washington Post*, January 11, 2021. https://www.washingtonpost.com/technology/2021/01/11/trump-twitter-ban/.

5. Associated Press, "The Latest: FBI Says Probe of Capitol Officer Death Ongoing," ABC News, March 2, 2021. https://abcnews.go.com/Politics/wireStory/latest-fbi-chief-calls-capitol-riot-domestic-terrorism-76204577.

6. Beswick, Emma, EuroNews, August 12, 2020. Viewed January 10, 2020, at https://www.euronews.com/2020/08/11/belarus-protesters-incited-to-change-tact-for-third-night-of-demonstrations.

7. Polityuk, Pavel. "Lukashenko Rivals Unite Behind Blogger's Wife to Fight Belarus Election," *Reuters*, July 16, 2020. Viewed September 22, 2020, at https://www.reuters.com/article/us-belarus-election/lukashenko-rivals-unite-behind-bloggers-wife-to-fight-belarus-election-idUSKCN24H2C2.

8. Abdurasulov, Abdujalil, "What's Happening in Belarus?" BBC News, September 8, 2020. Viewed November 20, 2020, at https://www.bbc.com/news/world-europe-53799065; and Scislowska, Monika, "2 Belarusian Journalists Sent to Prison for Covering Protest," Associated Press, February 18, 2021. https://apnews.com/article/alexander-lukashenko-belarus-journalists-elections-minsk-d5abad8bdc2909cb9327d77289da74f0?utm_source=Pew+Research+Center&utm_campaign=63a9d20178-EMAIL_CAMPAIGN_2021_02_18_02_14&utm_medium=email&utm_term=0_3e953b9b70-63a9d20178-399351245.

9. AP News, "Ukraine's Ousted President Testifies in Court," Associated Press, November 28, 2016. Viewed September 8, 2020, at https://apnews.com/article/9f3dab771d92490eb3f15cbd97a63dfd.

10. Press Release, "Human Rights Michelle Bachelet said that the situation with human rights in Belarus is getting worse," United Nations, Human Rights, Office of the Commissioner, 24 September 2021.

11. Associated Press, "Hundreds Arrested in Fresh Belarus Protests Against Lukashenko," *France 24*, December 12, 2020. https://www.france24.com/en/europe/20201206-hundreds-arrested-in-fresh-belarus-protests-against-lukashenko.

12. Herasimenka, Aliaksandr, "Belarus," case study within *Industrialized Disinformation: 2020 Global Inventory of Organized Social Media Manipulation* (separate citation below), January 13, 2021. https://comprop.oii.ox.ac.uk/wp-content/uploads/sites/127/2021/01/Cyber-Troop-Belarus-2020.pdf.

13. *Ibid.*

14. Tucker, Eric, "WATCH: FBI chief Chris Wray calls Jan. 6 'domestic terrorism,' defends intel," *PBS News Hour,* March 2 2021.

15. American Bar Association, Standing Committee on Election Law, "Current Litigation," March 4, 2021, viewed at https://www.americanbar.org/groups/public_interest/election_law/litigation/.

16. Abramson, Alana, and Abigail Abrams, "Here Are All the Lawsuits the Trump Campaign Has Filed Since Election Day—And Why Most Are Unlikely to Go Anywhere," *Time,* November 18, 2020. Viewed January 22, 2021, at https://time.com/5908505/trump-lawsuits-biden-wins/.

17. Rove, Karl, "Trump's Appeal Rings Hollow at CPAC," *Wall Street Journal,* March 3, 2021, https://www.wsj.com/articles/trumps-appeal-rings-hollow-at-cpac-11614812740.

18. Jenkins, Simon, "The World is Rocked by Protest—But Does Taking to the Streets Ever Work?" *The Guardian,* October 30, 2020. https://www.theguardian.com/commentisfree/2020/oct/30/demonstrations-protest-party-minsk-sao-paulo-protesters.

19. "Joint Statement from the ODNI, DOJ, FBI and DHS: Combating Foreign Influence in U.S. Elections," October 19, 2018, https://www.dni.gov/index.php/newsroom/press-releases/item/1915-joint-statement-from-the-odni-doj-fbi-and-dhs-combating-foreign-influence-in-u-s-elections.

20. Australian Associated Press, "China Is Seeking to 'Take Over' Australia's Political System, Former Asio Chief Claims," *The Guardian,* November 21, 2019. Viewed October 20, 2020, at https://www.theguardian.com/australia-news/2019/nov/22/china-is-seeking-to-take-over-australias-political-system-former-asio-chief-claims.

21. Li Xan Wong, Karen, and Amy Shields Dobson, "We're Just Data: Exploring China's Social Credit System in Relation to Digital Platform Ratings Cultures in Westernized Democracies," *Sage Journals,* June 18, 2019. Viewed January 15, 2021, at https://journals.sagepub.com/doi/full/10.1177/2059436419856090.

22. Leetaru, Kalev, "Social Media Companies Collect So Much Data Even They Can't Remember All the Ways They Surveil

Us," *Forbes,* October 25, 2018. Viewed January 22, 2021, at https://www.forbes.com/sites/kalevleetaru/2018/10/25/social-media-companies-collect-so-much-data-even-they-cant-remember-all-the-ways-they-surveil-us/?sh=77bd78ac7d0b.

23. Hamilton, Clive, and Marlene Ohlberg, *Hidden Hand: Exposing How the Chinese Communist Party is Reshaping the World* (London: Oneworld Books, 2020), 22–26.

24. McCauley, Kevin N., *Russian Influence Campaigns Against the West* (Charleston, SC: self-published 2016), 92–95.

25. U.S. Securities and Exchange Commission, "JP Morgan Chase Paying $264 Million to Settle FCPA Charges," press release 2016–241, November 17, 2016.

26. Brady, Anne-Marie, "Magic Weapons: China's Political Influence Activities Under Xi Jinping," conference paper for The Corrosion of Democracy Under China's Global Influence, Arlington, VA, September 16–17, 2017.

27. *Ibid.,* McCauley.

28. Andress, Jason, and Steve Winterfield, *Cyber Warfare: Techniques, Tactics and Tools for Security Practitioners* (New York: Elsevier, 2010), 4.

29. Benkler, Yochai, Rob Faris, Hal Roberts, and Nikki Bourassa, "Understanding Media and Information Quality in an Age of Artificial Intelligence, Automation, Algorithms and Machine Learning," Berkman Klein Center for Internet & Society, Harvard University, July 12, 2018.

30. Wallace, Chris, "Chris Wallace Interview with Russian President Vladimir Putin Earns Fox News First Ever Emmy Nomination," July 26, 2018, at https://www.foxnews.com/media/fox-news-nabs-first-emmy-nomination-for-chris-wallaces-interview-with-vladimir-putin.

31. Han, Bochen, "How Much Should We Read into China's New 'Core Socialist Values?'" Council on Foreign Relations, July 6, 2016. Viewed January 2020 at https://www.cfr.org/blog/how-much-should-we-read-chinas-new-core-socialist-values.

32. Partlett, William, "Can Russia Keep Faking Democracy?" The Brookings Institute, May 22, 2012. Viewed January 2020 at https://www.brookings.edu/opinions/can-russia-keep-faking-democracy/.

33. Diamond, Larry, and Orville Schell,

Chinese Influence and American Interests (Stanford, CA, The Hoover Institution Press, 2018), 5–6.

34. Bradshaw, Samantha, Philip Howard, and Hannah Bailey, "Industrialized Disinformation: 2020 Global Inventory of Organized Social Media Manipulation," University of Oxford, January 13, 2021, https://comprop.oii.ox.ac.uk/research/posts/industrialized-disinformation/#continue.

35. Director of National Intelligence, "Assessing Russian Activities and Intentions in Recent U.S. Election" (ICA 2017–01D), January 6, 2017, https://www.dni.gov/files/documents/ICA_2017_01.pdf; and "Joint Statement from the ODNI, DOJ, FBI and DHS: Combating Foreign Influence in U.S. Elections," October 19, 2018.

Chapter 1

1. Williams, Josette H., "The Information War in the Pacific, 1945," original not dated.

2. Hubert, Richard S.R., "The OWI Saipan Operation," The Official Report to the U.S. information Service, Washington 1946.

3. Smyth, Jamie, and Christian Shepherd, "Chinese App WeChat Censors Australian PM Scott Morrison's Post," *Financial Times*, December 3, 2020.

4. *Ibid.*

5. BBC News China, "Covid: What Do We Know about China's Coronavirus Vaccines?" January 14, 2021, viewed January 18, 2021, at https://www.bbc.com/news/world-asia-china-55212787.

6. Stubbs, Jack, "Hackers Steal Pfizer/BioNTech COVID-19 Vaccine Data in Europe, Companies Say," *Reuters*, December 9, 2020, viewed January 18, 2021, at https://www.reuters.com/article/us-ema-cyber/hackers-steal-pfizer-biontech-covid-19-vaccine-data-in-europe-companies-say-idUSKBN28J2Q7.

7. SANS NewsBites, "Stolen COVID Data Were Altered Before They Were Leaked," January 19, 2021, https://www.sans.org/newsletters/newsbites/xxiii-5/.

8. Gordon, Michael R., and Dustin Voltz, "Russian Disinformation Campaign Aims to Undermine Confidence in Pfizer, Other Covid-19 Vaccines, U.S. Officials Say," *Wall Street Journal*, March 7, 2021, https://www.wsj.com/articles/russian-disinformation-campaign-aims-to-undermine-confidence-in-pfizer-other-covid-19-vaccines-u-s-officials-say-11615129200?st=ir0lson-vyyrl7mp&reflink=article_email_share.

9. Goodin, Dan, "Hackers alter stolen regulatory data to sow mistrust in COVID-19 vaccine," *Ars Technica*, January 15 2021.

10. Devine, Michael, "Covert Action and Clandestine Activities of the Intelligence Community: Selected Definitions in Brief," Congressional Research Service, June 14, 2019. Viewed September 22, 2020, at https://fas.org/sgp/crs/intel/R45175.pdf, as quoted in Central Intelligence Agency, Glossary of Counterinsurgency Terms, May 19, 1962, at https://www.cia.gov/library/readingroom/docs/CIA-RDP80B01676R003000050019-6.pdf.

11. Brady, Anne-Marie, "Magic Weapons: China's political influence activities under Xi Jinping," Conference paper presented at the conference on "The Corrosion of Democracy under China's Global Influence," supported by the Taiwan Foundation for Democracy, and hosted in Arlington, Virginia, September 16-17, 2017.

12. Gupta, Anti, Brigadier, "Winning without Fighting: China's Video War Fails," *Indian Defence Review*, January 9, 2021, http://www.indiandefencereview.com/news/winning-without-fighting-chinas-video-war-fails/.

13. *Ibid.*

14. Gol, Jyar, "Iran Blasts: What Is Behind Mysterious Fires at Key Sites?" BBC News, July 6, 2020, viewed July 29, 2020, at https://www.bbc.com/news/world-middle-east-53305940.

15. Howard, Philip, "Social Media Manipulation by Political Actors an Industrial Scale Problem," University of Oxford report, January 13, 2021, https://www.ox.ac.uk/news/2021-01-13-social-media-manipulation-political-actors-industrial-scale-problem-oxford-report.

16. Myers, Steven, and Paul Mozur, "China Is Waging a Disinformation War Against Hong Kong Protesters," *New York Times*, August 13, 2019. Viewed December 4, 2020, at https://www.nytimes.com/2019/08/13/world/asia/hong-kong-protests-china.html.

17. Nimmo, Ben, and C. Shawn Eib, et

al., "Spamouflage Dragon Goes to America," Graphika, August 2020, https://public-assets.graphika.com/reports/graphika_report_spamouflage_dragon_goes_to_america.pdf.

18. Nimmo, Ben, C. Shawn Eib, and L. Tamora, "Cross-Platform Spam Network Targeted Hong Kong Protests," Graphika, September 2019. Viewed August 31, 2020, at https://public-assets.graphika.com/reports/graphika_report_spamouflage.pdf.

19. Al Jazeera News, "Saudi Accuses Iran of Potential 'Act of War,'" November 6, 2017.

20. *Ibid.*

21. Abaad Research Center, "The Terror of Iranian Weapons, Houthi Forces Threaten Gulf Security," July 19, 2019, p. 2, https://abaadstudies.org.

22. Shipler, David K., "Israeli Jets Destroy Iraqi Atomic Reactor; Attack Condemned by U.S. and Arab Nations," *New York Times*, June 9, 1981, https://www.nytimes.com/1981/06/09/world/israeli-jets-destroy-iraqi-atomic-reactor-attack-condemned-us-arab-nations.html.

23. Pirseyedi, Bobi, *Arms Control and Iranian Foreign Policy* (New York: Routledge, 2013), 120.

24. Farrell, Stephen, "Israel Admits Bombing Suspected Syrian Nuclear Reactor in 2007, Warns Iran," *Reuters*, March 20, 2018, https://www.reuters.com/article/us-israel-syria-nuclear/israel-admits-bombing-suspected-syrian-nuclear-reactor-in-2007-warns-iran-idUSKBN1GX09K.

25. Beck, Martin, "An International Relations Perspective on the Iran Nuclear Deal," August 8, 2018, viewed September 22, 2019, at https://www.e-ir.info/2018/08/08/an-international-relations-perspective-on-the-iran-nuclear-deal/.

26. Warrick, Joby, "Iran's Underground Nuclear Sites Not Immune to U.S. Bunker-Busters, Experts Say," *Washington Post*, February 29, 2012, https://www.washingtonpost.com/world/national-security/experts-irans-underground-nuclear-sites-not-immune-to-us-bunker-busters/2012/02/24/gIQAzWaghR_story.html?noredirect=on&utm_term=.aff40eb0df08.

27. Bergman, Ronen, "When Israel Hatched a Secret Plan to Assassinate Iranian Scientists," *Politico*, March 5, 2018, https://www.politico.com/magazine/story/2018/03/05/israel-assassination-iranian-scientists-217223.

28. Sanger, David E., *The Perfect Weapon* (New York: Crown Publishing Group, 2018), 7–12.

29. Karimi, Nasser, and Jon Gambrell, "Iran Says Israel Killed Military Nuclear Scientist Remotely," Associated Press, November 30, 2020, https://apnews.com/article/iran-israel-killed-mohsen-fakhrizadeh-88c2173048f77695af864d2055af54c6.

30. U.S. Department of Justice, Indictment in U.S. District of Columbia for the District February 16, 2018, p. 25. Viewed February 16, 2018, at https://www.justice.gov/file/1035477/download.

31. *Ibid.*, 5.

32. *Ibid.*, 1.

33. *Ibid.*, 6.

34. *Ibid.*, 26.

35. U.S. Department of Justice, Indictment in U.S. District of Columbia for the District February 16, 2018.

36. Schwirtz, Michael, "A Year After Skripal Poisoning, Russia Offers Defiant Face to Britain and the West," *New York Times*, March 4, 2019. Viewed August 24, 2019, at https://www.nytimes.com/2019/03/04/world/europe/russia-skripal-poisoning-britain.html.

37. Neufeld, Jennie, "Transcript: Trump and Putin's Joint Press Conference," National Public Radio, July 16, 2018. Viewed November 1, 2019, at https://www.npr.org/2018/07/16/629462401/transcript-president-trump-and-russian-president-putins-joint-press-conference.

38. Joint Statement from the Department of Homeland Security and Office of the Director of National Intelligence on Election Security, October 7, 2016. https://www.dhs.gov/news/2016/10/07/joint-statement-department-homeland-security-and-office-director-national.

39. U.S. Department of Justice, Indictment in U.S. District Court, Western District of Pennsylvania, unsealed October 15, 2020. https://www.justice.gov/opa/press-release/file/1328521/download.

Chapter 2

1. Director of National Intelligence, National Counterintelligence and Security

Center (NCSC), "National Counterintelligence Strategy of the United States of America 2020–2022," February 2020.

2. Cimpanu, Catalin, "Czech Republic Blames Russia for Multiple Government Network Hacks," *ZDNet*, December 3, 2018. Viewed September 2, 2019, at https://www.zdnet.com/article/czech-republic-blames-russia-for-multiple-government-network-hacks/.

3. Associated Press, "Czechs Blame Foreign State for Foreign Ministry Cyberattack," *Security Week*, August 14, 2019, viewed September 2020 at https://www.securityweek.com/czechs-blame-foreign-state-foreign-ministry-cyberattack.

4. Bowman, M.E., "Secrets in Plain View: Covert Action the U.S. Way," *International Law Studies*, vol. 72.

5. Dorn, Walter, "Plausible Deniability or How Leaders May Try to Conceal Their Roles," International Criminal Court/Office of the Prosecutor ICC/OTP, May 18, 2010.

6. Wallace, Chris, "Chris Wallace Interviews Russian President Vladimir Putin," Fox News, July 16, 2018, https://video.foxnews.com/v/5810009147001#sp=showclips.

7. Bradshaw, Samantha, and Philip N. Howard, "The Global Disinformation Disorder: 2019 Global Inventory of Organised Social Media Manipulation," Working Paper 2019.2., Oxford, UK, Project on Computational Propaganda, viewed January 15, 2021, https://comprop.oii.ox.ac.uk/wp-content/uploads/sites/93/2020/10/CyberTroop-Report19_V2NOV.pdf.

8. Vilmer, Jean-Baptiste Jeangène, "Successfully Countering Russian Electoral Interference," Center for Strategic and International Studies, June 21, 2018, https://www.csis.org/analysis/successfully-countering-russian-electoral-interference.

9. Conley, Heather, "Successfully Countering Russian Electoral Interference," Center for Strategic and International Studies, June 21, 2018, https://www.csis.org/analysis/successfully-countering-russian-electoral-interference.

10. Vilmer, "Successfully Countering…"

11. Rogers, Michael S., Admiral, "Statement Before the Senate Committee on Armed Services," May 9, 2017.

12. Greenburg, Andy, "The NSA Confirms It: Russia Hacked French Election 'Infrastructure,'" *Wired*, May 9, 2017.

Viewed November 8, 2018, at https://www.wired.com/2017/05/nsa-director-confirms-russia-hacked-french-election-infrastructure/.

13. Vilmer, Jean-Baptiste Jeangene, "The 'Macron Leaks' Operation: A Post-Mortem," *The Atlantic Council*, June 2019. Viewed November 6, 2020, at https://www.atlanticcouncil.org/wp-content/uploads/2019/06/The_Macron_Leaks_Operation-A_Post-Mortem.pdf.

14. McCauley, Kevin N., *Russian Influence Campaigns Against the West* (North Carolina: self-published, 2016), 87–88.

15. *Ibid.*, 367–368.

16. Statement by NCSC Director William Evanina: Election Threat Update for the American Public, July 20, 2020. Viewed July 14, 2020, https://www.dni.gov/index.php/ncsc-newsroom/item/2140-statement-by-ncsc-director-william-evanina-election-threat-update-for-the-american-public.

17. *Ibid.*

18. Press Release, Office of the Director National Intelligence, "DNI John Ratcliffe's Remarks at Press Conference on Election Security," 22 October 2020.

19. Singman, Brooke, "Barr: DOJ Yet to Find Widespread Voter Fraud that Could Have Changed 2020 Election," Fox News, December 2, 2020. https://www.foxnews.com/politics/william-barr-doj-fbi-voter-fraud-2020-election.

20. *United States of America vs Viktor Borisovich Netyksho, Boris Alekseyevich Antonov, Dmitriy Sergeyevich Badin, et al.,* Case 1:18-cr-00215-ABJ, Document 1, filed July 13, 2018, 26.

21. Hui, Mary, *China Has Completed Its Takeover of Hong Kong's Legislature, Quartz,* November 11, 2020. Viewed December 24, 2020, at https://qz.com/1931705/china-exerts-its-control-over-hong-kongs-legislative-council/; and Palmer, James, "Hong Kong's Violence Will Get Worse," *Foreign Policy*, November 11, 2019. Viewed September 7, 2020, at https://foreignpolicy.com/2019/11/11/police-killing-protests-beijing-lam-xi-hong-kong-violence-will-get-worse/.

22. Sherlock, Dr. Stephen, "Hong Kong and the Transfer to China: Issues and Prospects," Government of Australia Current Issues Brief 33 1996–97, 6–7.

23. Crowley, Michael, and Julia Ioffe,

"Why Putin hates Hillary," *Politico*, July 25, 2016, https://www.politico.com/story/2016/07/clinton-putin-226153.

24. Clayton, Mark, "Ukraine Election Narrowly Avoided 'Wanton Destruction' from Hackers," *Christian Science Monitor*, June 17, 2014; Committee to Protect Journalists, "Ukrainian Journalists Held by Pro-Russian Separatists" (contains several stories); Boyle, Jon, "Ukraine Hit by Cyberattacks: Head of Ukraine Security Service," *Reuters*, March 14, 2014; AFT/PTI News Service, "Ukraine Hit With Partial Power Outages," *Business Standard*, March 25, 2014; Erlanger, Steven, "Russia Ratchets Up Ukraine's Gas Bills in shift to an Economic Battlefield," *New York Times*, May 11 2014; Marcus, Lauri Lowenthal, "Jews Must Register Flyer in Ukraine and Echo of Babi Yar," *Jewish Press*, April 18, 2014.

25. U.S. Army Special Operations Command, "Little Green Men: A Primer on Modern Russian Unconventional Warfare, Ukraine 2013–2014."

26. Kofman, Michael, Katya Migacheva, Brian Nichiporuk, Andrew Radin, Olesya Tkacheva, and Jenny Oberholtzer, *Lessons from Russia's Operations in Crimea and Eastern Ukraine* (Santa Monica, CA: RAND Corporation, 2017), 90.

27. Murphy, Simon, "UK Report on Russian Interference: Key Points Explained," *The Guardian*, July 21, 2020. Viewed September 29, 2020, at https://www.theguardian.com/world/2020/jul/21/just-what-does-the-uk-russia-report-say-key-points-explained.

28. Sabbagh, Dan, and Luke Harding, "PM Accused of Cover-Up over Report on Russian Meddling in UK Politics," https://www.theguardian.com/politics/2019/nov/04/no-10-blocks-russia-eu-referendum-report-until-after-election.

29. *Ibid.*, Vilmer, Jean-Baptiste Jeangène.

30. Ewing, Philip, "The 2020 Election Was Attacked, But Not Severely Disrupted. Here's How," NPR, November 4, 2020, viewed November 6, 2020, at https://www.npr.org/2020/11/04/931090626/the-2020-election-was-attacked-but-not-severely-disrupted-heres-how.

31. Doshi, Rush, and Robert D. Williams, Is China Interfering in American Politics?" The Brookings Institution, 2 October 2, 2018, viewed July 2020 at https://www.brookings.edu/blog/order-from-chaos/2018/10/02/is-china-interfering-in-american-politics/.

32. Barr, William P., Transcript of Attorney General Barr's Remarks on China Policy at the Gerald R. Ford Presidential Museum, July 17, 2020, https://www.justice.gov/opa/speech/transcript-attorney-general-barr-s-remarks-china-policy-gerald-r-ford-presidential-museum.

33. Brady, Anne-Marie, "Magic Weapons: China's Political Influence Activities Under Xi Jinping," conference paper for *The Corrosion of Democracy Under China's Global Influence*, Arlington, VA, September 16–17, 2017.

34. *Ibid.*, McCauley, 8.

35. *Ibid.*, 88–93.

36. *Ibid.*, 136.

37. U.S. Department of Justice, U.S. District Court for the District of Columbia, *United States of America v. Victor Borisovich Netyksho, et al.*, July 13, 2018, 8–12, https://www.justice.gov/file/1080281/download.

38. Select Committee on Intelligence, U.S. Senate, "Russian Active Measure Campaigns and Interference in the 2016 U.S. Election, vol. 3: U.S. Government Response to Russian Activities," viewed November 2020 at https://www.intelligence.senate.gov/sites/default/files/documents/Report_Volume1.pdf.

39. *Ibid.*

40. *Ibid.*

41. U.S. Department of Justice, District Court for the Eastern District of Virginia, "Affidavit in Support of a Criminal Complaint and Arrest Warrant for Artem Mikhayovich Lifshits," Case No. 1:20-mj-256.

42. Wallace, Chris, Fox News, https://www.youtube.com/watch?v=R2CJ0PNLNKw.

43. Nakashima, Ellen, et al., "U.S. Government Concludes Iran Was Behind Threatening Emails Sent to Democrats," viewed October 29, 2020, at https://www.washingtonpost.com/technology/2020/10/20/proud-boys-emails-florida/.

Chapter 3

1. Robinson, Linda, Todd C. Helmus, Raphael S. Cohen, Alireza Nader, Andrew Radin, Madeline Magnuson, and Katya Migacheva, *The Growing Need to Focus on*

Modern Political Warfare (Santa Monica, CA: RAND Corporation, 2019), https://www.rand.org/pubs/research_briefs/RB10071.html.

2. Congressional Research Service, "Artificial Intelligence and National Security, November 21, 2019.

3. Urban, Mark, *The Skripal Files* (New York: Henry Holt and Co. 2018), 22–23.

4. *United States of America vs Viktor Borisovich Netyksho, Boris Alekseyevich Antonov, Dmitriy Sergeyevich Badin, et al.,* Case 1:18-cr-00215-ABJ, Document 1, filed July 13, 2018, 4.

5. *Ibid.*, 2, 5.

6. Theohary, Catherine A., "Information Warfare: Issues for Congress," Congressional Research Service, report number R45142, March 5, 2018, https://fas.org/sgp/crs/natsec/R45142.pdf.

7. Cheng, Dean, "Winning Without Fighting: Chinese Public Opinion Warfare and the Need for a Robust American Response," The Heritage Foundation, November 26, 2012, viewed January 20, 2013, at https://www.heritage.org/asia/report/winning-without-fighting-chinese-public-opinion-warfare-and-the-need-robust-american.

8. Rosenberg, Matthew, Nicole Perlroth, David E. Sanger, "'Chaos Is the Point': Russian Hackers and Trolls Grow Stealthier in 2020," *New York Times*, September 10, 2020. https://www.nytimes.com/2020/01/10/us/politics/russia-hacking-disinformation-election.html.

9. *Ibid.*

10. *Ibid.*

11. Federal Indictment, Internet Research Agency, U.S. District Court for the District of Columbia, February 2, 2018, https://www.justice.gov/file/1035477/.

12. Associated Press, "Twitter Deletes Accounts Linked to Foreign Governments," June 13, 2019, https://www.apnews.com/5581109be59b40d2ad18871d286e0898?utm_source=Pew+Research+Center&utm_campaign=ed0a7936c4-EMAIL_CAMPAIGN_2019_06_14_01_41&utm_medium=email&utm_term=0_3e953b9b70-ed0a7936c4-399351245.

13. Bradshaw, Samantha, Hannah Bailey, and Philip N. Howard, "Industrialized Disinformation: 2020 Global Inventory of Organized Social Media Manipulation," Oxford Internet Institute, University of Oxford. Viewed January 13, 2021, https://demtech.oii.ox.ac.uk/research/posts/industrialized-disinformation/.

14. *Ibid.*, 2.

15. Crowley, Michael, and Julia Ioffe, "Why Putin Hates Hillary," *Politico*, July 25, 2016. Viewed February 8, 2020, at https://www.politico.com/story/2016/07/clinton-putin-226153.

16. Tynan, Dan, "How Facebook Powers Money Machines for Obscure Political 'News' Sites," *The Guardian*, August 14, 2016. Viewed March 5, 2019, https://www.theguardian.com/technology/2016/aug/24/facebook-clickbait-political-news-sites-us-election-trump.

17. Director of National Intelligence, "Assessing Russian Activities and Intentions in Recent U.S. Elections," January 6, 2017.

18. Landay, Jonathan, and Mark Hosenball, "Russia, China, Iran Sought to Influence U.S. 2018 Elections: U.S. Spy Chief," *Reuters*, December 21, 2018, https://www.reuters.com/article/us-usa-election-interference/russia-china-iran-sought-to-influence-u-s-2018-elections-u-s-spy-chief-idUSKCN1OK2FS.

19. Eller, Donnelle, "Citing Ad in Des Moines Register, Trump Accuses China of Meddling in U.S. Elections," *Des Moines Register*, September 26, 2018, viewed January 21, 2021, at https://www.desmoinesregister.com/story/news/politics/2018/09/26/donald-trump-des-moines-register-ad-attack-china-meddling-united-nations-president-election/1434194002/.

20. Brown University, "Understanding the Iran-Contra Affairs," various dates and data files at https://www.brown.edu/Research/Understanding_the_Iran_Contra_Affair/n-contrasus.php.

21. Boffey, Daniel, and Martin Chulov, "Death of an Electrician: How Luck Run Out for Dissident Who Fled Iran In 1981," *The Guardian*, January 14, 2019, https://www.theguardian.com/world/2019/jan/14/a-dutch-electricians-raises-issues-of-trust-in-iran.

22. Unattributed article, "Iran Hit with Sanctions After Being Blamed for Killing Dissidents," *Aljazeera News*, January 8, 2019,

23. Finn, Peter, "Notorious Iranian Militant Has a Connection to Alleged Assassination Plot Against Saudi Envoy," *Washington Post*, October 14, 2011, https://

www.washingtonpost.com/world/national-security/notorious-iranian-militant-has-a-connection-to-alleged-assassination-plot-against-saudi-envoy/2011/10/14/gIQAJ3E6kL_story.html?utm_term=.2a472 4e3d203.

24. Trump, Donald, "Executive Order on Securing the Information and Communications Technology and Services Supply Chain," May 15, 2019.

25. Hayden, Michael, "Interview Regarding Edward Snowden, Cyber Security, and Transparency." *Australian Financial Review*, July 2013.

26. Sanger, David E., and Perlroth, Nicole, "N.S.A Breached Chinese Servers Seen as Security Threat," *New York Times*, March 22, 2014, https://www.nytimes.com/2014/03/23/world/asia/nsa-breached-chinese-servers-seen-as-spy-peril.html.

Chapter 4

1. Rosner, Max, and Esteban Ortiz-Ospina, "Literacy," OurWorldInData.org, January 2020, https://ourworldindata.org/literacy.

2. Gilens, Martin, and Benjamin I. Page, "Testing Theories of American Politics: Elites, Interest Groups, and Average Citizens," American Political Science Association, 2014; see also Gilens, Bartels 2008, https://www.cambridge.org/core/journals/perspectives-on-politics/article/testing-theories-of-american-politics-elites-interest-groups-and-average-citizens/62327F513959D0A304 D4893B382B992B#ref3, and Gilens 2012, https://www.cambridge.org/core/journals/perspectives-on-politics/article/testing-theories-of-american-politics-elites-interest-groups-and-average-citizens/62 327F513959D0A304D4893B382B992B# ref26, and Jacobs and Page 2005, https://www.cambridge.org/core/journals/perspectives-on-politics/article/testing-theories-of-american-politics-elites-interest-groups-and-average-citizens/62 327F513959D0A304D4893B382B992B# ref32, which indicates that the general public may have little or no influence on U.S. foreign policy, when the preferences of business leaders and other elites are taken into account.

3. Gilens and Page.

4. Feldman, Stanley, "Structure and Consistency in Public Opinion" *American Journal of Political Science*, Vol. 32, No. 2 (May, 1988), pp. 416-440.

5. Converse, Philip E., "The Nature of Belief Systems in Mass Publics," *Critical Review*, vol. 18, No. 1–3, 2006, originally published in David E. Apter, ed., *Ideology and Its Discontents* (New York: The Free Press of Glencoe). Republished by permission of the author and the editor.

6. *Ibid.*

7. Schank, Roger C., *Tell Me a Story* (New York: Charles Scribner's Sons, 1990), 30–31.

8. Diamond, Larry, and Orville Schell (eds.), *China's Influence and American Interests: Promoting Constructive Vigilance* (Stanford, CA: Hoover Institution Press, 2018), 7.

9. Schank, *Tell Me a Story*, 30-31.

10. Hamilton, Clive, and Marlene Ohlberg, *Hidden Hand: Exposing How the Chinese Communist Party is Reshaping the World* (London: Oneworld Books, 2020), 22.

11. Schank, *Tell Me a Story*, 30-31.

12. *Ibid.*

13. *Ibid.*

14. "Russian Spy Poisoning: What We Know So Far" BBC News, October 8, 2018. Viewed December 7, 2018, at https://www.bbc.com/news/uk-43315636.

15. Myers, Steven Lee, "China Spins Tale That the U.S. Army Started the Coronavirus Epidemic," *New York Times*, March 13, 2020. Viewed July 15, 2020, https://www.nytimes.com/2020/03/13/world/asia/coronavirus-china-conspiracy-theory.html.

16. Festinger, Leon, and James M. Carlsmith, "Cognitive Consequences of Forced Compliance," *Journal of Abnormal and Social Psychology*, no. 58, 203–210.

17. Schachter, Stanley, *Biographical Memoirs*, vol. 64, The National Academies of Sciences, Engineering, and Medicine, (Washington, D.C.: National Academy Press, 1994).

18. Petty, Richard E., and John T. Cacioppo, "The Elaboration Likelihood Model of Persuasion." *Advances in Experimental Social Psychology*, vol. 19, Academic Press. Inc., 1986.

19. Lapin, Denis, Olga Pavlova, Bianca Britton, and Sarah Dean, "Film Director

Oleg Sentsov and Mh17 Suspect Among Those Freed In Russia-Ukraine Prisoner Swap," CNN, September 7, 2019, https://www.cnn.com/2019/09/07/europe/ukraine-russia-prisoner-swap-intl/index.html.

20. Postman, Neil, and Charles Weingartner, *Teaching as a Subversive Activity* (New York: Dell Publishing,1969), 3.

21. U.S. Senate, "China's Impact on the U.S. Education System," Permanent Subcommittee on Investigations, February 22, 2019, https://www.hsgac.senate.gov/imo/media/doc/PSI%20Report%20China's%20Impact%20on%20the%20US%20Education%20System.pdf.

22. Reike, Richard D., and Malcom O. Sillars, "Argumentation and the Decision-Making Process" (New York: John Wiley & Son, 1975), 139.

23. Kumkale, Tarcan, Dolores Albarracin, and Paul J. Seignoourel, "The Effects of Source Credibility in the Presence or Absence of Prior Attitudes: Implications for the Design of Persuasive Communication Campaigns," *Journal of Applied Social Psychology*, June 1, 2010.

24. Gold, Ashley, and Sara Fischer, Facebook Takes Down Chinese Campaign Aimed at U.S. Election," *Axios*, September 22, 2020.

25. Grind, Kirsten, Sam Schechner, Robert McMillian, and John West, "How Google Interferes with Its Search Algorithms and Changes Your Results," *Wall Street Journal*, November 15, 2019. Viewed January 18, 2020, at https://www.wsj.com/articles/how-google-interferes-with-its-search-algorithms-and-changes-your-results-11573823753.

26. Milton, Joyce, "The Yellow Kids: Foreign Correspondents in the Heyday of Yellow Journalism" (New York: Harper Perennial, 1990), 67.

27. Library of Congress, "Remember the Maine!" https://www.loc.gov/item/today-in-history/february-15/.

28. Office of the Historian, U.S. Department of State, "U.S. Diplomacy and Yellow Journalism, 1895–1898." https://history.state.gov/milestones/1866-1898/yellow-journalism.

29. Fisher, Louis, "Destruction of the *Maine* (1898)," Law Library of Congress, August 2009, http://www.loufisher.org/docs/wi/434.pdf .

30. Phillips, Macon, White House Press Release, "TooManyWebsites.gov," June 13, 2011, https://obamawhitehouse.archives.gov/blog/2011/06/13/toomanywebsitesgov.

31. Breslow, Jason, "M. Colin Powell: U.N. Speech 'Was a Great Intelligence Failure,'" *Frontline* PBS, May 17, 2016, https://www.pbs.org/wgbh/frontline/article/colin-powell-u-n-speech-was-a-great-intelligence-failure/.

32. Commission on the Intelligence Capabilities of the United States Regarding Weapons of Mass Destruction, Congressional Commission on the Intelligence Capabilities of the United States Regarding Weapons of Mass Destruction," March 2005, p. 3.

33. Rosentiel, Tom, "Trends in Public Opinion about the War in Iraq, 2003–2007," Pew Research Center, March 2007.

34. Friedman, Norman, "The Vincennes Incident," *Proceedings of the Naval Institute*, May 1989.

35. Video posted by ODN News, supplied by Interior Ministry, Ukraine, https://www.youtube.com/watch?v=PsbC8yDeGUw (Comments from individual reviewers follow the story).

36. Pollock, John, "Russian Disinformation Technology," *MIT Technology Review*, April 13, 2017. Viewed October 8, 2019, https://www.technologyreview.com/s/604084/russian-disinformation-technology/.

37. Reuters News, "Families: Investigation Found MH17 Downed from Pro-Russia Rebel Held Territory," republished by CNBC News, September 28, 2016, https://www.cnbc.com/2016/09/28/families-investigation-found-mh17-downed-from-pro-russia-rebel-held-territory.html.

38. Weaver, Mathew, "MH17 Crash Report: Dutch Investigators Confirm Buk Missile Hit Plane," *The Guardian*, October 13, 2015, https://www.theguardian.com/world/live/2015/oct/13/mh17-crash-report-ukraine-live-updates.

39. Andersen, Kenneth, and Theodore Clevenger, Jr., "A Summary of Experimental Research in Ethos," Speech Monographs, June 30, 1963, 59–78; Andersen, Kenneth, *Persuasion: Theory and Practice* (Boston: Allyn & Bacon, 1971), 217–263; Bowers, John W., and William A. Phillips, "A Note on the Generality of Source Credibility

Scales," *Speech Monographs*, 34 (June 1967), 185–186; Giffin, Kim, "The Contributions of Studies of Source Credibility to a Theory of Interpersonal Trust in the Communications Process," *Psychological Bulletin*, 68 (August 1967), 104–120; McCroskey, James C., *An Introduction to Rhetorical Communication*, 2nd ed. (Englewood Cliffs, NJ: Prentice-Hall, 1972,) 63–8; Markham, David, "The Dimensions of Source Credibility in Television," *Newscasters Journal of Communication*, 18 (1968), 57–64; Hovland, Carl I., Irving Janis, and Harold H. Kelly, *Communication and Persuasion* (New Haven, CT: Yale University Press, 1953); as shown in Richard D. Rieke, and Malcolm O. Sillars, *Argumentation and the Decision Making Process* (New York: John Wiley & Sons, 1975), 144–155.

40. Caralle, Katelyn, "Google, China Create Search Engine that Tracks, Censors Searches and Links Them to Users' Phone Numbers," *Washington Examiner*, November 20, 2019, https://www.washingtonexaminer.com/news/google-china-create-search-engine-that-tracks-censors-searches-and-links-them-to-users-phone-numbers.

41. Doffman, Zak, "New Google Warning: 280M+ Android Users at Risk as China 'Manipulates' Play Store," *Forbes*, October 2, 2019, https://www.forbes.com/sites/zakdoffman/2019/10/02/new-google-play-warning-280m-users-at-risk-as-china-manipulates-top-vpns/.

42. Tung, Liam, "Google Boots China's Main Digital Certificate Authority CNNIC," *ZDNet*, April 2, 2015. Viewed August 15 at https://www.zdnet.com/article/google-banishes-chinas-main-digital-certificate-authority-cnnic/.

43. "China Internet Regulator Slams Google's Certificate Refusal," *Reuters*, April 2, 2015, viewed May 2016 at https://www.theguardian.com/technology/2015/apr/02/china-internet-regulator-slams-googles-certificate-refusal.

44. Marczak, Bill, et al., "China's Great Cannon," *The Citizen Lab*, University of Toronto, April 10, 2015. Viewed June 14, 2015, https://citizenlab.ca/2015/04/chinas-great-cannon/.

45. Westcott, Ben, "Huge Leaks Are Exposing Xinjiang's Re-Education Camps. But Don't Expect Beijing to Back Down," December 2, 2019. Viewed September 17, 2020, at https://www.cnn.com/2019/11/26/asia/china-xinjiang-leaks-analysis-intl-hnk/index.html.

46. Wee, Sui-Lee, "Giving In to China, U.S. Airlines Drop Taiwan (in Name at Least)," *New York Times*, July 25, 2018. Viewed October 16, 2019, https://www.nytimes.com/2018/07/25/business/taiwan-american-airlines-china.html.

47. Horton, Chris, "Taiwan's Status Is a Geopolitical Absurdity," *The Atlantic*, July 8, 2019, https://www.theatlantic.com/international/archive/2019/07/taiwans-status-geopolitical-absurdity/593371/.

48. Wee, Sui-lee, "Giving In to China, U.S. Airlines Drop Taiwan (in Name at Least)," *New York Times*, July 25, 2018. Viewed August 17, 2020, at https://www.nytimes.com/2018/07/25/business/taiwan-american-airlines-china.html.

49. Bessinger, Greg, "Google Maps Vary Depending on Who's Looking at Them," *Washington Post*, March 1, 2020, https://www.washingtonpost.com/technology/2020/02/14/google-maps-political-borders/.

50. Hille, Kathrin, and Victor Mallet, "China Accuses France of Illegally Sailing Warship in Taiwan Strait," *Financial Times*, April 25, 2019. Viewed September 25, 2020, at https://www.ft.com/content/12f4ff22-674d-11e9-9adc-98bf1d35a056. [Link not active]

51. East Asia Pacific, Voice of America, "U.S. Destroyer Sails Through Taiwan Strait, Provoking China," October 30, 2017. Viewed November 4, 2020, at https://www.voanews.com/east-asia-pacific/us-destroyer-sails-through-taiwan-strait-provoking-china.

52. Ruan, Lotus, Jeffrey Knockel, and Masashi Crete-Nishihata, "Censored Contagion," March 3, 2020. Viewed October 8, 2020, at https://citizenlab.ca/2020/03/censored-contagion-how-information-on-the-coronavirus-is-managed-on-chinese-social-media/.

53. *Ibid.*.

54. PEN America, "Made in Hollywood, Censored by Beijing," 2020. Viewed November 20, 2020, at https://pen.org/report/made-in-hollywood-censored-by-beijing/.

55. *Ibid.*, 6.

56. Ferris-Rotman, Amie, "Britain Regrets Russia's Lugovoy Elected to

Duma," *Reuters*, December 7, 2007, https://www.reuters.com/article/uk-russia-britain-lugovoy/britain-regrets-russias-lugovoy-elected-to-duma-idUKL0749585820071207.

57. Schwirtz, Michael, and Ellen Barry, "A Spy Story: Sergei Skripal Was a Little Fish. He Had a Big Enemy," *New York Times*, September 9, 2018., https://www.nytimes.com/2018/09/09/world/europe/sergei-skripal-russian-spy-poisoning.html.

58. BBC News, "Russian Spy Poisoning: What We Know So Far," October 8, 2018. Viewed July 2019, https://www.bbc.com/news/uk-43315636.

59. Urban, Mark, *The Skripal Files* (New York: Henry Holt & Co., 2018), 234–243.

60. Wallace, Chris, "Chris Wallace Interviews Russian President Vladimir Putin," Fox News, July 16, 2016. Viewed August 2, 2019, at https://video.foxnews.com/v/5810009147001/#sp=show-clips.

Chapter 5

1. Lozano, Alicia Victoria, "Secretary of State Pompeo Says Hack Was 'Pretty Clearly' Russian," NBC News, December 19, 2020. https://www.nbcnews.com/news/us-news/secretary-state-pompeo-says-hack-was-pretty-clearly-russian-n1251798.

2. Reichert, Corinne, and Laura Hautala. "Russia Blamed for Solarwinds Hack in Joint FBI, NSA and CISA Statement," CNET, January 5, 2021. https://www.cnet.com/tech/services-and-software/fbi-nsa-and-cisa-say-solarwinds-hack-was-likely-of-russian-origin/.

3. Deutch, John M., "Foreign Information Warfare Programs and Capabilities," June 25, 1996. Viewed February 7, 2020, at https://www.cia.gov/news-information/speeches-testimony/1996/dci_testimony_062596.html.

4. Bradshaw and Howard, op cit.

5. Walker, Christopher, and Jessica Ludwig, "The Meaning of Sharp Power," *Foreign Affairs*, November 16, 2017.

6. Barnes, Julian E., and Matthew Rosenberg, "Charges of Ukrainian Meddling? A Russian Operation, U.S. Intelligence Says," *New York Times*, November 26, 2019. Viewed December 26, 2019. https://www.nytimes.com/2019/11/22/us/politics/ukraine-russia-interference.html.

7. "China's Online Population Climbs to 772 Million," *The Economic Times*, Jan. 31, 2018 https://economictimes.indiatimes.com/news/international/world-news/chinas-online-population-climbs-to-772-million/articleshow/62726168.cms.

8. Mitchell, Amy, "Americans Still Prefer Watching to Reading the News—and Mostly Still Through Television," Pew Research, December 3, 2018. http://www.journalism.org/2018/12/03/americans-still-prefer-watching-to-reading-the-news-and-mostly-still-through-television/.

9. Shearer, Elisa, "Lessons Learned from More than 20 Years of Asking About Americans' Online News Habits," Pew Research Center, July 1, 2019. https://medium.com/pew-research-center-decoded/lessons-learned-from-more-than-20-years-of-asking-about-americans-online-news-habits-ba4b0dee578a.

10. Shearer, Elisa, and Jeffrey Gottfried, "News Use Across Social Media Platforms 2016," Pew Research, May 26, 2016. Viewed March 5, 2019, at https://www.journalism.org/2016/05/26/news-use-across-social-media-platforms-2016/.

11. *Ibid.*, Mitchell.

12. Li, Rouhan, and Ayoung Suh, "Factors Influencing Information Credibility on Social Media Platforms: Evidence from Facebook Pages, Information Systems International Conference (ISICO20)." Viewed September 10, 2020, at https://scholars.cityu.edu.hk/files/28155280/Factors_Influencing_Information_credibility_on_Social_Media_Platforms_Evidence_from_Facebook_Pages.pdf.

13. *Ibid.*

14. Benkler et al.

15. Adee, Sally, "What Are Deepfakes and How Are They Created?" IEEE Spectrum, April 29, 2020. https://spectrum.ieee.org/tech-talk/computing/software/what-are-deepfakes-how-are-they-created.

16. Winning, David, "Chinese 'Wolf Warrior' Diplomat Enrages Australia with Twitter Post," *Wall Street Journal*, November 30, 2020. https://www.wsj.com/articles/chinese-wolf-warrior-diplomat-enrages-australia-with-twitter-post-11606731906?st=zhin3x4dumqel03&reflink=article_email_share.

17. Varol, Onur, Emilio Ferrara, Clayton A. Davis, Filippo Menczer, and Alessandro Flammini, "Online Human-Bot

Interactions: Detection, Estimation, and Characterization," Proceedings of 11th Annual International AAAI Conference on Web and Social Media, 2017. Viewed December 24, 2020, at https://aaai.org/ocs/index.php/ICWSM/ICWSM17/paper/view/15587/14817.

18. U.S. Security and Exchange Commission website. Viewed December 31, 2020, at https://secsearch.sec.gov/search?utf8=%3F&affiliate=secsearch&query=bots+.

19. Varol, et al.

20. Noble, Safiya Umoja, *Algorithms of Oppression* (New York: NYU Press, 2018).

21. Herber, Patric, "140+ Search Engines and Directories," *Mashable*, October 22, 2007. Viewed August 21, 2020, at https://mashable.com/2007/10/22/140-search-engines/#:~:text=Search%2C%20the%20holy%20grail%20that,is%20still%20coveted.

22. Grind, Kirsten, Sam Schechner, Robert McMillian, and John West, "How Google Interferes with Its Search Algorithms and Changes Your Results," *Wall Street Journal*, November 15, 2019. Viewed January 18, 2020, at https://www.wsj.com/articles/how-google-interferes-with-its-search-algorithms-and-changes-your-results-11573823753

23. *Ibid.*

24. Goldman, Eric, "Search Engine Bias and the Demise of Search Engine Utopianism," *Yale Journal of Law and Technology*, vol. 8, issue 1, 2006.

25. Shelton, Kelly, "The Value of Search Results Rankings," *Forbes*, October 2017. Viewed September 20, 2020, at https://www.forbes.com/sites/forbesagencycouncil/2017/10/30/the-value-of-search-results-rankings/?sh=61818d4d44d3.

26. Ahmari, Sohrab, "Meet your (Chinese) Facebook Censors," *New York Post*, October 20, 2020. Viewed November 7, 2020, at https://nypost.com/2020/10/20/meet-your-chinese-facebook-censors/.

27. Rothschild, Neal ,and Sara Fisher, "NY Post Story Goes Massive on Social Media Despite Crackdowns," *Axios*, October 20, 2020. https://www.axios.com/new-york-post-hunter-biden-facebook-twitter-censor-bf8d9f32-f8cb-444e-bc12-c3b5e8694e84.html.

28. Rachman, Gideon, "Chinese Censorship Is Spreading Beyond Its Borders,"

Financial Times, October 14, 2019. https://www.ft.com/content/cda1efbc-ee5a-11e9-ad1e-4367d8281195.

29. Gregg, A.P., B. Seibt, and "M.R. Banaji, Easier Done Than Undone: Asymmetry in the Malleability of Implicit Preferences," *Journal of Personality and Social Psychology* (2006), 1–20.

30. Ukrainian Election Task Force, "Ukrainian Election Task Force Foreign Interference in Ukraine's Democracy," The Atlantic Council, 2019. Viewed January 4, 2020, at https://www.atlanticcouncil.org/wp-content/uploads/2019/05/Foreign_Interference_in_Ukraines_Election.pdf.

31. Popken, Ben, "Russian Trolls Duped Global Media and Nearly 40 Celebrities," NBC News, November 3, 2017. Viewed November 30, 2020, at https://www.nbcnews.com/tech/social-media/trump-other-politicians-celebs-shared-boosted-russian-troll-tweets-n817036.

32. Paul, Christopher and Miriam Matthews, "The Russian 'Firehose of Falsehood' Propaganda Model," The RAND Corporation, https://www.rand.org/pubs/perspectives/PE198.html.

33. Shirvanian, Maliheh, Nitesh Saxena, and Dibya Mukhopadhyay. "Short Voice Imitation Man-in-the-Middle Attacks on Crypto Phones: Defeating Humans and Machines." *IOS Press*, January 1, 2018, 311–333. https://content.iospress.com/articles/journal-of-computer-security/jcs17970.

34. Burt, Tom, "New Cyberattacks Targeting U.S. Elections," Microsoft, September 10, 2020. Viewed January 13, 2021, at https://blogs.microsoft.com/on-the-issues/2020/09/10/cyberattacks-us-elections-trump-biden/.

35. U.S. Election Assistance Commission website. Viewed December 4, 2020, at https://www.eac.gov/.

36. CISA Alert (AA20–283A), "APT Actors Chaining Vulnerabilities Against SLTT, Critical Infrastructure, and Elections Organizations." Viewed December 4, 2020, at https://us-cert.cisa.gov/ncas/alerts/aa20-283a.

37. U.S. District Court, Western District of Pennsylvania, *United States of America vs. Yuriy Sergeyevich Andrienko, et al.*, indictment, October 15, 2020. https://www.justice.gov/opa/press-release/file/1328521/download.

38. Voltz, Dustin, Aruna Viswanatha, and Kate O'Keeffe, "U.S. Charges Chinese Nationals in Cyberattacks on More Than 100 Companies," *Wall Street Journal*, September 16, 2020. https://www.wsj.com/articles/justice-department-unseals-indictments-alleging-chinese-hacking-against-u-s-international-firms-11600269024.

39. *Ibid.*

40. McWhorter, Dan, "Mandiant Exposes APT1—One of China's Cyber Espionage Units & Releases 3,000 Indicators," *FireEye*, February 19, 2013. https://www.fireeye.com/blog/threat-research/2013/02/mandiant-exposes-apt1-chinas-cyber-espionage-units.html.

41. Crowdstrike Global Intelligence Team, Crowdstrike Intelligence Report (Putter Panda), May 2, 2014. https://cdn0.vox-cdn.com/assets/4589853/crowdstrike-intelligence-report-putter-panda.original.pdf.

42. Anthony, Sebastian, "DARPA Shows Off 1.8-Gigapixel Surveillance Drone, Can Spot a Terrorist From 20,000 Feet," *Extreme Tech*, January 28, 2013. Viewed January 26, 2021, at https://www.extremetech.com/extreme/146909-darpa-shows-off-1-8-gigapixel-surveillance-drone-can-spot-a-terrorist-from-20000-feet.

43. Winter, Tom, and Kevin Collier, "DOJ Says Five Chinese Nationals Hacked into 100 U.S. Companies," *Yahoo News*, September 16, 2020. Viewed October 10, 2020, at https://news.yahoo.com/doj-says-five-chinese-nationals-152220554.html.

44. Clement, J., "Cyber Crime: Number of Breaches and Records Exposed 2005–2020," *Statista*, October 1, 2020. Viewed January 11, 2021, at https://www.statista.com/statistics/273550/data-breaches-recorded-in-the-united-states-by-number-of-breaches-and-records-exposed/.

45. Fruhlinger, Josh, "The OPM Hack Explained: Bad Security Practices Meet China's Captain America." *CSO Digital Magazine*, February 12, 2020. Viewed January 10, 2021, at https://www.csoonline.com/article/3318238/the-opm-hack-explained-bad-security-practices-meet-chinas-captain-america.html.

46. Adler, Seth, "Top Breaches: Part III, 2020–12–29," *Cyber Security Hub*. Viewed December 2020 at https://www.cshub.com/content-hub/incident-of-the-week.

47. Zetter, Kim, "Access Software on Systems Sold to States," *Vice*, July 17, 2018. Viewed December 8, 2020, at https://www.vice.com/en/article/mb4ezy/top-voting-machine-vendor-admits-it-installed-remote-access-software-on-systems-sold-to-states.

48. *Ibid.*

49. *Ibid.*

50. Geller, Eric, "U.S.: Russian Hackers Targeting State, Local Governments on Eve of Election." Viewed January 11, 2021, at https://www.politico.com/news/2020/10/22/russian-hackers-state-local-governments-431327.

51. Department of Justice, United States District Court for the District of Columbia, indictment, Case 1:18-cr-00215-ABJ Filed 07/13/18. Viewed at https://www.justice.gov/file/1080281/download.

52. Robertson, Jordan, and Michael Riley, "The Big Hack: How China Used a Tiny Chip to Infiltrate U.S. Companies," *Bloomberg Business*, October 4, 2018. Viewed November 4, 2020, at https://www.bloomberg.com/news/features/2018-10-04/the-big-hack-how-china-used-a-tiny-chip-to-infiltrate-america-s-top-companies.

53. *Ibid.*

54. Volz, Dustin, "U.S. Agencies Hacked in Foreign Cyber Espionage Campaign Linked to Russia," *Wall Street Journal*, December 13, 2020. https://www.wsj.com/articles/agencies-hacked-in-foreign-cyber-espionage-campaign-11607897866?st=7hnrqwraz2u73rr&reflink=article_email_share.

55. Mandia, Kevin, "Transcript: Kevin Mandia on 'Face the Nation,'" December 20, 2020.

56. Krebs, Brian, "U.S. Treasury, Commerce Depts. Hacked Through SolarWinds Compromise," *Krebs on Security*, December 14, 2020. https://krebsonsecurity.com/2020/12/u-s-treasury-commerce-depts-hacked-through-SolarWindss-compromise/.

57. *Ibid.*

58. Sheperd, Brittany, "Biden Says U.S. Will 'Respond in Kind' for Solarwinds Hack Blamed on Russia," *Yahoo News*, December 22, 2020. https://news.yahoo.com/biden-says-us-will-respond-in-kind-for-solar-wind-hacking-blamed-on-russia-215116852.html.

59. Grenell, Richard, interview on *Varney & Company,* December 22, 2020.

60. Tucker, Eric, and Frank Bajak, "Justice Department, Federal Court System Hit by Russian Hack," Associated Press, January 6, 2020, at https://apnews.com/article/russia-hacking-justice-department-6290618f08cad5b11c4dd0263ef6820b.

61. Stubbs, Jack, Joseph Menn, and Christopher Bing, "Inside the West's Failed Fight Against China's 'Cloud Hopper' Hackers," *Reuters*, June 26, 2020. https://www.reuters.com/investigates/special-report/china-cyber-cloudhopper/.

62. Katz, Justin, "Biden Promises 'Overwhelming Focus' on Hack Recovery," *FCW*, December 22, 2020. https://fcw.com/articles/2020/12/22/biden-cyber-SolarWindss-hack-attribute.aspx.

63. Zhong, Raymond, Paul Mozur, and Aron Knolik, at *New York Times* and Kao, Jeff, at *ProPublica*. Published jointly by *The New York Times* and *ProPublica*, 19 December 2020

64. Krebs, Brian, "Who Else Was Hit by the RSA Attackers Krebs On Security," Krebs on Security, http//krebsonsecurity.com/2011/10/who-else-was-hit-by-the-RSA;attackers/; "Capability of the People's Republic of China to Conduct Cyber Warfare and Computer Network Exploitation," U.S.-China Economic & Security Review Commission, October 9, 2009; and Meyer, Carl, "Are Chinese Spies Getting an Easy Ride?" *Embassy*, July 27, 2011.

65. Weller, Amanda J., "Design Thinking for a User-Centered Approach to Artificial Intelligence," *The Journal of Design, Economics, and Innovation*, vol. 5, no. 4, Winter 2019. Viewed December 15, 2020, at https://reader.elsevier.com/reader/sd/pii/S2405872619300887?token=B21B6C06E5C411FA9C36BDEB242BE12F76ED61ECC8264BABA8459E936AEA947B8F8B13AB22CFC62D6FE446785CF04CBB.

66. Lapowsky, Issie, "How Cambridge Analytica Sparked the Great Privacy Awakening," *Wired*, March 17, 2019. https://www.wired.com/story/cambridge-analytica-facebook-privacy-awakening/; and "The Man Who Saw the Dangers of Cambridge Analytica Years Ago," June 19, 2018. Viewed December 14, 2020, at https://www.wired.com/story/the-man-who-saw-the-dangers-of-cambridge-analytica/

67. Lapowsky.

68. *Ibid.*

69. Westerheide, Fabian, "China—The First Artificial Intelligence Superpower," *Forbes*, January 14, 2020. Viewed December 25, 2020, at https://www.forbes.com/sites/cognitiveworld/2020/01/14/china-artificial-intelligence-superpower/?sh=6a1ae6542f05.

70. Associated Press, "Exposed Chinese Database Reveals Scope of Citizen Surveillance," *New York Post*, February 19, 2019. Viewed December 14, 2020, at https://nypost.com/2019/02/19/exposed-chinese-database-reveals-scope-of-citizen-surveillance/.

71. Mitchell, Anna, and Larry Diamond, "China's Surveillance State Should Scare Everyone," *The Atlantic*, February 2, 2018. Viewed December 15, 2020, at https://www.theatlantic.com/international/archive/2018/02/china-surveillance/55220 3/.

72. Beckett, Lois, "Yes, Companies are Harvesting—and Selling—Your Facebook Profile," November 9, 2012. Viewed December 14, 2020, at https://www.propublica.org/article/yes-companies-are-harvesting-and-selling-your-social-media-profiles.

Chapter 6

1. Seppelt, Hajo, "Geheimsache Doping—Wie Russland seine Sieger macht," WDR/ARD Sportschau, 2014. News documentary.

2. McLaren, Dr. Richard, "McLaren Independent Investigation Report, Part 1," World Anti-Doping Agency, July 18, 2016.

3. Grove, Thomas, and Sara Germano, "Putin Blasts Olympic Committee for Banning Russia From 2018 Games," *Wall Street Journal*, December 6, 2017. Viewed November 20, 2017, at https://www.wsj.com/articles/russia-voices-regret-over-2018-winter-olympics-ban-1512558515.

4. U.S. Justice Department, "U.S. Charges Russian GRU Officers with International Hacking and Related Influence and Disinformation Operations," press release, October 4, 2018.

5. McLaren, Richard H. "Report to the President of WADA (the World Anti-Doping Agency) by the Independent Person," July 16, 2016, https://www.wadaama.org/sites/default/files/resources/files/20160718_ip_report_newfinal.pdf.

6. Kumar, Mohit, "How to Hack WiFi Password Easily Using New Attack on WPA/WPA2," November 25, 2018. Viewed January 25, 2020, at https://thehackernews.com/2018/08/how-to-hack-wifi-password.html.

7. U.S. Justice Department, "U.S. Charges Russian GRU Officers with International Hacking and Related Influence and Disinformation Operations," press release, October 4, 2018.

8. *Ibid.*

9. Sanders-Zakre, Alicia, "Russia Charged with OPCW Hacking Attempt," Arms Control Association, November 2018. Viewed September 20, 2020, at https://www.armscontrol.org/act/2018-11/news/russia-charged-opcw-hacking-attempt.

10. Nimmo, Ben, "#PutinAtWar: WADA Hack Shows Kremlin Full-Spectrum Approach," The Atlantic Council Digital Forensic Research Lab, October 14, 2018. Viewed August 24, 2019, https://medium.com/dfrlab/putinatwar-wada-hack-shows-kremlin-full-spectrum-approach-21dd495f2e91.

11. The Fancy Bear moniker was first coined by the U.S. cybersecurity firm Crowdstrike, and later adopted by the pro-Russian hackers. The group is also thought to be responsible for previous hacks, including the 2016 attack on the Democratic National Committee in 2016, the French elections, and German Parliament, as well as organizations perceived as hostile to Russian interests, including the World Anti-Doping Agency.

12. Nimmo.

13. "WADA's Controversial Informant Rodchenkov Changes Look for Camera, Thinks Kremlin is After Him," *RT*, February 9, 2018, https://www.rt.com/news/418374-rodchenkov-interview-60-minutes/.

14. "WADA Reveals Worst Doping Cheaters in 2016, Russia Not Even in Top 5," *RT*, April 8, 2018. Viewed September 21, 2019, at https://www.rt.com/sport/425395-worst-doping-cheaters-wada/.

15. *Ibid.*

16. U.S. Justice Department, indictment, p. 17.

17. Associated Press, "Russia Banned from Using Its Name, Flag at Next Two Olympics," *Sportsnet*, December 17, 2020. https://www.sportsnet.ca/olympics/article/russia-banned-using-name-flag-next-2-olympics/.

18. Conley, Heather, "Successfully Countering Russian Electoral Interference," Center for Strategic and International Studies, June 21, 2018. https://www.csis.org/analysis/successfully-countering-russian-electoral-interference.

19. Bulckaert, Ninon, "How France Successfully Countered Russian Interference During the Presidential Election," *Euractiv*, September 2017. Viewed November 8, 2018, at https://www.euractiv.com/section/elections/news/how-france-successfully-countered-russian-interference-during-the-presidential-election/.

20. Stelzenmuller, Constanze. "The Impact of Russian Interference on Germany's 2017 Elections," testimony before the U.S. Senate Select Committee on Intelligence, June 28, 2017. Also found at https://www.brookings.edu/testimonies/the-impact-of-russian-interference-on-germanys-2017-elections/.

21. U.S. Department of the Treasury, notice, Office of Foreign Assets Control Notice of OFAC Sanctions Actions, AGENCY: Office of Foreign Assets Control, Treasury.

Chapter 7

1. Aaltola, Mika, "Democracy's Eleventh Hour: Safeguarding Democratic Elections against Cyber-Enabled Autocratic Meddling," Briefing Paper 226, Helsinki: Finnish Institute of International Affairs, November 2017. https://storage.googleapis.com/upi-live/2017/11/bp226_democracys_eleventh_hour.pdf.

2. U.S. Senate, Committee on Foreign Relations, "Putin's Asymmetric Assault on Democracy in Russia and Europe: Implications for U.S. National Security," press release, January 10, 2018. https://www.foreign.senate.gov/imo/media/doc/FinalRR.pdf.

3. U.S. Justice Department, "Six Russian GRU Officers Charged in Connection with Worldwide Deployment of Destructive Malware and Other Disruptive Actions in Cyberspace," press release, October 19, 2020. https://www.justice.gov/opa/pr/six-russian-gru-officers-charged-connection-worldwide-deployment-destructive-malware-and.

4. U.S. Justice Department, *United States of America, v. Yuriy Sergeyevich Andrienko, et al.*, unsealed indictment, October 15, 2020. Viewed December 7, 2020, at https://www.justice.gov/opa/press-release/file/1328521/download.

5. Hickey, Adam S., "Election Interference: Ensuring Law Enforcement is Equipped to Target Those Seeking to Do Harm, Testimony Before the Senate Judiciary Committee," June 12, 2018 and; U.S. Senate, Select Committee on Intelligence, "Russian Targeting of Election Infrastructure During the 2016 Election: Summary of Initial Findings and Recommendations," May 2018.

6. U.S. Senate, Select Committee on Intelligence, "Russian Targeting of Election Infrastructure During the 2016 Election: Summary of Initial Findings and Recommendations" (May 2018).

7. BallotPedia, 2020 Election Help. Viewed January 6, 2020, at https://ballotpedia.org/Who_runs_elections_in_the_United_States%3F_(2020) .

8. Cybersecurity and Infrastructure Security Agency, "Critical Infrastructure Security and Resilience Note," July 28, 2020. Viewed January 6, 2021, at https://www.cisa.gov/sites/default/files/publications/cisa-election-infrastructure-cyber-risk-assessment_508.pdf.

9. Koerner, Brendan, "Inside the Cyberattack that Shocked the U.S. Government," *Wired*, October 23, 2016. Viewed October 10, 2020, at https://www.wired.com/2016/10/inside-cyberattack-shocked-us-government/.

10. U.S. Justice Department, Grand Jury for the District of Columbia, *United States of America v. Viktor Borisovich Netyksho, et al.*, (Case 1:18-cr-00215-ABJ) 07/13/18. Viewed October 2018 at https://www.justice.gov/file/1080281/download.

11. *Ibid.*

12. Mueller, Special Counsel Robert S., "Report on the Investigation into Russian Interference in the 2016 Presidential Election," U.S. Department of Justice, March 2019, p. 167.

13. Parkinson, Joe, and Georgi Kantchev, "Document: Russia Uses Rigged Polls, Fake News to Sway Foreign Elections," *Wall Street Journal*, March 23, 2017. https://www.wsj.com/articles/how-does-russia-meddle-in-elections-look-at-bulgaria-1490282352.

14. Nimmo, Ben, "Putin's Media are Pushing Britain for the Brexit," *The Interpreter*, February 12, 2016. https://www.interpretermag.com/putins-media-are-pushing-britain-for-the-brexit/; Ministry of Foreign Affairs of the Russian Federation, Tweet, https://twitter.com/mfa—russia/status/748231648936869888, June 29, 2016.

15. Piper, Elizabeth and James, William *UK government failed to find out whether Russia meddled in Brexit vote: report*, Reuters, 21 July 2020.

16. Kerbaj, Richard, "Russia Steps Up Cyber-Attacks on UK," *The Times*, February 12, 2017. https://www.thetimes.co.uk/article/russia-steps-up-cyber-attacks-on-uk-rl262pnlb.

17. United Kingdom National Cyber Security Centre, "Cyber Security: Fixing the Present So We Can Worry About the Future," November 15, 2017.

18. Minority Report, "Putin's Asymmetric Assault on Democracy in Russia and Europe: Implications for U.S. National Security," January 10, 2018, https://www.foreign.senate.gov/imo/media/doc/FinalRR.pdf.

19. Nixon, Mattew, "Leaked Report Says Russian May Have Affected Brexit Referendum Result," *The New European*, November 19, 2019.

20. Adam, Karla, and William Booth, "Rising Alarm in Britain Over Russian Meddling in Brexit Vote," *Washington Post*, November 17, 2017. https://www.washingtonpost.com/world/europe/rising-alarm-in-britain-over-russian-meddling-in-brexit-vote/2017/11/17/2e987a30-cb34-11e7-b506-8a10ed11ecf5_story.html.

21. Polonski, Vyacheslav, "Impact of Social Media on the Outcome of the EU Referendum," EU Referendum Analysis, Loughboro University, June 2016.

22. Stelzenmueller, Dr. Constanze, "The Impact of Russian Interference on Germany's 2017 Elections," testimony before the U.S. Senate Select Committee on Intelligence, Brookings Institute, June 28, 2017. https://www.brookings.edu/testimonies/the-impact-of-russian-interference-on-germanys-2017-elections/#footnote-1.

23. *Ibid.*

24. Alandete, David, and Daniel Verdu, "How Russian Networks Worked to Boost the Far Right in Italy," *El Pais*, March 1,

2018. https://elpais.com/elpais/2018/03/01/inenglish/1519922107_909331.html.

25. Buickaert, Nimon, "How France Successfully Countered Russian Interference During the Presidential Election," *Euractiv Networks*, July 17, 2018, https://www.euractiv.com/section/elections/news/how-france-successfully-countered-russian-interference-during-the-presidential-election/.

26. Vilmer, Jean-Baptiste Jeangene. "The 'Macron Leaks' Operation: A Post-Mortem." The Atlantic Council, June 2019. Viewed November 6, 2020, at https://www.atlanticcouncil.org/wp-content/uploads/2019/06/The_Macron_Leaks_Operation-A_Post-Mortem.pdf.

27. Federal Indictment, February 2, 2018.

28. Timmons, Heather, Lucia Murkani and Diane Bartz. "Trump Campaign Aide Pushed Ukraine Hacking Theory: Documents," *National Post*, November 2, 2019. https://nationalpost.com/pmn/news-pmn/politics-news-pmn/trump-campaign-aide-pushed-ukraine-hacking-theory-documents.

29. Eltagouri, Marwa, "The Rise of 'Putin's Chef,' the Russian Oligarch Accused of Manipulating the U.S. Election." *Washington Post*, June 21, 2020. https://www.washingtonpost.com/news/worldviews/wp/2018/02/16/the-rise-of-putins-chef-yevgeniy-prigozhin-the-russian-accused-of-manipulating-the-u-s-election/.

30. Federal Indictment, Internet Research Agency, U.S. District Court for the District of Columbia, February 2, 2018, https://www.justice.gov/file/1035477/.

31. *Ibid.*

32. *Ibid.*

33. Fattah, Hassan H. "Attack on Saudi Oil Facility Thwarted," *New York Times*, February 24, 2006. Viewed October 8, 2019, at https://www.nytimes.com/2006/02/24/international/middleeast/attack-on-saudi-oil-facility-thwarted.html.

34. George, Roger Z., and James B. Bruce (eds.), *Analyzing Intelligence* (Washington D.C.: Georgetown University Press, 2014), 201.

35. Director of National Intelligence, "Assessing Russian Activities and Intentions in Recent U.S. Election" (ICA 2017–01D), January 6, 2017. https://www.dni.gov/files/documents/ICA_2017_01.pdf.

36. Singman, Brooke, "DNI Declassifies Brennan Notes, CIA Memo on Hillary Clinton 'Stirring Up' Scandal Between Trump, Russia," Fox News, October 7, 2020. https://www.foxnews.com/politics/dni-brennan-notes-cia-memo-clinton.

37. Nieves, Alexander, "Poll: 60 Percent of Americans Say Russia Meddled in 2016 Election," *Politico*, July 18, 2018. https://www.politico.com/story/2018/07/18/poll-russia-meddling-election-mueller-investigation-730529.

38. Joint Statement from the ODNI, DOJ, FBI and DHS, "Combating Foreign Influence in U.S. Elections," October 2018. https://www.dni.gov/index.php/newsroom/press-releases/item/1915-joint-statement-from-the-odni-doj-fbi-and-dhs-combating-foreign-influence-in-u-s-elections.

39. Redden, Elizabeth, "Closing Confucius Institutes," *Inside Higher Education*, January 9, 2019. Viewed October 7, 2020, at https://www.insidehighered.com/news/2019/01/09/colleges-move-close-chinese-government-funded-confucius-institutes-amid-increasing.

40. Wong, Edward, "China Threatens to Detain Americans if U.S. Prosecutes Chinese Scholars," *New York Times*, October 18, 2020. https://www.nytimes.com/2020/10/18/us/politics/china-us-threats-detain.html.

41. Diamond, Larry, and Orville Schell, *Chinese Influence and American Interests*, Stanford, CA: The Hoover Institution, 2019), 33.

42. Cave, Damien, "Australian Politician's Home Raided in Chinese Influence Inquiry," *New York Times*, June 26, 2020. Viewed October 7, 2020, at https://www.nytimes.com/2020/06/26/world/australia/politician-home-raid-china-influence.html.

43. Davies, Anne, and Daniel Hurst, "Asio Raids Home of NSW Labor MP Shaoquett Moselmane Over Alleged Links to China," *The Guardian*, June 26, 2020. Viewed October 7, 2020, at https://www.theguardian.com/australia-news/2020/jun/26/asio-raids-home-nsw-labor-mp-shaoquett-moselmane-links-china.

44. "Australia Formally Names China in Foreign Interference Investigation," *South China Morning Post*. Viewed October 7, 2020, at https://www.scmp.com/

news/asia/australasia/article/3101774/
australia-formally-names-china-foreign-
interference.

45. Searight, Amy, "Countering China's
Influence Operations: Lessons from Australia," Center for Strategic and International
Studies, May 8, 2020. Viewed October 7,
2020, at https://www.csis.org/analysis/
countering-chinas-influence-operations-
lessons-australia.

46. U.S. Justice Department, District
Court for the District of Columbia, indictment of the Internet Research Agency, et
al., February 16, 2018.

47. Burr, Richard, "Open Hearing:
Social Media Influence in the 2016 U.S.
Election," Senate Select Committee on
Intelligence, November 1, 2017. https://
www.intelligence.senate.gov/hearings/
open-hearing-social-media-influence-
2016-us-elections#.

48. Government of Canada, "Measuring Results of Advertising," updated
May 5, 2018. https://canadabusiness.ca/
managing-your-business/marketing-and-
sales/promoting-and-advertising-your-
business/measuring-the-results-of-your-
advertising/.

49. Eldelman, Gilad, "The Pre-Election
Polls Were Wrong. The Exit Polls Are
Worse," Wired, November 11 2020. https://
www.wired.com/story/the-pre-election-
polls-were-wrong-the-exit-polls-are-
worse/.

50. Office of the Director of National
Intelligence, "Background to Assessing Russian Activities and Intentions in
Recent U.S. Elections: The Analytic Process and Cyber Incident Attribution," January 6, 2017. https://www.dni.gov/files/
documents/ICA_2017_01.pdf.

Chapter 8

1. Talley, Ian, "U.S. Steps Up Pressure on
China Over North Korean Coal Exports,"
Wall Street Journal, December 8, 2020.
https://www.wsj.com/articles/u-s-steps-
up-pressure-on-china-over-north-korean-
coal-exports-11607464646?st=3ixkwgj8d9
yfw4b&reflink=article_email_share.

2. Farmer, Brit McCandless, "How
China Can Spy on Your Electronics—Even
in the U.S.," CBS News, August 11, 2019.

3. Getz, Bill, "State Department

Cancels China-Paid Junkets for Congressional Staff," Washington Times, December 4, 2020. https://www.washingtontimes.
com/news/2020/dec/4/state-department-
cancels-china-paid-junkets-congre/.

4. Seldin, Jeff, "Outgoing U.S. Intel Chief
Warns China Seeking Global Domination," Voice of America, December 3, 2020.
https://www.voanews.com/usa/outgoing-
us-intel-chief-warns-china-seeking-global-
domination.

5. Seibt, Sebastian, "Is China Provoking
a Diplomatic Fight with Australia?" France
24, January 12, 2020. Viewed November
4, 2020, at https://www.france24.com/en/
asia-pacific/20201201-is-china-provoking-
a-diplomatic-fight-with-australia.

6. Barrett, Eamon, "China Is Ramping Up Its Other Big Trade War," Fortune, November 4, 2020. https://fortune.
com/2020/11/04/china-australia-trade-
war/.

7. Davidson, Helen, "More Than 50
Australian Coal Ships Remain Stranded
Off China's Coast Despite Power Blackouts," The Guardian, December 24, 2020.
https://www.theguardian.com/world/2020/
dec/24/more-than-50-australian-coal-
ships-remain-stranded-off-china-coast-
despite-power-blackouts.

8. Wong, Jacky, "China's Sour Grapes
Spell Trouble for Australian Wine," Wall
Street Journal, November 30, 2020. https://
www.wsj.com/articles/chinas-sour-
grapes-spell-trouble-for-australian-wine-
11606733275?page=1.

9. Jennings, Peter, "Australia Is Not the
Only Country Asking Questions About
the Origins of Coronavirus, and China Is
Not Happy," The Guardian, May 15, 2020.
Viewed November 6, 2020, at https://www.
theguardian.com/commentisfree/2020/
may/15/australia-is-not-the-only-country-
asking-questions-about-the-origins-of-
coronavirus-and-china-is-not-happy.

10. Brady, op cit.

11. Graham-McLay, "What Next for
New Zealand's National Party and Its
Embattled Leader?" The Guardian, October 18, 2020. Viewed December 10, 2020, at
https://www.theguardian.com/world/2020/
oct/18/what-next-for-new-zealands-
national-party-and-its-embattled-leader-
judith-collins.

12. Brady, Anne-Marie, "Magic Weapons: China's Political Influence Activities

Under Xi Jinping," conference paper for The Corrosion of Democracy Under China's Global Influence, Arlington, VA, September 16–17, 2017.

13. Dorfman, Zach, "How Silicon Valley Became a Den of Spies," *Politico*, July 27, 2018. Viewed June 2019, at https://www.politico.com/magazine/story/2018/07/27/silicon-valley-spies-china-russia-219071.

14. *Ibid.*

15. Allen-Ebrahimian, Bethany and Zach Dorfman, "Exclusive: Suspected Chinese Spy Targeted California Politicians," *Axios*, December 8, 2020.

16. Hamilton and Ohlberg, pp. 100–105.

17. Securities and Exchange Commission, press release, November 17, 2010.

18. Mullen, Jethro, "China Blocks New York Times Website After Story on Leader's Family Wealth," October 26, 2012. Viewed January 5, 2014, at https://www.cnn.com/2012/10/26/world/asia/china-times-website-blocked/index.html.

19. Forsythe, Michael, "Panama Papers Tie More of China's Elite to Secret Accounts," *New York Times*, April 6, 2016. https://www.nytimes.com/2016/04/07/world/asia/china-panama-papers.html.

20. Mishra, Sahil, "How the Global Push-back Against China Is Gathering Pace," *The Taiwan Times*, September 8, 2020. Viewed November 6, 2020, at https://thetaiwantimes.com/how-the-global-push-back-against-china-is-gathering-pace/5153.

21. Standish, Reid, "China's Path Forward Is Getting Bumpy," *The Atlantic*, October 1, 2019. Viewed November 6, 2020, at https://www.theatlantic.com/international/archive/2019/10/china-belt-road-initiative-problems-kazakhstan/597853/.

22. Sudworth, John, "China's Hidden Camps," BBC News, October 24, 2018. Viewed September 5, 2019, at https://www.bbc.co.uk/news/resources/idt-sh/China_hidden_camps.

23. Neely, Amber, "Apple Supplier O-Film Tech Accused of Human Rights Violations in China," *Apple Insider*, August 2020. Viewed November 6, 2020, at https://appleinsider.com/articles/20/07/20/apple-supplier-o-film-tech-accused-of-human-rights-violations-in-china#:~:text=Apple%20supplier%20O%2Dfilm%20Tech%20accused%20of%20human%20rights%20violations%20i.

24. France 24, "'A Huge Game-Changer': Report Says More Than 570,000 Uighurs Forced to Pick Cotton," *France 24*, April 14, 2020.

25. These stories may be viewed at: Xinjiang think tank unveils Adrian Zenz as swindler under academic disguise and https://news.cgtn.com/news/2020-09-14/Six-lies-in-Adrian-Zenz-s-Xinjiang-report-of-genocide--TMIv2qWemA/index.html https://news.cgtn.com/news/2020-09-14/Six-lies-in-Adrian-Zenz-s-Xinjiang-report-of-genocide--TMIv2qWemA/index.html and https://www.globaltimes.cn/content/1197187.shtml

26. Lynch, Colum, and Robbie Gramer, "Outfoxed and Outgunned: How China Routed the U.S. in a U.N. Agency," *Foreign Policy*, October 23, 2019.

27. Alexander, Keith, and Jamil N. Jaffer, "China Is Waging Economic War on America. The Pandemic Is an Opportunity to Turn the Fight Around," *Barron's*, August 4, 2020. Viewed November 4, 2020, at https://www.barrons.com/articles/china-is-waging-cyber-enabled-economic-war-on-the-u-s-how-to-fight-back-51596587400.

28. Northern Miner Staff, "Chinese Rare Earth Metals Surge in Price," December 3, 2020. https://www.mining.com/chinese-rare-earth-metals-surge-in-price/.

29. U.S.-China Economic and Security Review Commission, report to Congress, December 2020, p. 258.

30. Reuters Staff, "Huawei Pleads Not Guilty to New U.S. Criminal Charges in 2018 Case," *Reuters*, March 4, 2020. Viewed May 10, 2020, at https://www.reuters.com/article/us-china-huawei-tech/huawei-pleads-not-guilty-to-new-u-s-criminal-charges-in-2018-case-idUSKBN20R2Y8.

31. "U.S. Accuses China's Huawei of Helping Iran Track Protesters," Radio Free Europe, February 14, 2020.

32. Ramey, Corinne, and Kate O'Keeffe, "China's Huawei Charged with Racketeering, Stealing Trade Secrets," *Wall Street Journal*, February 13, 2020. Viewed December 4, 2020, at https://www.wsj.com/articles/chinas-huawei-charged-with-racketeering-11581618336?st=9r5u2ts82s6o4lx&reflink=article_email_share.

33. U.S. Department of Justice, "Chinese Telecommunications Conglomerate Huawei and Subsidiaries Charged in Racketeering Conspiracy and Conspiracy

to Steal Trade Secrets," press release, February 13, 2020. Viewed December 4, 2020, at https://www.justice.gov/usao-edny/pr/chinese-telecommunications-conglomerate-huawei-and-subsidiaries-charged-racketeering.

34. Ratcliffe, John, Fox News, December 7 and 8, 2020.

35. U.S. Department of Justice, ZTE Factual Resume, filing to the U.S. District Court for the Northern District of Texas, Dallas Division, March 7, 2017. https://www.justice.gov/opa/press-release/file/946281.

36. U.S. Department of Justice, plea agreement filing to the U.S. District Court of the Northern District of Texas, Dallas Division, March 7, 2017. https://www.justice.gov/opa/press-release/file/946276/download.

37. Delaney, Robert, "U.S. Slaps China's ZTE with 7-Year Components Ban for Breaching Terms of Sanctions Settlement," *South China Morning Post*, April 16, 2016, https://www.scmp.com/business/companies/article/2142002/us-slaps-zte-seven-year-components-ban-breaching-terms-sanctions.

38. Elis, Niv, "Trump Says ZTE Support Followed Request from Chinese President," *The Hill*, March 17, 2018. https://thehill.com/policy/finance/388199-trump-says-zte-support-followed-request-from-xi.

39. Rauhala, Emily, "Huawei Executive Wanted by U.S. Faces Fraud Charges Related to Iran Sanctions, Could Face 30 Years in Prison." *Washington Post*, December 7, 2018.

40. Patrick, Margot, and Julie Steinberg, "Some Global Banks Break Ties with Huawei," *Wall Street Journal*, December 20, 2018, https://www.wsj.com/articles/some-global-banks-break-ties-with-huawei-11545321306.

41. Sanger, David E., and Nichole Perlroth, "N.S.A. Breached Chinese Servers Seen as Security Threat," *New York Times*, March 22, 2014, https://www.nytimes.com/2014/03/23/world/asia/nsa-breached-chinese-servers-seen-as-spy-peril.html.

42. Trump, Donald, "Executive Order on Securing the Information and Communications Technology and Services Supply Chain," May 15, 2019.

43. Hayden, Michael, "Interview Regarding Edward Snowden, Cyber Security, And Transparency," *Australian Financial Review*, July 2013.

44. Sanger, David E. and Nicole Perlroth, "N.S.A Breached Chinese Servers Seen as Security Threat," *New York Times*, March 22, 2014. https://www.nytimes.com/2014/03/23/world/asia/nsa-breached-chinese-servers-seen-as-spy-peril.html.

45. Panettieri, Joe, "Huawei: Banned and Permitted in Which Countries? List and FAQ," *Channele2e*, updated December 15, 2020. https://www.channele2e.com/business/enterprise/huawei-banned-in-which-countries/2/.

46. U.S. Justice Department, "Chinese Telecommunications Device Manufacturer and Its U.S. Affiliate Indicted for Theft of Trade Secrets, Wire Fraud, and Obstruction of Justice," press release, January 28, 2019.

47. Lee, Timothy B., "U.S. Indicts Huawei for Stealing T-Mobile Robot Arm, Selling U.S. Tech to Iran," *Ars Technica*, January 28, 2019. Viewed December 1, 2020, at https://arstechnica.com/tech-policy/2019/01/us-indicts-huawei-for-stealing-t-mobile-robot-selling-us-tech-to-iran/.

48. Shepardson, David, "U.S. Agency Votes 5–0 to Bar China's Huawei, ZTE from Government Subsidy Program," *Reuters*, November 22, 2019. Viewed April 24, 2020, at https://www.reuters.com/article/us-usa-china-huawei-tech/u-s-agency-votes-5-0-to-bar-chinas-huawei-zte-from-government-subsidy-program-idUSKBN1XW1TC.

49. Pham, Sherisse, "U.S. Judge Rejects Huawei Lawsuit Challenging a Ban on Its Products," CNN Business, February 19, 2020. Viewed December 8, 2020, at https://www.cnn.com/2020/02/19/tech/huawei-us-lawsuit-rejected/index.html.

50. Shields, Todd, "FCC Moves Against China Telecom and Huawei, Citing Security," *Bloomberg Technology*, December 10, 2020.

51. Pancevski, Bojan, and Matthew Dalton, "Spy Case Linked to China Raises Red Flags for Poland and the U.S.," *Wall Street Journal*, January 24, 2019, https://www.wsj.com/articles/spy-case-linked-to-china-raises-red-flags-for-poland-and-the-u-s-11548357192.

52. Tanner, Murray Scot, "Beijing's New National Intelligence Law: From Defense to Offense," *Lawfare Blog*, July 20, 2017. Viewed December 7, 2020, at https://www.lawfareblog.com/beijings-new-national-intelligence-law-defense-offense.

53. *Ibid.*

54. White House, "Remarks by President Obama and President Xi of the People's Republic of China in Joint Press Conference," press release, September 25, 2015. https://obamawhitehouse.archives.gov/the-press-office/2015/09/25/remarks-president-obama-and-president-xi-peoples-republic-china-joint.

55. Goodwin, Dan, "Citing BGP Hijacks and Hack Attacks, Feds Want China Telecom Out of the U.S.," *Ars Technica*, April 10, 2020. Viewed December 20, 2020, at https://arstechnica.com/tech-policy/2020/04/citing-bgp-hijacks-and-hack-attacks-feds-want-china-telecom-out-of-the-us/.

56. Kubota, Yoko, and Liza Lin, "Beijing Orders Agencies to Swap Out Foreign Tech for Chinese Gear," *Wall Street Journal*, December 9, 2019. https://www.wsj.com/articles/beijing-orders-agencies-to-swap-out-foreign-tech-for-chinese-gear-11575921277.

57. Huawei Cyber Security Evaluation Centre (HCSEC) Oversight Board Annual Report 2019, report to the National Security Adviser of the United Kingdom, March 2019, pp. 3, 7.

58. Kelion, Leo, "Huawei 5G Kit Must Be Removed from UK by 2027," BBC News, July 14, 2020. Viewed December 14, 2020, at https://www.bbc.com/news/technology-53403793.

59. *Ibid.*

60. Layton, Roslyn, "Stealing from States: China's Power Play in IT Contracts," *China Tech Threat*, March 20, 2020. Viewed January 3, 2021, at https://chinatechthreat.com/wp-content/uploads/2020/02/CTT-Report-Stealing-From-States-Chinas-Power-Play-in-IT-Contracts.pdf.

61. U.S. Senate, Permanent Subcommittee on Investigations, "Threats to U.S. Networks: Oversight of Chinese Government-Owned Carriers," June 9, 2020, 10. https://www.hsgac.senate.gov/imo/media/doc/2020-06-09%20PSI%20Staff%20Report%20-%20Threats%20to%20U.S.%20Communications%20Networks.pdf.

62. U.S. Department of Justice, "Executive Branch Agencies Recommend the FCC Revoke and Terminate China Telecom's Authorizations to Provide International Telecommunications Services in the United States," press release, April 9, 2020, at https://www.justice.gov/opa/pr/executive-branch-agencies-recommend-fcc-revoke-and-terminate-china-telecom-s-authorizations.

63. U.S. Senate, Permanent Subcommittee on Investigations, 23.

64. *Ibid.*, 11.

65. *Ibid.*, 9.

66. U.S. Senate, Homeland Security & Government Affairs, Permanent Subcommittee on Investigations, "Portman, Carper: Bipartisan Report Reveals How Three Chinese Government-Owned Telecoms Operated in the U.S. for Nearly 20 Years with Little-to-No Oversight from the Federal Government," press release, June 9, 2020. Viewed January 5, 2020, at https://www.hsgac.senate.gov/subcommittees/investigations/media/portman-carper-bipartisan-report-reveals-how-three-chinese-government-owned-telecoms-operated-in-the-us-for-nearly-20-years-with-little-to-no-oversight-from-the-federal-government.

67. U.S.-China Economic and Security Review Commission, report to Congress, December 2020, p. 52.

68. U.S.-China Econom

69. ic and Security Rev

70. iew Comm

71. ission, report to Congress, December 2020, p. 52.

nitions, https://gdpr-info.eu/art-4-gdpr/.

72. Shahbaz, Adrian, Allie Funk, and Andrea Hackl, "User Privacy or Cyber Sovereignty?," *Freedom House*, 2020 Special Report. Viewed December 1, 2020, at https://freedomhouse.org/report/special-report/2020/user-privacy-or-cyber-sovereignty#footnote1_3ojp0cs.

73. Potter, Robert, and David Robinson, "Exposing Mystery and Menace of Chinese Communist Party Membership," *The Australian*, December 18, 2020. https://www.theaustralian.com.au/commentary/exposing-mystery-and-menace-of-chinese-communist-party-membership/news-story/ef3e79d1e3d9022388f5e4fdcce14895.

74. *Ibid.*

Chapter 9

1. Diamond, Larry, and Orville Schell, "Chinese Influence and American

Interests," Hoover Institution Press, November 29, 2018. Viewed August 2019 at https://www.hoover.org/research/chinas-influence-american-interests-promoting-constructive-vigilance.

2. Bureau of Economic Analysis, "Direct Investment by Country and Industry, 2018." Viewed January 10, 2020, at https://www.bea.gov/news/2019/direct-investment-country-and-industry-2018.

3. U.S.-China Economic and Security Review Commission, report to Congress, December 2020, 214.

4. Dunbar, John, "The Citizens United Decision and Why it Matters," Center for Public Integrity, October 18, 2012. Viewed January 6, 2021, at https://publicintegrity.org/politics/the-citizens-united-decision-and-why-it-matters/.

5. Jackson, James K., "The Committee on Foreign Investment in the United States (CFIUS)," Congressional Research Service, February 14, 2020. Viewed January 5, 2021, at https://fas.org/sgp/crs/natsec/RL33388.pdf.

6. James Jackson, The Committee on Foreign Investment in the United States (CFIUS), Congressional Research Service, February 14, 2020. Viewed on March 3, 2020, at https://fas.org/sgp/crs/natsec/RL33388.pdf.

7. Morrison/Foerster, Client Alert: CFIUS Means Business, Unwinding Non-Notified Transactions and Penalizing Non-Compliance with Mitigation Agreements, Morrison & Foerster LLP.

8. Jackson, James K., "The Committee on Foreign Investment."

9. Trump, Donald, "Executive Order on Addressing the Threat Posed by WeChat, & Executive Order on Addressing the Threat Posed by TikTok," August 6, 2020. Viewed August 7, 2020, at https://www.whitehouse.gov/presidential-actions/executive-order-addressing-threat-posed-wechat/, and https://www.whitehouse.gov/presidential-actions/executive-order-addressing-threat-posed-tiktok/.

10. Sherman, Alex, "Tiktok Reveals Detailed User Numbers for the First Time," CNBC News, August 24, 2020. Viewed February 17, 2020, at https://www.cnbc.com/2020/08/24/tiktok-reveals-us-global-user-growth-numbers-for-first-time.html.

11. Kelly, Heather, and Emily Rauhala. "What a WeChat Ban Could Mean for Millions of U.S. Users." Washington Post, September 18, 2020. Viewed February 17, 2020, at https://www.washingtonpost.com/technology/2020/09/18/wechat-ban-faq/.

12. Yang, Jing, "WeChat Becomes a Powerful Surveillance Tool Everywhere in China," Wall Street Journal, December 22, 2020. https://www.wsj.com/articles/wechat-becomes-a-powerful-surveillance-tool-everywhere-in-china-11608633003.

13. Schroeder, Pete, "U.S. Congress Bans Anonymous Shell Companies," Reuters, December 20, 2020. Viewed January 21, 2021, at https://www.reuters.com/article/us-usa-congress-banks/u-s-congress-bans-anonymous-shell-companies-idUSKBN28L2NV.

14. Luce, Edward, "How Money Laundering Is Poisoning American Democracy," Financial Times, November 28, 2019. Viewed August 13, 2020, at https://www.ft.com/content/99bf2b62-1162-11ea-a225-db2f231cfeae.

15. Federal Election Commission website at https://www.fec.gov/legal-resources/.

16. ACAMS, "Weekly Roundup: Trump Private Bankers Quit Deutsche Bank, FinCEN Targets Private Cryptocurrency Wallets, and More," December 23, 2020. https://www.moneylaundering.com/news/weekly-roundup-trump-private-bankers-quit-deutsche-bank-fincen-targets-private-cryptocurrency-wallets-and-more/.

17. Hickey, Adam S., "Testimony Before House Judiciary Committee at Hearing Titled 'Securing America's Elections Part II: Oversight of Government Agencies,'" October 22, 2019. Viewed December 1, 2020, at https://www.justice.gov/opa/speech/deputy-assistant-attorney-general-adam-s-hickey-testifies-house-judiciary-committee.

18. Straus, Jacob R., Congressional Research Service, "Foreign Agents Registration Act: An Overview," updated March 7, 2019. https://sgp.fas.org/crs/misc/IF10499.pdf.

19. U.S. Department of Justice, "Court Finds RM Broadcasting Must Register as a Foreign Agent," press release, May 13, 2019. Viewed February 12, 2020, at https://www.justice.gov/opa/pr/court-finds-rm-broadcasting-must-register-foreign-agent.

20. MacFarquhar, Neil, "Playing on Kansas City Radio: Russian Propaganda," New

York Times, February 13, 2020. https://www.nytimes.com/2020/02/13/us/russian-propaganda-radio.html.

21. Katz, Justin, "Biden Promises 'Overwhelming Focus' on Hack Recovery," *Federal Computer Week*, December 22, 2020.

22. Mazarr, Michael J., *Understanding Deterrence*, Santa Monica, CA: RAND Corporation, 2018. Viewed December 23, 2020, at https://www.rand.org/pubs/perspectives/PE295.html.

23. Marczak, Bill, and Nicholas Weaver, et al., "China's Great Cannon," Citizen Lab, Munk School of Global Affairs, University of Toronto, April 10, 2015. Viewed August 2019 at https://citizenlab.ca/2015/04/chinas-great-cannon/.

24. *Ibid.*

25. *Ibid.*

26. Weaver, Nicolas, "A Close Look at the NSA's Most Powerful Internet Attack Tool," March 13, 2014. Viewed August 2019 at https://www.wired.com/2014/03/quantum/.

27. U.S. Justice Department, U.S. District Court for the District of Columbia, *United States of America v. Internet Research Agency*, filing, February 16, 2018, Case 1:18-cr-00032-DLF. https://www.justice.gov/file/1035477/download.

28. Turnbull, Malcom "Speech Introducing the National Security Legislation Amendment (Espionage and Foreign Interference) Bill 2017," *MalcolmTurnbull.com*, December 7, 2017. https://www.malcolmturnbull.com.au/media/speech-introducing-the-national-security-legislation-amendment-espionage-an.

29. *Ibid.*

30. Wray, Christopher, "China's Attempt to Influence U.S. Institutions," The Hudson Institute, August 6 2020. Viewed November 22, 2020, at https://digitalguardian.com/blog/2500-fbis-counterintelligence-cases-linked-china; and "The Threat Posed by the Chinese Government and the Chinese Communist Party to the Economic and National Security of the United States," The Hudson Institute July 7, 2020. Viewed November 22, 2020, at https://www.fbi.gov/news/speeches/the-threat-posed-by-the-chinese-government-and-the-chinese-communist-party-to-the-economic-and-national-security-of-the-united-states.

31. *Ibid.*

32. Wang, Vivian, and Edward Wong, "U.S. Hits Back at China with New Visa Restrictions on Journalists," *New York Times*, May 9, 2020. Viewed November 22, 2020, at https://www.nytimes.com/2020/05/09/us/politics/china-journalists-us-visa-crackdown.html.

33. Bing, Christopher, "Exclusive: Twitter Deletes Over 10,000 Accounts that Sought to Discourage U.S. Voting," *Reuters*, November 2, 2018. Viewed September 28, 2019, at https://www.reuters.com/article/us-usa-election-twitter-exclusive/exclusive-twitter-deletes-over-10000-accounts-that-sought-to-discourage-u-s-voting-idUSKCN1N72FA.

34. Romo, Vanessa, "Facebook Removed Nearly 3.4 Billion Fake Accounts in 6 Months," National Public Radio, May 23, 2019. Viewed September 28, 2019, at https://www.npr.org/2019/05/23/726353723/facebook-removed-nearly-3-2-billion-fake-accounts-in-last-six-months.

35. Gouarie, Chava, "Censorship in the Social Media Age," *Columbia Journalism Review*, January 21, 2016. Viewed August 31, 2020, at https://www.cjr.org/analysis/censorship_in_the_social_media_age.php.

Bibliography

Aaltola, Mika. "Democracy's Eleventh Hour: Safeguarding Democratic Elections Against Cyber-Enabled Autocratic Meddling." Briefing Paper 226. Helsinki: Finnish Institute of International Affairs, 2017. https://storage.googleapis.com/upi-live/2017/11/bp226_democracys_eleventh_hour.pdf.

Abaad Research Center. "The Terror of Iranian Weapons: Houthi Forces Threaten Gulf Security." July 19, 2019, 2. https://abaadstudies.org.

Abdurasulov, Abdujalil. "What's Happening in Belarus?" BBC News, September 8, 2020. Viewed November 20, 2020, at https://www.bbc.com/news/world-europe-53799065.

Abramson, Alana, and Abigail Abrams. "Here Are All the Lawsuits the Trump Campaign Has Filed Since Election Day—And Why Most Are Unlikely to Go Anywhere" *Time*, November 18, 2020. Viewed January 22, 2021, at https://time.com/5908505/trump-lawsuits-biden-wins/.

ACAMS, "Weekly Roundup: Trump Private Bankers Quit Deutsche Bank, FinCEN Targets Private Cryptocurrency Wallets, and More." Moneylaundering.com, December 23, 2020. https://www.moneylaundering.com/news/weekly-roundup-trump-private-bankers-quit-deutsche-bank-fincen-targets-private-cryptocurrency-wallets-and-more/.

Adam, Karla, and William Booth. "Rising Alarm in Britain Over Russian Meddling in Brexit Vote." *Washington Post*, November 17, 2017.

Adee, Sally. "What Are Deepfakes and How Are They Created?" *IEEE Spectrum*, April 29, 2020. https://spectrum.ieee.org/tech-talk/computing/software/what-are-deepfakes-how-are-they-created.

Adler, Seth. "Top Breaches: Part III, 2020-12-29." *Cyber Security Hub*. Viewed December 2020 at https://www.cshub.com/content-hub/incident-of-the-week.

AFP. "U.S. Destroyer Sails Through Taiwan Strait, Provoking China." *Voice of America*, October 30, 2017. Viewed November 4, 2020, at https://www.voanews.com/east-asia-pacific/us-destroyer-sails-through-taiwan-strait-provoking-china.

AFT/PTI News Service. "Ukraine Hit with Partial Power Outages." *Business Standard*, March 25, 2014.

Ahmari, Sohrab. "Meet Your (Chinese) Facebook Censors." *New York Post*, October 20, 2020. Viewed November 7, 2020, at https://nypost.com/2020/10/20/meet-your-chinese-facebook-censors/.

Al Jazeera News, "Saudi Accuses Iran of Potential 'Act of War.'" November 6, 2017. https://www.aljazeera.com/news/2017/11/6/saudi-accuses-iran-of-potential-act-of-war.

Alandete, David, and Daniel Verdu. "How Russian Networks Worked to Boost the Far Right in Italy." *El Pais*, 1 March 1, 2018.

Alexander, Keith, and Jamil N. Jaffer. "China Is Waging Economic War on America. The Pandemic Is an Opportunity to Turn the Fight Around." Barron's, August 4, 2020. Viewed November 4, 2020, at https://www.barrons.com/articles/china-is-waging-cyber-enabled-economic-war-on-the-u-s-how-to-fight-back-51596587400.

Allen-Ebrahimian, Bethany, and Zach Dorfman. "Exclusive: Suspected Chinese Spy Targeted California Politicians." *Axios*, December 8, 2020.

American Bar Association. "Standing Committee on Election Law." *Current Litigation*, March 4, 2021. https://www.americanbar.org/groups/public_interest/election_law/litigation/.

Andersen, Kenneth. *Persuasion: Theory and Practice*. Boston: Allyn & Bacon, 1971, 217–263.

Andersen, Kenneth, and Theodore Clevenger, Jr. "A Summary of Experimental Research in Ethos." *Speech Monographs*, June 30, 1963, 59–78.

Andress, Jason, and Steve Winterfield. *Cyber Warfare*. New York: Elsevier, Inc., 2010, 4.

Anthony, Sebastian. "Darpa Shows Off 1.8-Gigapixel Surveillance Drone, Can Spot a Terrorist from 20,000 Feet." *Extreme Tech*, January 28, 2013. Viewed January 26, 2021, at https://www.extremetech.com/extreme/146909-darpa-shows-off-1-8-gigapixel-surveillance-drone-can-spot-a-terrorist-from-20000-feet.

AP News. "Ukraine's Ousted President Testifies in Court." Associated Press, November 28, 2016. Viewed September 8, 2020, at https://apnews.com/article/9f3dab771d92490e b3f15cbd97a63dfd.

Associated Press, "Czechs Blame Foreign State for Foreign Ministry Cyberattack." *Security Week*, August 14, 2019. Viewed September 2020 at https://www.securityweek.com/czechs-blame-foreign-state-foreign-ministry-cyberattack.

Associated Press. "Exposed Chinese Database Reveals Scope Of Citizen Surveillance." *New York Post*, February 19, 2019. Viewed December 14, 2020, at https://nypost.com/2019/02/19/exposed-chinese-database-reveals-scope-of-citizen-surveillance/.

Associated Press. "Hundreds Arrested in Fresh Belarus Protests Against Lukashenko." *French 24*, December 12, 2020. Viewed December 22, 2020, at https://www.france24.com/en/europe/20201206-hundreds-arrested-in-fresh-belarus-protests-against-lukashenko.

Associated Press. "Russia Banned from Using Its Name, Flag at Next Two Olympics." *Sportsnet*, December 17, 2020. https://www.sportsnet.ca/olympics/article/russia-banned-using-name-flag-next-2-olympics/.

Associated Press. "The Latest: FBI Says Probe of Capitol Officer Death Ongoing." ABC News, March 2, 2021. https://abcnews.go.com/Politics/wireStory/latest-fbi-chief-calls-capitol-riot-domestic-terrorism-76204577.

"Australia Formally Names China in Foreign Interference Investigation." *South China Morning Post*, September 16, 2020. Viewed October 7, 2020, at https://www.scmp.com/news/asia/australasia/article/3101774/australia-formally-names-china-foreign-interference.

Australian Associated Press. "China Is Seeking to 'Take Over' Australia's Political System, Former Asio Chief Claims." Published in *The Guardian*, November 21, 2019.

BallotPedia. "2020 Election Help." Viewed January 6, 2020, at https://ballotpedia.org/Who_runs_elections_in_the_United_States%3F_(2020).

Barnes, Julian E., and Matthew Rosenberg. "Charges of Ukrainian Meddling? A Russian Operation, U.S. Intelligence Says." *New York Times*, November 26, 2019. Viewed November 22, 2020, at https://www.nytimes.com/2019/11/22/us/politics/ukraine-russia-interference.html.

Barr, William P. "Transcript of Attorney General Barr's Remarks on China Policy at the Gerald R. Ford Presidential Museum." July 17 2020. https://www.justice.gov/opa/speech/transcript-attorney-general-barr-s-remarks-china-policy-gerald-r-ford-presidential-museum.

Barrett, Eamon. "China Is Ramping Up Its Other Big Trade War." *Fortune*, November 4, 2020. https://fortune.com/2020/11/04/china-australia-trade-war/.

BBC News. "Russian Spy Poisoning: What We Know So Far." October 8, 2018. Viewed July 2019 at https://www.bbc.com/news/uk-43315636.

BBC News China. "COVID: What Do We Know About China's Coronavirus Vaccines?" January 14, 2021. https://www.bbc.com/news/world-asia-china-55212787.

Beck, Martin. "An International Relations Perspective on the Iran Nuclear Deal." *E-International Relations*, August 8, 2018. Viewed September 22, 2019, at https://www.e-ir.info/2018/08/08/an-international-relations-perspective-on-the-iran-nuclear-deal/.

Beckett, Lois. "Yes, Companies Are Harvesting—and Selling—Your Facebook Profile." *ProPublica*, November 9, 2012. Viewed December 14, 2020, at https://www.propublica.org/article/yes-companies-are-harvesting-and-selling-your-social-media-profiles.

Benkler, Yochai, Rob Faris, Hal Roberts, and Nikki Bourassa. "Understanding Media and

Information Quality in an Age of Artificial Intelligence, Automation, Algorithms and Machine Learning." Berkman Klein Center for Internet and Society, Harvard University, July 12, 2018.

Bergman, Ronen. "When Israel Hatched a Secret Plan to Assassinate Iranian Scientists." *Politico*, March 5, 2018. https://www.politico.com/magazine/story/2018/03/05/israel-assassination-iranian-scientists-217223.

Bessinger, Greg. "Google Maps Vary Depending on Who's Looking at Them." *Washington Post*, March 1, 2020. Viewed April 5, 2020, at https://www.washingtonpost.com/technology/2020/02/14/google-maps-political-borders/.

Beswick, Emma. "Belarus: Second Protester Dies and 6,000 Arrested in Demonstrations." *EuroNews*, August 12, 2020. Viewed January 10, 2020, at https://www.euronews.com/2020/08/11/belarus-protesters-incited-to-change-tact-for-third-night-of-demonstrations.

Bing, Christopher. "Exclusive: Twitter Deletes over 10,000 Accounts That Sought to Discourage U.S. Voting." *Reuters*, November 2, 2018. Viewed September 28, 2019, at https://www.reuters.com/article/us-usa-election-twitter-exclusive/exclusive-twitter-deletes-over-10000-accounts-that-sought-to-discourage-u-s-voting-idUSKCN1N72FA.

Bowers, John W., and Phillips, William A. "A Note on the Generality of Source Credibility Scales." *Speech Monographs*, 34 (June 1967), 185–186.

Bowman, M.E. "Secrets in Plain View: Covert Action the U.S. Way." *International Law Studies*, vol. 72. Viewed November 14, 2020, at https://digital commons.usnwc.edu/cgi/viewcontent.cgi?referer=https://www.google.com/&httpsredir=1&article=1470&context=il.

Boyle, Jon. "Ukraine Hit by Cyberattacks: Head of Ukraine Security Service." *Reuters*, March 14, 2014. Viewed at https://www.reuters.com/article/us-ukraine-crisis-telecoms-id USBREA230Q920140304.

Bradshaw, Samantha, and Philip N. Howard. "The Global Disinformation Disorder: 2019 Global Inventory of Organised Social Media Manipulation." Working Paper 2019.2. Oxford, UK: Project on Computational Propaganda. Viewed January 15, 2021, at https://comprop.oii.ox.ac.uk/wp-content/uploads/sites/93/2020/10/CyberTroop-Report19_V2NOV.pdf

Bradshaw, Samantha, Philip Howard, and Hannah Bailey. *Industrialized Disinformation*. Oxford Internet Institute, University of Oxford, January 13, 2021. https://comprop.oii.ox.ac.uk/research/posts/industrialized-disinformation/#continue.

Brady, Anne-Marie. "Magic Weapons: China's Political Influence Activities Under Xi Jinping." Conference paper for "The Corrosion of Democracy Under China's Global Influence." Arlington, VA, September 16–17, 2017.

Breslow, Jason M. "Colin Powell: U.N. Speech 'Was a Great Intelligence Failure." *Frontline* PBS, May 17, 2016. https://www.pbs.org/wgbh/frontline/article/colin-powell-u-n-speech-was-a-great-intelligence-failure/.

Bulckaert, Ninon. "How France Successfully Countered Russian Interference During the Presidential Election." *Euractiv*, September 2017. Viewed November 8, 2018, at https://www.euractiv.com/section/elections/news/how-france-successfully-countered-russian-interference-during-the-presidential-election/.

Bureau of Economic Analysis. "Direct Investment by Country and Industry, 2018." Viewed January 10, 2020, at https://www.bea.gov/news/2019/direct-investment-country-and-industry-2018.

Burr, Richard. "Open Hearing: Social Media Influence in the 2016 U.S. Election." Senate Select Committee on Intelligence, November 1, 2017. https://www.intelligence.senate.gov/hearings/open-hearing-social-media-influence-2016-us-elections#.

Burt, Tom. *New cyberattacks targeting U.S. elections*, Microsoft, September 10, 2020 Viewed January 13, 2021, at https://blogs.microsoft.com/on-the-issues/2020/09/10/cyberattacks-us-elections-trump-biden/

Caralle, Katelyn. "Google, China Create Search Engine that Tracks, Censors Searches and Links Them To Users' Phone Numbers." *Washington Examiner*, November 20, 2019. Viewed November 20, 2019, at https://www.washingtonexaminer.com/news/google-china-create-search-engine-that-tracks-censors-searches-and-links-them-to-users-phone-numbers.

Cave, Damien. "Australian Politician's Home Raided in Chinese Influence Inquiry." *New York Times*, June 26, 2020. Viewed October 7, 2020, at https://www.nytimes.com/2020/06/26/world/australia/politician-home-raid-china-influence.html.

"China's Online Population Climbs to 772 Million." *Economic Times*, January 31, 2018. Viewed October 20, 2020, at https://economictimes.indiatimes.com/news/international/world-news/chinas-online-population-climbs-to-772-million/articleshow/62726168.cms?utm_source=contentofinterest&utm_medium=text&utm_campaign=cppst.

Cimpanu, Catalin. "Czech Republic Blames Russia for Multiple Government Network Hacks." *ZDNet*, December 3, 2018. Viewed September 2, 2019, at https://www.zdnet.com/article/czech-republic-blames-russia-for-multiple-government-network-hacks/.

CISA Alert (AA20–283A). "APT Actors Chaining Vulnerabilities Against SLTT, Critical Infrastructure, and Elections Organizations." Viewed December 4, 2020, at https://us-cert.cisa.gov/ncas/alerts/aa20-283a.

Clayton, Mark. "Ukraine Election Narrowly Avoided 'Wanton Destruction' from Hackers." *Christian Science Monitor*, June 17, 2014.

Clement, J. "Cyber Crime: Number of Breaches and Records Exposed 2005–2020." *Statista*, October 1, 2020. Viewed January 11, 2020, at https://www.statista.com/statistics/273550/data-breaches-recorded-in-the-united-states-by-number-of-breaches-and-records-exposed/.

Commission on the Intelligence Capabilities of the United States Regarding Weapons of Mass Destruction. "Congressional Commission on the Intelligence Capabilities of the United States Regarding Weapons of Mass Destruction March 2005," p. 3.

Committee on Foreign Relations, U.S. Senate Minority Report. "Putin's Asymmetric Assault on Democracy in Russia and Europe: Implications for U.S. National Security." January 10, 2018. https://www.foreign.senate.gov/imo/media/doc/FinalRR.pdf.

Committee to Protect Journalists. "Ukrainian Journalists, Held by Pro-Russian Separatists." July 1, 2014. https://cpj.org/2014/07/ukrainian-journalists-held-by-pro-russian-separati/.

Conley, Heather. "Successfully Countering Russian Electoral Interference." Center for Strategic and International Studies, June 21, 2018. https://www.csis.org/analysis/successfully-countering-russian-electoral-interference.

Converse, Philip E. "The Nature of Belief Systems in Mass Publics." *Critical Review*, vol. 18, no. 1–3, 2006. Originally published in David E. Apter (ed.), *Ideology and Its Discontents*. New York: The Free Press of Glencoe.

Crowdstrike Global Intelligence Team. "Crowdstrike Intelligence Report (Putter Panda)." May 2, 2014. https://cdn0.vox-cdn.com/assets/4589853/crowdstrike-intelligence-report-putter-panda.original.pdf.

Crowley, Michael, and Julia Ioffe. "Why Putin Hates Hillary." *Politico*, July 25, 2016. Viewed 2017 at https://www.politico.com/story/2016/07/clinton-putin-226153.

Cybersecurity and Infrastructure Security Agency. "Critical Infrastructure Security and Resilience Note." July 28, 2020. Viewed January 6, 2021, at https://www.cisa.gov/sites/default/files/publications/cisa-election-infrastructure-cyber-risk-assessment_508.pdf.

Davidson, Helen. "More Than 50 Australian Coal Ships Remain Stranded Off China's Coast Despite Power Blackouts." *The Guardian*, December 24, 2020. https://www.theguardian.com/world/2020/dec/24/more-than-50-australian-coal-ships-remain-stranded-off-china-coast-despite-power-blackouts.

Davies, Anne, and Daniel Hurst. "ASIO Raids Home of NSW Labor MP Shaoquett Moselmane over Alleged Links to China." *The Guardian*, June 26, 2020. Viewed October 7, 2020, at https://www.theguardian.com/australia-news/2020/jun/26/asio-raids-home-nsw-labor-mp-shaoquett-moselmane-links-china.

Delaney, Robert. "U.S. Slaps China's ZTE with 7-Year Components Ban for Breaching Terms of Sanctions Settlement." *South China Morning Post*, April 16, 2016. https://www.scmp.com/business/companies/article/2142002/us-slaps-zte-seven-year-components-ban-breaching-terms-sanctions.

Devine, Michael. "Covert Action and Clandestine Activities of the Intelligence Community: Selected Definitions in Brief." Congressional Research Service, June 14, 2019.

Diamond, Larry, and John M. Deutch. "Foreign Information Warfare Programs and

Capabilities." June 25, 1996. Viewed February 7, 2020, at https://www.cia.gov/news-information/speeches-testimony/1996/dci_testimony_062596.html.

Diamond, Larry, and Orville Schell. "Chinese Influence and American Interests." The Hoover Institution, Stanford University, p. 33. Viewed August 2019 at https://www.hoover.org/research/chinas-influence-american-interests-promoting-constructive-vigilance.

Dimock, Michael, and Richard Wike. "America Is Exceptional in the Nature of Its Political Divide." Pew Research Center, November 13, 2020. https://www.pewresearch.org/fact-tank/2020/11/13/america-is-exceptional-in-the-nature-of-its-political-divide/.

Director of National Intelligence. "Assessing Russian Activities and Intentions in Recent U.S. Election." (ICA 2017–01D), January 6, 2017. https://www.dni.gov/files/documents/ICA_2017_01.pdf.

Director of National Intelligence. The National Counterintelligence and Security Center (NCSC) *National Counterintelligence Strategy of the United States of America 2020–2022*, February 2020.

Doffman, Zak. "New Google Warning: 280M+ Android Users at Risk as China 'Manipulates' Play Store." *Forbes*, October 2, 2019. Viewed April 12, 2020, at https://www.forbes.com/sites/zakdoffman/2019/10/02/new-google-play-warning-280m-users-at-risk-as-china-manipulates-top-vpns/?sh=c260866149bb.

Dorfman, Zach. "How Silicon Valley Became a Den of Spies." *Politico*, July 27, 2018. Viewed June 2019 at https://www.politico.com/magazine/story/2018/07/27/silicon-valley-spies-china-russia-219071.

Dorn, Walter. "Plausible Deniability or How Leaders May Try to Conceal Their Roles." International Criminal Court/Office of the Prosecutor ICC/OTP, May 18, 2010.

Doshi, Rush, and Robert D. Williams. "Is China interfering in American politics?" The Brookings Institution, October 2, 2018. Viewed July 2020 at https://www.brookings.edu/blog/order-from-chaos/2018/10/02/is-china-interfering-in-american-politics/.

Dunbar, John. "The Citizens United Decision and Why it Matters." Center for Public Integrity, October 18, 2012. Viewed January 2021 at https://publicintegrity.org/politics/the-citizens-united-decision-and-why-it-matters/.

Eldelman, Gilad. "The Pre-Election Polls Were Wrong. The Exit Polls Are Worse." *Wired*, November 11, 2020. Viewed November 14, 2020, at https://www.wired.com/story/the-pre-election-polls-were-wrong-the-exit-polls-are-worse/.

Elis, Niv. "Trump Says ZTE Support Followed Request from Chinese President." *The Hill*, March 17, 2018. https://thehill.com/policy/finance/388199-trump-says-zte-support-followed-request-from-xi.

Eltagouri, Marwa. "The Rise of 'Putin's Chef,' the Russian Oligarch Accused of Manipulating the U.S. Election." *Washington Post*, June 21, 2020. https://www.washingtonpost.com/news/worldviews/wp/2018/02/16/the-rise-of-putins-chef-yevgeniy-prigozhin-the-russian-accused-of-manipulating-the-u-s-election/.

Erlanger, Steven. "Russia Ratchets up Ukraine's Gas Bills in Shift to an Economic Battlefield." *New York Times*, May 11, 2014.

Evanina, William. "Statement by NCSC Director William Evanina: Election Threat Update for the American Public." National Counterintelligence and Security Center, July 20, 2020. https://www.dni.gov/index.php/ncsc-newsroom/item/2140-statement-by-ncsc-director-william-evanina-election-threat-update-for-the-american-public.

Ewing, Philip. "The 2020 Election Was Attacked, but Not Severely Disrupted. Here's How." NPR, November 4, 2020. https://www.npr.org/2020/11/04/931090626/the-2020-election-was-attacked-but-not-severely-disrupted-heres-how.

Farmer, Brit McCandless. "How China Can Spy on Your Electronics—Even in the U.S." CBS News, August 11, 2019.

Farrell, Stephen. "Israel Admits Bombing Suspected Syrian Nuclear Reactor in 2007, Warns Iran." *Reuters*, March 20, 2018, https://www.reuters.com/article/us-israel-syria-nuclear/israel-admits-bombing-suspected-syrian-nuclear-reactor-in-2007-warns-iran-idUSKB-N1GX09K.

Fattah, Hassan H. "Attack on Saudi Oil Facility Thwarted." *New York Times*, February 24, 2006.

Federal Election Commission website. https://www.fec.gov/legal-resources/.

Feldman, Stanley. "Structure and Consistency in Public Opinion." University of Kentucky, 1988, 3.

Ferris-Rotman, Amie, "Britain Regrets Russia's Lugovoy Elected to Duma." *Reuters*, December 7, 2007. https://www.reuters.com/article/uk-russia-britain-lugovoy/britain-regrets-russias-lugovoy-elected-to-duma-idUKL0749585820071207.

Festinger, Leon, and James M. Carlsmith. "Cognitive Consequences of Forced Compliance." *Journal of Abnormal and Social Psychology*, no. 58, 203–210.

Fisher, Louis. "Destruction of the *Maine* (1898)." Law Library of Congress, August 4, 2009, http://www.loufisher.org/docs/wi/434.pdf.

Forsythe, Michael. "Panama Papers Tie More of China's Elite to Secret Accounts." *New York Times*, April 6, 2016. Viewed November 24, 2020, at https://www.nytimes.com/2016/04/07/world/asia/china-panama-papers.html.

France 24, "A Huge Game-Changer': Report Says More Than 570,000 Uighurs Forced to Pick Cotton." *France 24*, April 14, 2020. Viewed December 14, 2020, at https://www.france24.com/en/asia-pacific/20201215-a-huge-game-changer-report-says-more-than-570-000-uighurs-forced-to-pick-cotton.

Friedman, Norman. "The Vincennes Incident." Proceedings of the Naval Institute, May 1989. https://www.usni.org/magazines/proceedings/1989/may/vincennes-incident.

Fruhlinger, Josh. "The OPM Hack Explained: Bad Security Practices Meet China's Captain America." *CSO Digital Magazine*, February 12, 2020. Viewed January 10, 2021, at https://www.csoonline.com/article/3318238/the-opm-hack-explained-bad-security-practices-meet-chinas-captain-america.html.

Geller, Eric. "U.S.: Russian Hackers Targeting State, Local Governments on Eve of Election." *Politico*, October 22, 2020. Viewed January 11, 2021, at https://www.politico.com/news/2020/10/22/russian-hackers-state-local-governments-431327.

General Data Protection Regulation (GDPR), Article 4, available at https://gdpr-info.eu/art-4-gdpr/.

George, Roger Z., and James B. Bruce (eds.) *Analyzing Intelligence*. Washington D.C.: Georgetown University Press, 2014, 201.

Getz, Bill. "State Department Cancels China-Paid Junkets for Congressional Staff." *Washington Times*, December 4, 2020. Viewed December 4, 2020, at https://www.washingtontimes.com/news/2020/dec/4/state-department-cancels-china-paid-junkets-congre/.

Giffin, Kim. "The Contributions of Studies of Source Credibility to a Theory of Interpersonal Trust in the Communications Process." *Psychological Bulletin*, 68 (August 1967), 104–120.

Gilens, Martin, and Benjamin I. Page. "Testing Theories of American Politics: Elites, Interest Groups, and Average Citizens." American Political Science Association, 2014; and Gilens and Bartels 2008, Gilens 2012, Jacobs and Page, 2005, which indicates that the general public may have little or no influence on U.S. foreign policy, when the preferences of business leaders and other elites are taken into account.

Gol, Jyar. "Iran Blasts: What Is Behind Mysterious Fires at Key Sites?" BBC News, July 6, 2020. Viewed July 29, 2020 at https://www.bbc.com/news/world-middle-east-53305940.

Gold, Ashley, and Sara Fischer. "Facebook Takes Down Chinese Campaign Aimed at U.S. Election." *Axios*, September 22, 2020.

Goldman, Eric. "Search Engine Bias and the Demise of Search Engine Utopianism." *Yale Journal of Law and Technology*, vol. 8, issue 1, 2006.

Goodin, Dan. "Citing BGP Hijacks and Hack Attacks, Feds Want China Telecom out of the U.S." *ArsTechnica*, April 10, 2020. Viewed December 20, 2020, at https://arstechnica.com/tech-policy/2020/04/citing-bgp-hijacks-and-hack-attacks-feds-want-china-telecom-out-of-the-us/.

Gordon, Michael R., and Dustin Volz. "Russian Disinformation Campaign Aims to Undermine Confidence in Pfizer, Other Covid-19 Vaccines, U.S. Officials Say." *Wall Street Journal*, March 7, 2021. https://www.wsj.com/articles/russian-disinformation-campaign-aims-to-undermine-confidence-in-pfizer-other-covid-19-vaccines-u-s-officials-say-11615129200?st=ir0lsonvyyrl7mp&reflink=article_email_share.

Gottfried, Jeffrey, and Elisa Shearer. "News Use Across Social Media Platforms 2016." Pew

Research, May 26, 2016. Viewed March 5, 2019, at https://www.journalism.org/2016/05/26/news-use-across-social-media-platforms-2016/.

Gouarie, Chava. "Censorship in the Social Media Age." *Columbia Journalism Review*, January 21, 2016. Viewed August 21, 2020, at https://www.cjr.org/analysis/censorship_in_the_social_media_age.php.

Government of Canada. "Measuring Results of Advertising." Updated May 18, 2018. https://canadabusiness.ca/managing-your-business/marketing-and-sales/promoting-and-advertising-your-business/measuring-the-results-of-your-advertising/.

Graham-McLay. "What Next for New Zealand's National Party and Its Embattled Leader?" *The Guardian*, October 18, 2020. December 10, 2020, at https://www.theguardian.com/world/2020/oct/18/what-next-for-new-zealands-national-party-and-its-embattled-leader-judith-collins.

Greenburg, Andy. "The NSA Confirms It: Russia Hacked French Election 'Infrastructure.'" *Wired*, May 9, 2017. Viewed November 8, 2018, at https://www.wired.com/2017/05/nsa-director-confirms-russia-hacked-french-election-infrastructure/.

Gregg, A.P., B. Seibt, and M.R. Banaji. Easier Done than Undone: Asymmetry in the Malleability of Implicit Preferences." *Journal of Personality and Social Psychology* (2006), 1–20.

Grenell, Rick. "Trump's 'America First' Agenda Won't Go Away." Fox News, interview on *Varney & Co.*, December 22, 2020. https://video.foxbusiness.com/v/6221366667001#sp=show-clips.

Grind, Kirsten, Sam Schechner, Robert McMillian, and John West. "How Google Interferes with Its Search Algorithms and Changes Your Results." *Wall Street Journal*, November 15, 2019. Viewed January 18, 2020, at https://www.wsj.com/articles/how-google-interferes-with-its-search-algorithms-and-changes-your-results-11573823753.

Grove, Thomas, and Sara Germano. "Putin Blasts Olympic Committee for Banning Russia From 2018 Games." *Wall Street Journal*, December 6, 2017. Viewed November 20, 2017. https://www.wsj.com/articles/russia-voices-regret-over-2018-winter-olympics-ban-1512558515.

The Guardian. "China Internet Regulator Slams Google's Certificate Refusal." April 2, 2015. Viewed May 2016 at https://www.theguardian.com/technology/2015/apr/02/china-internet-regulator-slams-googles-certificate-refusal.

Gupta, Anti, Brigadier. Winning Without Fighting: China's Video War Fails." *Indian Defence Review*, January 9, 2021. http://www.indiandefencereview.com/news/winning-without-fighting-chinas-video-war-fails/.

Hamilton, Clive, and Marlene Ohlberg. *Hidden Hand: Exposing How the Chinese Communist Party is Reshaping the World*. London: Oneworld Books, 2020, 22–26.

Han, Bochen. "How Much Should We Read Into China's New 'Core Socialist Values.'" Council on Foreign Relations, July 6, 2016. Viewed January 2020 at https://www.cfr.org/blog/how-much-should-we-read-chinas-new-core-socialist-values.

Hayden, Michael. "Interview Regarding Edward Snowden, Cyber Security, and Transparency." *Australian Financial Review*, July 2013.

Herasimenka, Aliaksandr. *Belarus*. Case study within *Industrialized Disinformation: 2020 Global Inventory of Organized Social Media Manipulation*, January 14, 2021. https://comprop.oii.ox.ac.uk/wp-content/uploads/sites/127/2021/01/Cyber-Troop-Belarus-2020.pdf.

Herber, Patric. "Search Engines." *Mashable*, October 22, 2007. Viewed August 21, 2020, at https://mashable.com/2007/10/22/140-search-engines/#:~:text=Search%2C%20the%20holy%20grail%20that,is%20still%20coveted.

Hickey, Adam S. "Election Interference: Ensuring Law Enforcement Is Equipped to Target Those Seeking to Do Harm." Testimony before Senate Judiciary Committee, June 12, 2018.

Hickey, Adam S. "Securing America's Elections Part II: Oversight of Government Agencies." Testimony before House Judiciary Committee, October 22, 2019. Viewed December 1, 2020, at https://www.justice.gov/opa/speech/deputy-assistant-attorney-general-adam-s-hickey-testifies-house-judiciary-committee.

Hille, Kathrin, and Victor Mallet. "China Accuses France of Illegally Sailing Warship in Taiwan Strait." *Financial Times*, April 25, 2019. Viewed September 25, 2020, at https://www.ft.com/content/12f4ff22-674d-11e9-9adc-98bf1d35a056.

Horton, Chris. "Taiwan's Status Is a Geopolitical Absurdity." *The Atlantic*, July 8, 2019. Viewed August 14, 2019, at https://www.theatlantic.com/international/archive/2019/07/taiwans-status-geopolitical-absurdity/593371/.

Hovland, Carl I., Irving Janis, and Harold H. Kelly. *Communication and Persuasion*. New Haven: Yale University Press, 1953. As shown in Richard D. Rieke, and Malcolm O. Sillars. *Argumentation and the Decision-Making Process*. New York: John Wiley & Sons, 1975, 144–155.

Howard, Philip. "Social Media Manipulation by Political Actors an Industrial Scale Problem." Oxford University report, January 13, 2021. Viewed January 13, 2021, at https://www.ox.ac.uk/news/2021-01-13-social-media-manipulation-political-actors-industrial-scale-problem-oxford-report.

Huawei Cyber Security Evaluation Centre (HCSEC). Oversight Board Annual Report, 2019. A report to the National Security Adviser of the United Kingdom, March 2019, pp. 3, 7.

Hubert, Richard S. R. "The OWI Saipan Operation." The Official Report to the U.S. Information Service, Washington 1946. https://www.cia.gov/static/dd7ad3b-72f8a2a23244a734857a35b09/Information-War-in-Pacific.pdf.

Hui, Mary. "China Has Completed Its Takeover of Hong Kong's Legislature." *Quartz*, November 11, 2020. Viewed December 24, 2020, at https://qz.com/1931705/china-exerts-its-control-over-hong-kongs-legislative-council/.

Jackson, James K. "The Committee on Foreign Investment in the United States (CFIUS)." Congressional Research Service, February 14, 2020. Viewed January 5, 2021, at https://fas.org/sgp/crs/natsec/RL33388.pdf.

Jenkins, Simon. "The World Is Rocked by Protest—But Does Taking to the Streets Ever Work?" *The Guardian*. Viewed October 30, 2020, at https://www.theguardian.com/commentisfree/2020/oct/30/demonstrations-protest-party-minsk-sao-paulo-protesters.

Jennings, Peter. "Australia Is Not the Only Country Asking Questions About the Origins Of Coronavirus, and China Is Not Happy." The Guardian, May 15, 2020. Viewed November 6, 2020, at https://www.theguardian.com/commentisfree/2020/may/15/australia-is-not-the-only-country-asking-questions-about-the-origins-of-coronavirus-and-china-is-not-happy.

Joint Statement from the ODNI, DOJ, FBI and DHS: Combating Foreign Influence in U.S. Elections. October 19, 2018. https://www.dni.gov/index.php/newsroom/press-releases/item/1915-joint-statement-from-the-odni-doj-fbi-and-dhs-combating-foreign-influence-in-u-s-elections.

Joint Statement from the Department of Homeland Security and Office of the Director of National Intelligence on Election Security. October 7, 2016. https://www.dhs.gov/news/2016/10/07/joint-statement-department-homeland-security-and-office-director-national.

Karimi, Nasser, and Jon Gambrell. "Iran Says Israel Killed Military Nuclear Scientist Remotely." Associated Press, November 30, 2020. https://apnews.com/article/iran-israel-killed-mohsen-fakhrizadeh-88c2173048f77695af864d2055af54c6.

Katz, Justin. "Biden Promises 'Overwhelming Focus' on Hack Recovery." *Federal Computer Week (FCW)*, December 22, 2020.

Kelion, Leo. "Huawei 5G Kit Must Be Removed from UK by 2027." BBC News, July 14, 2020. Viewed December 14, 2020. https://www.bbc.com/news/technology-53403793.

Kerbaj, Richard. "Russia Steps Up Cyber-Attacks on UK." *The Times*, February 12, 2017. Viewed November 22, 2020. https://www.thetimes.co.uk/article/russia-steps-up-cyber-attacks-on-uk-rl262pnlb.

Koerner, Brendan. "Inside the Cyberattack That Shocked the U.S. Government." *Wired*, October 23, 2016. Viewed October 10, 2020, at https://www.wired.com/2016/10/inside-cyberattack-shocked-us-government/.

Kofman, Michael, Katya Migacheva, Brian Nichiporuk, Andrew Radin, Olesya Tkacheva, and Jenny Oberholtzer. "Lessons from Russia's Operations in Crimea and Eastern Ukraine." RAND Corporation, 2017, p. 90.

Krebs, Brian. "U.S. Treasury, Commerce Depts. Hacked Through SolarWinds Compromise." *Krebs on Security*, December 14, 2020. https://krebsonsecurity.com/2020/12/u-s-treasury-commerce-depts-hacked-through-SolarWindss-compromise/.

Krebs, Brian. "Who Else Was Hit by the RSA Attackers?" Krebs on Security, October 2011. https://krebsonsecurity.com/2011/10/who-else-was-hit-by-the-RSA;attackers/.

Kubota, Yoko, and Liza Lin. "Beijing Orders Agencies to Swap Out Foreign Tech for Chinese Gear." *Wall Street Journal,* December 9, 2019. https://www.wsj.com/articles/beijing-orders-agencies-to-swap-out-foreign-tech-for-chinese-gear-11575921277.

Kumar, Mohit. "How to Hack WiFi Password Easily Using New Attack On WPA/WPA2." November 25, 2018. Viewed January 25, 2020, at https://thehackernews.com/2018/08/how-to-hack-wifi-password.html.

Kumkale, Tarcan, Dolores Albarracin, and Paul J. Seignoourel. "The Effects of Source Credibility in the Presence or Absence of Prior Attitudes: Implications for the Design of Persuasive Communication Campaigns." *Journal of Applied Social Psychology,* June 1, 2010.

Lapin, Denis, Olga Pavlova, Bianca Britton, and Sarah Dean. "Film Director Oleg Sentsov and MH17 Suspect Among Those Freed in Russia-Ukraine Prisoner Swap." CNN, September 7, 2019.

Lapowsky, Issie. "How Cambridge Analytica Sparked the Great Privacy Awakening." *Wired,* March 17, 2019. https://www.wired.com/story/cambridge-analytica-facebook-privacy-awakening/; and "The Man Who Saw the Dangers of Cambridge Analytica Years Ago." *Wired,* June 19, 2018. https://www.wired.com/story/the-man-who-saw-the-dangers-of-cambridge-analytica/.

Layton, Roslyn, PhD. "Stealing from States: China's Power Play in IT Contracts." *China Tech Threat,* March 20, 2020. Viewed January 3, 2021, at https://chinatechthreat.com/wp-content/uploads/2020/02/CTT-Report-Stealing-From-States-Chinas-Power-Play-in-IT-Contracts.pdf.

Lee, Timothy B. U.S. Indicts Huawei for Stealing T-Mobile Robot Arm, Selling U.S. Tech to Iran." *ARS Technica,* January 28, 2019. Viewed December 1, 2020, at https://arstechnica.com/tech-policy/2019/01/us-indicts-huawei-for-stealing-t-mobile-robot-selling-us-tech-to-iran/.

Leetaru, Kalev. "Social Media Companies Collect So Much Data Even They Can't Remember All the Ways They Surveil Us." *Forbes,* October 25, 2018. Viewed January 22, 2021, at https://www.forbes.com/sites/kalevleetaru/2018/10/25/social-media-companies-collect-so-much-data-even-they-cant-remember-all-the-ways-they-surveil-us/?sh=77b-d78ac7d0b.

Li Xan Wong, Karen, and Amy Shields Dobson. "We're Just Data: Exploring China's Social Credit System in Relation to Digital Platform Ratings Cultures in Westernized Democracies." *Sage Journals,* June 18, 2019. Viewed January 15, 2021, at https://journals.sagepub.com/doi/full/10.1177/2059436419856090.

Li, Rouhan and Ayoung Suh. "Factors Influencing Information credibility on Social Media Platforms: Evidence from Facebook Pages, Information Systems International Conference (ISICO20)." City University of Hong Kong, 2015. Viewed September 10, 2020, at https://scholars.cityu.edu.hk/files/28155280/Factors_Influencing_Information_credibility_on_Social_Media_Platforms_Evidence_from_Facebook_Pages.pdf.

Library of Congress History. "Remember the Maine!" https://www.loc.gov/item/today-in-history/february-15/.

Lozano, Alicia Victoria. "Secretary of State Pompeo Says Hack Was 'Pretty Clearly' Russian." NBC News, December 19, 2020. https://www.nbcnews.com/news/us-news/secretary-state-pompeo-says-hack-was-pretty-clearly-russian-n1251798.

Luce, Edward. Editorial. *Financial Times,* December 3, 2020.

Luce, Edward. "How Money Laundering Is Poisoning American Democracy." *Financial Times,* November 28, 2019.

Lynch, Colum, and Robbie Gramer. "Outfoxed and Outgunned: How China Routed the U.S. in a U.N. Agency." *Foreign Policy,* October 23, 2019. Viewed November 24, 2020, at https://foreignpolicy.com/2019/10/23/china-united-states-fao-kevin-moley/.

MacFarquhar, Neil. "Playing on Kansas City Radio: Russian Propaganda." *New York Times,* February 3, 2020, https://www.nytimes.com/2020/02/13/us/russian-propaganda-radio.html.

Mandia, Kevin. "Transcript: Kevin Mandia on 'Face the Nation.'" CBS News, December 20, 2020.

Marcus, Lauri Lowenthan. "Jews Must Register Flyer in Ukraine and Echo of Babi Yar." *Jewish Press*, April 18, 2014.

Marczak, Bill, and Nicholas Weaver, et al. "China's Great Cannon." Citizen Lab, Munk School of Global Affairs, University of Toronto, April 10, 2015. Viewed August 2019 at https://citizenlab.ca/2015/04/chinas-great-cannon/.

Markham, David. "The Dimensions of Source Credibility in Television Newscasters." *Journal of Communication*, 18 (1968), pp. 57–64.

Mazarr, Michael J. *Understanding Deterrence.* Santa Monica, CA: RAND Corporation, 2018. Viewed December 23, 2020, at https://www.rand.org/pubs/perspectives/PE295.html.

McCauley, Kevin N. "Russian Influence Campaigns Against the West. North Carolina: self-published, 2016, 87–88, 92–95.

McCroskey, James C. *An Introduction to Rhetorical Communication*, 2nd ed. Englewood Cliffs, NJ: Prentice-Hall,1972, 63–68.

McLaren, Richard, Dr. "McLaren Independent Investigation Report, Part 1." World Anti-Doping Agency, July 18, 2016. https://www.wada-ama.org/en/resources/doping-control-process/mclaren-independent-investigation-report-part-i.

McWhorter, Dan. "Mandiant Exposes APT1—One of China's Cyber Espionage Units & Releases 3,000 Indicators." *FireEye*, February 19, 2013. https://www.fireeye.com/blog/threat-research/2013/02/mandiant-exposes-apt1-chinas-cyber-espionage-units.html.

Meyer, Carl. "Are Chinese Spies getting an Easy Ride?" *Embassy*, July 2011. Viewed November 23, 2020, at http://www.embassymag.ca/page/printpage/spies-07-27-2011.

Milton, Joyce. *The Yellow Kids: Foreign Correspondents in the Heyday of Yellow Journalism.* New York: Harper Perennial, 1990, 67.

Mishra, Sahil. "How the Global Push-back Against China Is Gathering Pace." *The Taiwan Times*, September 8, 2020. Viewed November 6, 2020, at https://thetaiwantimes.com/how-the-global-push-back-against-china-is-gathering-pace/5153.

Mitchell, Amy. "Americans Still Prefer Watching to Reading the News—and Mostly Still Through Television." Pew Research, December 3, 2018. Viewed at http://www.journalism.org/2018/12/03/americans-still-prefer-watching-to-reading-the-news-and-mostly-still-through-television/.

Mitchell, Anna, and Larry Diamond. "China's Surveillance State Should Scare Everyone." *The Atlantic*, February 2, 2018. Viewed December 15, 2020, at https://www.theatlantic.com/international/archive/2018/02/china-surveillance/552203/.

Morrison/Foerster. "Client Alert: CFIUS Means Business, Unwinding Non-Notified Transactions and Penalizing Non-Compliance with Mitigation Agreements." Morrison & Foerster LLP. https://www.mofo.com/resources/insights/190415-cfius-mitigation-agreements.html.

Mueller, Special Counsel Robert S. Report on the Investigation into Russian Interference in the 2016 Presidential Election." U.S. Department of Justice, March 2019, p. 167.

Mullen, Jethro. "China Blocks New York Times Website After Story on Leader's Family Wealth." CNN, October 26, 2012. Viewed January 5, 2014, at https://www.cnn.com/2012/10/26/world/asia/china-times-website-blocked/index.html.

Murphy, Simon. "UK Report on Russian Interference: Key Points Explained." *The Guardian*, July 21, 2020. Viewed September 29, 2020, at https://www.theguardian.com/world/2020/jul/21/just-what-does-the-uk-russia-report-say-key-points-explained.

Myers, Steven Lee. "China Spins Tale that the U.S. Army Started the Coronavirus Epidemic." *New York Times*, March 13, 2020. Viewed July 15, 2020, at https://www.nytimes.com/2020/03/13/world/asia/coronavirus-china-conspiracy-theory.html.

Myers, Steven, and Paul Mozur. "China Is Waging a Disinformation War Against Hong Kong Protesters." *New York Times*, August 13, 2019.

Nakashima, Ellen, et al. "U.S. Government Concludes Iran Was Behind Threatening Emails Sent to Democrats." *Washington Post*, October 10, 2020.

Neely, Amber. "Apple Supplier O-film Tech Accused of Human Rights Violations in China." *Apple Insider*, July 7, 2020. Viewed November 6, 2020, at https://appleinsider.com/articles/20/07/20/apple-supplier-o-film-tech-accused-of-human-rights-violations-in-china#:~:text=Apple%20supplier%20O%2Dfilm%20Tech%20accused%20of%20human%20rights%20violations%20i.

Neufeld, Jennie. "Read the Full Transcript of the Helsinki Press Conference." NPR, July 17, 2018. Viewed November 1, 2019, at https://www.npr.org/2018/07/16/629462401/transcript-president-trump-and-russian-president-putins-joint-press-conference.

Nieves, Alexander. "Poll: 60 Percent of Americans Say Russia Meddled in 2016 Election." Politico, July 18 2018, https://www.politico.com/story/2018/07/18/poll-russia-meddling-election-mueller-investigation-730529

Nimmo, Ben."#PutinAtWar: WADA Hack Shows Kremlin Full-Spectrum Approach." The Atlantic Council Digital Forensic Research Lab, October 14, 2018. https://medium.com/dfrlab/putinatwar-wada-hack-shows-kremlin-full-spectrum-approach-21dd495f2e91.

Nimmo, Ben, C. Shawn Eib, and L. Tamora. "Cross-Platform Spam Network Targeted Hong Kong Protests." *Graphika*, September 21, 2019. August 3, 2020, at https://public-assets.graphika.com/reports/graphika_report_spamouflage.pdf.

Nimmo, Ben, C. Shawn Eib, et al. "Spamouflage Dragon Goes to America." *Graphika*, August 2020. https://public-assets.graphika.com/reports/graphika_report_spamouflage_dragon_goes_to_america.pdf.

Nimmo, Ben. "Putin's Media are Pushing Britain for the Brexit." *The Interpreter*, Febrary 12, 2016; Ministry of Foreign Affairs of the Russian Federation, Tweet, https://twitter.com/mfa—russia/status/748231648936869888, June 29, 2016.

Nixon, Mattew. "Leaked Report Says Russian May Have Affected Brexit Referendum Result." *The New European*, November 18, 2019.

Noble, Safiya Umoja. *Algorithms of Oppression*. New York: NYU Press, New York, 18.

Northern Miner Staff. "Chinese Rare Earth Metals Surge in Price." December 3, 2020. Viewed December 4, 2020, at https://www.mining.com/chinese-rare-earth-metals-surge-in-price/.

Office of the Director of National Intelligence. "Background to Assessing Russian Activities and Intentions in Recent U.S. Elections: The Analytic Process and Cyber Incident Attribution." January 2017. https://www.dni.gov/files/documents/ICA_2017_01.pdf.

Office of the Historian, U.S. Department of State. "U.S. Diplomacy and Yellow Journalism, 1895–1898." https://history.state.gov/milestones/1866-1898/yellow-journalism.

Palmer, James. "Hong Kong's Violence Will Get Worse." *Foreign Policy*, November 11, 2019. Viewed September 7, 2020, at https://foreignpolicy.com/2019/11/11/police-killing-protests-beijing-lam-xi-hong-kong-violence-will-get-worse/.

Pancevski, Bojan, and Matthew Dalton. "Spy Case Linked to China Raises Red Flags for Poland and the U.S." *Wall Street Journal*, January 24, 2019. https://www.wsj.com/articles/spy-case-linked-to-china-raises-red-flags-for-poland-and-the-u-s-11548357192.

Panettieri, Joe. "Huawei: Banned and Permitted in Which Countries." *Channele2e*, updated December 15, 2020. https://www.channele2e.com/business/enterprise/huawei-banned-in-which-countries/2/.

Parkinson, Joe, and Georgi Kantchev. "Document: Russia Uses Rigged Polls, Fake News to Sway Foreign Elections." *Wall Street Journal*, March 23, 2017. https://www.wsj.com/articles/how-does-russia-meddle-in-elections-look-at-bulgaria-1490282352.

Partlett, William. "Can Russia Keep Faking Democracy?" The Brookings Institution, May 22, 2012. Viewed January 2020 at https://www.brookings.edu/opinions/can-russia-keep-faking-democracy/.

Patrick, Margot, and Julie Steinberg. "Some Global Banks Break Ties with Huawei." *Wall Street Journal*, December 20, 2018. https://www.wsj.com/articles/some-global-banks-break-ties-with-huawei-11545321306.

Paul, Christopher, and Miriam Matthews. "The Russian "Firehose of Falsehood" Propaganda Model: Why It Might Work and Options to Counter It." Santa Monica, CA: RAND Corporation, 2016. Viewed October 2020 at https://www.rand.org/pubs/perspectives/PE198.html.

PEN America. "Made in Hollywood, Censored by Beijing 2020. Viewed November 9, 2020, at https://pen.org/report/made-in-hollywood-censored-by-beijing/.

Petty, Richard E., and John T. Cacioppo. "The Elaboration Likelihood Model of Persuasion." *Advances in Experimental Social Psychology*, vol. 19, 1986.

Pham, Sherisse. "U.S. Judge Rejects Huawei Lawsuit Challenging a Ban on Its Products." CNN Business, February 19, 2020. Viewed December 8, 2020, at https://www.cnn.com/2020/02/19/tech/huawei-us-lawsuit-rejected/index.html.

Phillips, Macon. "TooManyWebsites.gov." White House press release, June 13, 2011. https://obamawhitehouse.archives.gov/blog/2011/06/13/toomanywebsitesgov.

Pirseyedi, Bobi. *Arms Control and Iranian Foreign Policy*. New York: Routledge: 2013, 120.

Polityuk, Pavel. "Lukashenko Rivals Unite Behind Blogger's Wife to Fight Belarus Election." *Reuters*, July 16, 2020.Viewed September 22, 2020, at https://www.reuters.com/article/us-belarus-election/lukashenko-rivals-unite-behind-bloggers-wife-to-fight-belarus-election-idUSKCN24H2C2.

Pollock, John. "Russian Disinformation Technology." *MIT Technology Review*, April 13, 2017. Viewed October 8, 2019, at https://www.technologyreview.com/s/604084/russian-disinformation-technology/.

Polonski, Vyacheslav. "Impact of Social Media on the Outcome of the EU Referendum." EU Referendum Analysis 2016, Loughboro University, June 2016.

Popken, Ben. "Russian Trolls Duped Global Media and Nearly 40 Celebrities." NBC News, November 3, 2017. Viewed November 30, 2020, at https://www.nbcnews.com/tech/social-media/trump-other-politicians-celebs-shared-boosted-russian-troll-tweets-n817036.

Postman, Neil, and Charles Weingartner. "Teaching as a Subversive Activity." New York: Dell Publishing, 1969, 3.

Potter, Robert, and David Robinson. "Exposing Mystery and Menace of Chinese Communist Party Membership." *The Australian*, December 18, 2020. https://www.theaustralian.com.au/commentary/exposing-mystery-and-menace-of-chinese-communist-party-membership/news-story/ef3e79d1e3d9022388f5e4fdcce14895.

U.S. Justice Department. "U.S. Charges Russian GRU Officers with International Hacking and Related Influence and Disinformation Operations." Press release, October 4, 2018, https://www.justice.gov/opa/pr/us-charges-russian-gru-officers-international-hacking-and-related-influence-and.

Rachman, Gideon. "Chinese Censorship Is Spreading Beyond Its Borders." *The Financial Times*, October 14, 2019. https://www.ft.com/content/cda1efbc-ee5a-11e9-ad1e-4367d8281195.

Ramey, Corinne, and Kate O'Keeffe. "China's Huawei Charged with Racketeering, Stealing Trade Secrets." *Wall Street Journal*, February 13, 2020. Viewed December 4, 2020, at https://www.wsj.com/articles/chinas-huawei-charged-with-racketeering-11581618336?st=-9r5u2ts82s6o4lx&reflink=article_email_share.

Ratcliffe, John. "Trump Administration to Increase Intelligence Spending." Fox News, December 7 and 8, 2020. https://www.foxnews.com/transcript/ratcliffe-warns-of-china-using-gene-editing-to-boost-military.

Rauhala, Emily. "Huawei Executive Wanted by U.S. Faces Fraud Charges Related to Iran Sanctions, Could Face 30 Years in Prison." *Washington Post*, December 7, 2018.

Redden, Elizabeth. "Closing Confucius Institutes." *Inside Higher Education*, January 9, 2019. Viewed October 7, 2020, at https://www.insidehighered.com/news/2019/01/09/colleges-move-close-chinese-government-funded-confucius-institutes-amid-increasing.

Reichert, Corinne, and Laura Hautala. "Russia Blamed for Solarwinds Hack in Joint FBI, NSA And CISA Statement." CNET, January 5, 2021. https://www.cnet.com/tech/services-and-software/fbi-nsa-and-cisa-say-solarwinds-hack-was-likely-of-russian-origin/.

Reike, Richard D. and Malcom O. Sillars. *Argumentation and the Decision Making Process*. New York: John Wiley, 1975, 139–141.

Reuters News, republished by CNBC News. "Families: Investigation Found MH17 Downed from Pro-Russia Rebel Held Territory." September 28, 2016, https://www.cnbc.com/2016/09/28/families-investigation-found-mh17-downed-from-pro-russia-rebel-held-territory.html.

Reuters Staff. "Huawei Pleads Not Guilty to New U.S. Criminal Charges in 2018 Case." *Reuters*, March 4, 2020. Viewed May 10, 2020, at https://www.reuters.com/article/us-china-huawei-tech/huawei-pleads-not-guilty-to-new-u-s-criminal-charges-in-2018-case-idUSKBN20R2Y8.

Robertson, Jordan, and Michael Riley. "The Big Hack: How China Used a Tiny Chip to Infiltrate U.S. Companies" *Bloomberg Business*, October 4, 2018.

Rogers, Admiral Michael S. "Statement Before the Senate Committee on Armed Services." C-Span, May 9, 2017.

Romm, Tony, and Elizabeth Dwoskin. "Twitter Purged More than 70,000 Accounts Affiliated with Qanon Following Capitol Riot." *Washington Post*, January 2021. https://www.washingtonpost.com/technology/2021/01/11/trump-twitter-ban/.

Romo, Vanessa. "Facebook Removed Nearly 3.4 Billion Fake Accounts in 6 Months." NPR, May 23, 2019. Viewed September 28, 2019, at https://www.npr.org/2019/05/23/726353723/facebook-removed-nearly-3-4-billion-fake-accounts-in-last-six-months.

Rosentiel, Tom. "Trends in Public Opinion about the War in Iraq, 2003–2007." Pew Research Center, March 2007. Viewed November 3, 2020, at https://www.pewresearch.org/2007/03/15/trends-in-public-opinion-about-the-war-in-iraq-20032007/.

Rosner, Max, and Esteban Ortiz-Ospina. "Literacy." OurWorldInData.org, viewed January 2020. https://ourworldindata.org/literacy.

Rothschild, Neal, and Sara Fisher. "NY Post Story Goes Massive on Social Media Despite Crackdowns." *Axios*, October 20, 2020. Viewed October 30, 2020, at https://www.axios.com/new-york-post-hunter-biden-facebook-twitter-censor-bf8d9f32-f8cb-444e-bc12-c3b5e8694e84.html.

Rove, Karl. "Trump's Appeal Rings Hollow at CPAC." *Wall Street Journal*, March 3, 2021. Viewed March 3, 2021, at https://www.wsj.com/articles/trumps-appeal-rings-hollow-at-cpac-11614812740.

RT. Unattributed article, April 28, 2018. Viewed September 21, 2019. https://www.rt.com/sport/425395-worst-doping-cheaters-wada/. Article no longer available online.

RT. "WADA's Controversial Informant Rodchenkov Changes Look for Camera, Thinks Kremlin Is After Him." February 9, 2018. https://www.rt.com/news/418374-rodchenkov-interview-60-minutes/.

Ruan, Lotus, Jeffrey Knockel, and Masashi Crete-Nishihata. "Censored Contagion: How Information on the Coronavirus is Managed on Chinese Social Media." The Citizen Lab, March 3, 2020. Viewed October, 8, 2020, at https://citizenlab.ca/2020/03/censored-contagion-how-information-on-the-coronavirus-is-managed-on-chinese-social-media/.

Sabbagh, Dan, and Luke Harding. "PM Accused of Cover-Up Over Report on Russian Meddling in UK Politics." *The Guardian*, January 5, 2021, at https://www.theguardian.com/politics/2019/nov/04/no-10-blocks-russia-eu-referendum-report-until-after-election.

Sanders-Zakre, Alicia. "Russia Charged with OPCW Hacking Attempt." *Arms Control Association*, November 2018. Viewed September 20, 2020, at https://www.armscontrol.org/act/2018-11/news/russia-charged-opcw-hacking-attempt.

Sanger, David E., and Nichole Perlroth. "N.S.A. Breached Chinese Servers Seen as Security Threat." *New York Times*, March 22, 2014. https://www.nytimes.com/2014/03/23/world/asia/nsa-breached-chinese-servers-seen-as-spy-peril.html.

Sanger, David E. *The Perfect Weapon*. New York: Crown Publishing Group, 2018, 7–12.

SANS News. "Stolen COVID Data Were Altered Before They Were Leaked." *Security and Network Security*, January 19, 2021. Subscription required: newsbites@email.sans.org.

Schachter, Stanley. *Biographical Memoirs*, vol. 64. The National Academies of Sciences, Engineering, and Medicine. Washington, D.C.: National Academy Press; 1994.

Schank, Roger C. *Tell Me a Story*. New York: Charles Scribner's Sons, 1990, 30–31.

Schell, Orville (ed.). *China's Influence and American Interests: Promoting Constructive Vigilance*. Stanford, CA: Hoover Institution Press, 2018.

Schroeder, Pete. "U.S. Congress Bans Anonymous Shell Companies." *Reuters*, December 20, 2020. Viewed January 21, 2021, at https://www.reuters.com/article/us-usa-congress-banks/u-s-congress-bans-anonymous-shell-companies-idUSKBN28L2NV.

Schwirtz, Michael, and Ellen Barry. "A Spy Story: Sergei Skripal Was a Little Fish. He Had a Big Enemy." *New York Times*, September 9, 2018. Viewed November 18, 2020, at https://www.nytimes.com/2018/09/09/world/europe/sergei-skripal-russian-spy-poisoning.html.

Schwirtz, Michael. "A Year After Skripal Poisoning, Russia Offers Defiant Face to Britain and the West." *New York Times*, March 4, 2019. Viewed August 24, 2019, https://www.nytimes.com/2019/03/04/world/europe/russia-skripal-poisoning-britain.html.

Scislowska, Monika. "2 Belarusian Journalists Sent to Prison for Covering Protest."

Associated Press, February 18, 2021. https://apnews.com/article/alexander-lukashen-ko-belarus-journalists-elections-minsk-d5abad8bdc2909cb9327d77289da74f0?utm_source=Pew+Research+Center&utm_campaign=63a9d20178-EMAIL_CAM-PAIGN_2021_02_18_02_14&utm_medium=email&utm_term=0_3e953b9b70-63a9d20178-399351245.

Searight, Amy. "Countering China's Influence Operations: Lessons from Australia." Center for Strategic and International Studies, May 8, 2020. Viewed October 7, 2020, at https://www.csis.org/analysis/countering-chinas-influence-operations-lessons-australia.

Securities and Exchange Commission, press release, November 17, 2016.

Seibt, Sebastian. "Is China Provoking a Diplomatic Fight with Australia?" *France 24*, January 12, 2020. Viewed November 4, 2020, at https://www.france24.com/en/asia-pacific/20201201-is-china-provoking-a-diplomatic-fight-with-australia.

Seldin, Jeff. "Outgoing U.S. Intel Chief Warns China Seeking Global Domination." *Voice of America*, December 3, 2020. Viewed December 4, 2020, at https://www.voanews.com/usa/outgoing-us-intel-chief-warns-china-seeking-global-domination.

Seppelt, Hajo. "Geheimsache Doping—Wie Russland Seine Sieger Macht." WDR/ARD Sportschau, 2014. News documentary.

Shahbaz, Adrian, Allie Funk, and Andrea Hackl. "User Privacy or Cyber Sovereignty?" *Freedom House*, special report, 2020. Viewed December 1, 2020, at https://freedomhouse.org/report/special-report/2020/user-privacy-or-cyber-sovereignty#footnote1_3ojp0cs.

Shearer, Elisa. "Lessons Learned from More Than 20 Years of Asking About Americans' Online News Habits." Pew Research Center, July 1, 2019. Viewed July 3, 2019, at https://medium.com/pew-research-center-decoded/lessons-learned-from-more-than-20-years-of-asking-about-americans-online-news-habits-ba4b0dee578a.

Shelton, Kelly. "The Value of Search Results Rankings." *Forbes*, October 2017. Viewed September 20, 2020, at https://www.forbes.com/sites/forbesagencycouncil/2017/10/30/the-value-of-search-results-rankings/?sh=61818d4d44d3.

Shepardson, David. "U.S. Agency Votes 5–0 to Bar China's Huawei, ZTE From Government Subsidy Program." *Reuters*, November 22, 2019. Viewed April 24, 2020, at https://www.reuters.com/article/us-usa-china-huawei-tech/u-s-agency-votes-5-0-to-bar-chinas-huawei-zte-from-government-subsidy-program-idUSKBN1XW1TC.

Sheperd, Brittany. "Biden Says U.S. Will 'Respond in Kind' for Solarwinds Hack Blamed on Russia." Yahoo News, December 22, 2020. https://news.yahoo.com/biden-says-us-will-respond-in-kind-for-solar-wind-hacking-blamed-on-russia-215116852.html.

Sherlock, Stephen. "Hong Kong and the Transfer to China: Issues and Prospects." Parliament of Australia, Current Issues Brief 33, 1996–97, 6–7. Viewed January 23, 2021, at https://www.aph.gov.au/About_Parliament/Parliamentary_Departments/Parliamentary_Library/Publications_Archive/CIB/CIB9697/97cib33.

Shields, Todd. "FCC Moves Against China Telecom and Huawei." *Bloomberg Technology*, December 10, 2020.

Shipler, David K. "Israeli Jets Destroy Iraqi Atomic Reactor; Attack Condemned by U.S. and Arab Nations." *New York Times*, June 9, 1981. Viewed November 22, 2020, at https://www.nytimes.com/1981/06/09/world/israeli-jets-destroy-iraqi-atomic-reactor-attack-condemned-us-arab-nations.html.

Shirvanian, Maliheh, Nitesh Saxena, and Dibya Mukhopadhyay. "Short Voice Imitation Man-in-the-middle Attacks on Crypto Phones: Defeating Humans and Machines." January 1, 2018, 311–333.

Singman, Brooke. "Barr: DOJ Yet to Find Widespread Voter Fraud that Could Have Changed 2020 Election." Fox News, December 2, 2020.

Singman, Brooke. "DNI Declassifies Brennan Notes, CIA Memo on Hillary Clinton 'Stirring Up' Scandal Between Trump, Russia." Fox News, October 7, 2020. https://www.foxnews.com/politics/dni-brennan-notes-cia-memo-clinton.

Smyth, Jamie, and Christian Shepherd. "Chinese App WeChat Censors Australian PM Scott Morrison's Post." *Financial Times*, December 3, 2020. viewed at https://www.ft.com/content/9c5376e5-5d94-4942-ba3c-e553a75508cb

Standish, Reid. "China's Path Forward is Getting Bumpy." *The Atlantic*, October 1, 2019.

Viewed November 6, 2020, at https://www.theatlantic.com/international/archive/2019/10/china-belt-road-initiative-problems-kazakhstan/597853/.

Stelzenmuller, Constanze. "The Impact of Russian Interference on Germany's 2017 Elections." Brookings Institution. Testimony before the U.S. Senate Select Committee on Intelligence, June 28, 2017. https://www.brookings.edu/testimonies/the-impact-of-russian-interference-on-germanys-2017-elections/.

Straus, Jacob R. "Foreign Agents Registration Act: An Overview." Congressional Research Service, updated March 7, 2019.

Stubbs, Jack. "Hackers Steal Pfizer/Biontech COVID-19 Vaccine Data in Europe, Companies Say." *Reuters*, December 9, 2020. Viewed January 18, 2021, at https://www.reuters.com/article/us-ema-cyber/hackers-steal-pfizer-biontech-covid-19-vaccine-data-in-europe-companies-say-idUSKBN28J2Q7.

Stubbs, Jack, Joseph Menn, and Christopher Bing. "Inside the West's Failed Fight Against China's 'Cloud Hopper' Hackers." *Reuters*, June 26, 2020. https://www.reuters.com/investigates/special-report/china-cyber-cloudhopper/.

Sudworth, John. "China's Hidden Camps." BBC News, October 24, 2018. Viewed September 5, 2019, at https://www.bbc.co.uk/news/resources/idt-sh/China_hidden_camps.

"Summary, Election 2020: How Trump and Biden Compare on the Key Issues." *Wall Street Journal*, November 2, 2020.

Talley, Ian. "U.S. Steps up Pressure on China over North Korean Coal Exports." *Wall Street Journal*, December 8, 2020. Viewed December 8, 2020, at https://www.wsj.com/articles/u-s-steps-up-pressure-on-china-over-north-korean-coal-exports-11607464646?st=3ixkw-gj8d9yfw4b&reflink=article_email_share.

Tanner, Murray Scot. "Beijing's New National Intelligence Law: From Defense to Offense." *Lawfare Blog*, July 20, 2017. Viewed December 7, 2020, at https://www.lawfareblog.com/beijings-new-national-intelligence-law-defense-offense.

Timmons, Heather, Lucia Murkani, and Diane Bartz. "Trump Campaign Aide Pushed Ukraine Hacking Theory: Documents." *National Post*, November 2019. Viewed at https://nationalpost.com/pmn/news-pmn/politics-news-pmn/trump-campaign-aide-pushed-ukraine-hacking-theory-documents.

Trump, Donald. "Executive Order on Addressing the Threat Posed by WeChat, & Executive Order on Addressing the Threat Posed by TikTok." August 6, 2020. https://www.whitehouse.gov/presidential-actions/executive-order-addressing-threat-posed-wechat/; and https://www.whitehouse.gov/presidential-actions/executive-order-addressing-threat-posed-tiktok/.

Trump, Donald. "Executive Order on Securing the Information and Communications Technology and Services Supply Chain," May 15, 2019.

Tucker, Eric, and Frank Bajak. "Justice Department, Federal Court System Hit by Russian Hack." Associated Press, January 6, 2021. https://apnews.com/article/russia-hacking-justice-department-6290618f08cad5b11c4dd0263ef6820b.

Tung, Liam. "Google Boots China's Main Digital Certificate Authority CNNIC." *ZDNet*, April 2, 2015. viewed August 2016 at https://www.zdnet.com/article/google-banishes-chinas-main-digital-certificate-authority-cnnic/.

Turnbull, Malcom "Speech Introducing the National Security Legislation Amendment (Espionage and Foreign Interference) Bill 2017," Malcolmturnbull.com, December 7, 2017. https://www.malcolmturnbull.com.au/media/speech-introducing-the-national-security-legislation-amendment-espionage-an.

Ukrainian Election Task Force. *Ukrainian Election Task Force Foreign Interference in Ukraine's Democracy*, The Atlantic Council, 2019. Viewed January 4, 2020, at https://www.atlantic-council.org/wp-content/uploads/2019/05/Foreign_Interference_in_Ukraines_Election.pdf.

United Kingdom National Cyber Security Centre. "Cyber Security: Fixing the Present so We Can Worry About the Future," November 14, 2017. https://www.ncsc.gov.uk/news/cyber-security-fixing-present-so-we-can-worry-about-future.

Urban, Mark. *The Skripal Files*. New York: Henry Holt & Co., 2018, p234–243.

U.S. Army Special Operations Command. "Little Green Men: A Primer on Modern Russian

Unconventional Warfare, Ukraine 2013–2014." Fort Bragg, North Carolina: United States Army Special Operations Command, 2015.

U.S.-China Economic and Security Review Commission. Report to Congress, December 2020.

U.S. Department of Justice. Case 1:18-cr-00032-DLF, filing. https://www.justice.gov/file/1035477/download.

U.S. Department of Justice. "Chinese Telecommunications Conglomerate Huawei and Subsidiaries Charged in Racketeering Conspiracy and Conspiracy to Steal Trade Secrets." Press release, February 13, 2020. Viewed December 4, 2020, at https://www.justice.gov/usao-edny/pr/chinese-telecommunications-conglomerate-huawei-and-subsidiaries-charged-racketeering.

U.S. Department of Justice. "Chinese Telecommunications Device Manufacturer and its U.S. Affiliate Indicted for Theft of Trade Secrets, Wire Fraud, and Obstruction of Justice." Press release, January 28, 2019.

U.S. Department of Justice. "Court Finds RM Broadcasting Must Register as a Foreign Agent." Press release, May 13, 2019. Viewed February 12, 2020, https://www.justice.gov/opa/pr/court-finds-rm-broadcasting-must-register-foreign-agent.

U.S. Department of Justice. "Executive Branch Agencies Recommend the FCC Revoke and Terminate China Telecom's Authorizations to Provide International Telecommunications Services in the United States." Press release, April 9, 2020. https://www.justice.gov/opa/pr/executive-branch-agencies-recommend-fcc-revoke-and-terminate-china-telecom-s-authorizations.

U.S. Department of Justice. Indictment in the U.S. District Court for the District of Columbia. Case 1:18-cr-00215-ABJ, filed 07/13/18. Viewed at https://www.justice.gov/file/1080281/download.

U.S. Department of Justice. Indictment in the U.S. District Court for the District of Columbia. February 16, 2018, p. 25. Viewed February 16, 2018, at https://www.justice.gov/file/1035477/download.

U.S. Department of Justice. Indictment in the U.S. District Court for the District of Columbia. Internet Research Agency, February 16, 2018. Viewed at https://www.justice.gov/file/1035477/download.

U.S. Justice Department. United States District Court for the District of Columbia. *United States of America v. Victor Borisovich Netyksho, et al.*, July 13, 2018, p. 8–12. https://www.justice.gov/file/1080281/download.

U.S. Department of Justice. Indictment in U.S. District Court, Western District of Pennsylvania. *United States of America v. Yuriy Sergeyevich Andrienko, et al.* Unsealed October 15, 2020. https://www.justice.gov/opa/press-release/file/1328521/download.

U.S. Department of Justice. "Six Russian GRU Officers Charged in Connection with Worldwide Deployment of Destructive Malware and Other Disruptive Actions in Cyberspace." Press release, October 19, 2020. https://www.justice.gov/opa/pr/six-russian-gru-officers-charged-connection-worldwide-deployment-destructive-malware-and.

U.S. Department of Justice. The Grand Jury for the District of Columbia (Case 1:18-cr-00215-ABJ), 07/13/18. Viewed October 2018 at https://www.justice.gov/file/1080281/download.

U.S. Department of Justice. *United States of America v. Viktor Borisovich Netyksho, Boris Alekseyevich Antonov, Dmitriy Sergeyevich Badin, et al.* Case 1:18-cr-00215-ABJ Document 1. Filed July 13, 2018, p. 26.

U.S. Department of Justice. *United States of America v. Yuriy Sergeyevich Andrienko, et al.* Indictment, October 15, 2020. Viewed December 7, 2020, at https://www.justice.gov/opa/press-release/file/1328521/download.

U.S. Department of Justice. *United States of America v. ZTE Corporation.* Plea agreement filing to the U.S. District Court of the Northern District of Texas, Dallas Division, March 7, 2017. https://www.justice.gov/opa/press-release/file/946276/download.

U.S. Department of Justice. "ZTE Factual Resume." Filing to the U.S. District Court for the Northern District of Texas, Dallas Division, March 17, 2017. https://www.justice.gov/opa/press-release/file/946281.

U.S. Department of the Treasury Notice, Office of Foreign Assets Control Notice of OFAC Sanctions Actions Agency: Office of Foreign Assets Control, Treasury.

U.S. Election Assistance Commission website. Viewed December 4, 2020, at https://www.eac.gov/.

U.S. Securities and Exchange Commission. "JPMorgan Chase Paying $264 Million to Settle FCPA Charges." Press release, November 17, 2016.

U.S. Securities and Exchange Commission website. Viewed December 31, 2020, at https://secsearch.sec.gov/search?utf8=%3F&affiliate=secsearch&query=bots+.

U.S. Senate, Homeland Security & Government Affairs Permanent Subcommittee on Investigations. Press release, June 9, 2020. https://www.hsgac.senate.gov/subcommittees/investigations/media/portman-carper-bipartisan-report-reveals-how-three-chinese-government-owned-telecoms-operated-in-the-us-for-nearly-20-years-with-little-to-no-oversight-from-the-federal-government.

U.S. Senate. Permanent Subcommittee on Investigations. "China's Impact on The U.S. Education System." February 22, 2019. https://www.hsgac.senate.gov/imo/media/doc/PSI%20Report%20China's%20Impact%20on%20the%20US%20Education%20System.pdf.

U.S. Senate. Permanent Subcommittee on Investigations. "Threats to U.S. Networks: Oversight of Chinese Government-Owned Carriers." Staff Report, June 9, 2020, 10. https://www.hsgac.senate.gov/imo/media/doc/2020-06-09%20PSI%20Staff%20Report%20-%20Threats%20to%20U.S.%20Communications%20Networks.pdf.

U.S. Senate, Select Committee on Intelligence. *Russian Active Measure Campaigns and Interference in the 2016 U.S. Election*, vol. 3. U.S. Government Response to Russian Activities. Viewed November 2020 at https://www.intelligence.senate.gov/sites/default/files/documents/Report_Volume1.pdf.

U.S. Senate Select Committee on Intelligence. "Russian Targeting of Election Infrastructure During the 2016 Election: Summary of Initial Findings and Recommendations (May 2018)." https://www.intelligence.senate.gov/sites/default/files/documents/Report_Volume1.pdf

U.S.-China Economic & Security Review Commission. "Capability of the People's Republic of China to Conduct Cyber Warpp.re and Computer Network Exploitation." Report, October 9, 2009. https://www.uscc.gov/testimonies-speeches/chinas-approach-cyber-operations-implications-united-states-0.

Varol, Onur, Emilio Ferrara, Clayton A. Davis, Filippo Menczer, and Alessandro Flammini. "Online Human-Bot Interactions: Detection, Estimation, and Characterization." International AAAI Conference on Web and Social Media. Viewed December 24, 2020, at https://aaai.org/ocs/index.php/ICWSM/ICWSM17/paper/view/15587/14817.

Video posted by ODN News, supplied by Interior Ministry, Ukraine. https://www.youtube.com/watch?v=PsbC8yDeGUw. Comments from individual reviewers follow the story.

Vilmer, Jean-Baptiste Jeangène. "Successfully Countering Russian Electoral Interference." Center for Strategic and International Studies, June 21, 2018. https://www.csis.org/analysis/successfully-countering-russian-electoral-interference.

Vilmer, Jean-Baptiste Jeangene. "The 'Macron Leaks' Operation: A Post-Mortem." The Atlantic Council, June 2019. Viewed November 6, 2020, at https://www.atlanticcouncil.org/wp-content/uploads/2019/06/The_Macron_Leaks_Operation-A_Post-Mortem.pdf.

Volz, Dustin. "U.S. Agencies Hacked in Foreign Cyber Espionage Campaign Linked to Russia." *Wall Street Journal*, December 13, 2020. https://www.wsj.com/articles/agencies-hacked-in-foreign-cyber-espionage-campaign-11607897866?st=7hnrqwraz2u73r-r&reflink=article_email_share.

Volz, Dustin, Aruna Viswanatha, and Kate O'Keeffe. "U.S. Charges Chinese Nationals in Cyberattacks on More Than 100 Companies." *Wall Street Journal*, September 16, 2020. Viewed September 2020 at https://www.wsj.com/articles/justice-department-unseals-indictments-alleging-chinese-hacking-against-u-s-international-firms-11600269024.

Walker, Christopher, and Jessica Ludwig. "The Meaning of Sharp Power." *Foreign Affairs*, November 16, 2017. Viewed October 12, 2020, at https://www.foreignaffairs.com/articles/china/2017-11-16/meaning-sharp-power.

Wallace, Chris. "Chris Wallace Interviews Russian President Vladimir Putin." Fox News, 2018. https://www.foxnews.com/media/fox-news-nabs-first-emmy-nomination-for-chris-wallaces-interview-with-vladimir-putin.

Wallace, Chris. "Chris Wallace Grills Pelosi on Her Own Disregard for Social Distancing." Video originally aired on Fox News. Viewed December 3, 2020, at https://www.youtube.com/watch?v=R2CJ0PNLNKw.

Wang, Vivian, and Edward Wong. "U.S. Hits Back at China with New Visa Restrictions on Journalists." *New York Times*, May 9, 2020. Viewed November 20, 2020, at https://www.nytimes.com/2020/05/09/us/politics/china-journalists-us-visa-crackdown.html.

Warrick, Joby. "Iran's Underground Nuclear Sites Not Immune to U.S. Bunker-Busters, Experts Say." *Washington Post*, February 29, 2012. https://www.washingtonpost.com/world/national-security/experts-irans-underground-nuclear-sites-not-immune-to-us-bunker-busters/2012/02/24/gIQAzWaghR_story.html?noredirect=on&utm_term=.aff40eb0df08.

Weaver, Mathew. "MH17 Crash Report: Dutch Investigators Confirm Buk Missile Hit Plane." *The Guardian*, October 13, 2015. https://www.theguardian.com/world/live/2015/oct/13/mh17-crash-report-ukraine-live-updates.

Weaver, Nicolas. "A Close Look at the NSA's Most Powerful Internet Attack Tool." *Wired*, March 13, 2014. Viewed August 2019 at https://www.wired.com/2014/03/quantum/.

Wee, Sui-lee. "Giving In to China, U.S. Airlines Drop Taiwan (in Name at Least)." *New York Times*, July 25, 2018. Viewed August 17, 2020, at https://www.nytimes.com/2018/07/25/business/taiwan-american-airlines-china.html.

Weller, Amanda J. "Design Thinking for a User-Centered Approach to Artificial Intelligence." Journal of Design, Economics, and Innovation, vol. 5, no. 4, Winter 2019. Viewed December 15, 2020, at https://reader.elsevier.com/reader/sd/pii/S2405872619300887?token=B21B6C06E5C411FA9C36BDEB242BE12F76ED61ECC8264BABA8459E936AE-A947B8F8B13AB22CFC62D6FE446785CF04CBB.

Westcott, Ben. "Huge Leaks are Exposing Xinjiang's Re-Education Camps. But Don't Expect Beijing to Back Down." CNN, December 2, 2019. Viewed September 17, 2020, at https://www.cnn.com/2019/11/26/asia/china-xinjiang-leaks-analysis-intl-hnk/index.html.

Westerheide, Fabian. "China—The First Artificial Intelligence Superpower." *Forbes*, January 14, 2020. Viewed December 25, 2020, at https://www.forbes.com/sites/cognitiveworld/2020/01/14/china-artificial-intelligence-superpower/?sh=6a1ae6542f05.

White House Press Release, remarks by President Obama and President Xi of the People's Republic of China in Joint Press Conference, September 25, 2015. https://obamawhitehouse.archives.gov/the-press-office/2015/09/25/remarks-president-obama-and-president-xi-peoples-republic-china-joint.

Williams, Josette H. "The Information War in the Pacific, 1945." Original not dated, viewed February 8, 2020, at https://www.cia.gov/library/center-for-the-study-of-intelligence/kent-csi/vol46no3/pdf/v46i3a07p.pdf.

Winning, David. "Chinese 'Wolf Warrior' Diplomat Enrages Australia with Twitter Post." *Wall Street Journal*, November 30 2020. https://www.wsj.com/articles/chinese-wolf-warrior-diplomat-enrages-australia-with-twitter-post-11606731906?st=zhin3x-4dumqel03&reflink=article_email_share.

Winter, Tom, and Kevin Collier. "DOJ Says Five Chinese Nationals Hacked into 100 U.S. Companies." *Yahoo News*, September 16, 2020. Viewed October 10, 2020, at https://news.yahoo.com/doj-says-five-chinese-nationals-152220554.html.

Wong, Edward. "China Threatens to Detain Americans if U.S. Prosecutes Chinese Scholars." *New York Times*, October 18, 2020. Viewed 20 October 2020 at https://www.nytimes.com/2020/10/18/us/politics/china-us-threats-detain.html

Wong, Jacky. "China's Sour Grapes Spell Trouble for Australian Wine." *Wall Street Journal*, November 30, 2020. https://www.wsj.com/articles/chinas-sour-grapes-spell-trouble-for-australian-wine-11606733275?page=1.

Wray, Christopher. "China's Attempt to Influence U.S. Institutions." The Hudson Institute, August 6, 2020. Viewed November 22, 2020, at https://digitalguardian.com/blog/2500-fbis-counterintelligence-cases-linked-china; and "The Threat Posed by the Chinese Government and the Chinese Communist Party to the Economic and National Security of the United States." The Hudson Institute, July 7, 2020. Viewed November 22, 2020, at https://www.fbi.gov/news/speeches/the-threat-posed-by-the-chinese-government-and-the-chinese-communist-party-to-the-economic-and-national-security-of-the-united-states.

"Xinjiang Think Tank Unveils Adrian Zenz as Swindler Under Academic Disguise." *The Global Times*. August 9, 2020. https://www.globaltimes.cn/content/1197187.shtml.

Yang, Jing. "WeChat Becomes a Powerful Surveillance Tool Everywhere in China." *Wall Street Journal*, December 22, 2020. https://www.wsj.com/articles/wechat-become -a-powerful-surveillance-tool-everywhere-in-china-11608633003?st=36pxjeoztgn7mou&reflink=article_email_share.

Zetter, Kim. "Access Software on Systems Sold to States." *Vice*, July 17, 2018. Viewed December 8, 2020, at https://www.vice.com/en/article/mb4ezy/top-voting-machine-vendor-admits-it-installed-remote-access-software-on-systems-sold-to-states.

Zhong, Raymond, Paul Mozur, Aron Knolik, and Jeff Kao. "Leaked Documents Show How China's Army of Paid Internet Trolls Helped Censor the Coronavirus." *Propublica*, December 19, 2020. https://www.propublica.org/article/leaked-documents-show-how-chinas-army-of-paid-internet-trolls-helped-censor-the-coronavirus.

Index